浙江省普通本科高校“十四五”重点立项建设教材

跨境电商信文与实务

双语版

Cross-border E-commerce Correspondence and Practice

隋月红　许可欣　石凯含　主编

中国轻工业出版社

图书在版编目（CIP）数据

跨境电商信文与实务 / 隋月红，许可欣，石凯含主编. -- 北京 : 中国轻工业出版社，2025. 8. -- ISBN 978-7-5184-5558-4

Ⅰ. F713. 365. 2

中国国家版本馆 CIP 数据核字第 20257RE373 号

责任编辑：李寅寅
策划编辑：崔丽娜　　责任终审：劳国强　　封面设计：锋尚设计
版式设计：砚祥志远　　责任校对：朱　慧　朱燕春　　责任监印：张京华

出版发行：中国轻工业出版社（北京鲁谷东街 5 号，邮编：100040）
印　　刷：北京君升印刷有限公司
经　　销：各地新华书店
版　　次：2025 年 8 月第 1 版第 1 次印刷
开　　本：787×1092　1/16　印张：16
字　　数：380 千字
书　　号：ISBN 978-7-5184-5558-4　定价：59. 00 元
邮购电话：010-85119873
发行电话：010-85119832　010-85119912
网　　址：http://www. chlip. com. cn
Email:　club@ chlip. com. cn

242171J1X101ZBW

PREFACE 前言

当前，数字经济改变了跨境贸易信息传递方式，数字贸易等新业态增长率超过 15%，吸引了大量年轻人就业。然而，通过对国内外相关教材市场的追踪与调研发现，现有教材在支持国际贸易实务的信息与文字传输上，仍以传统的函电为主，缺乏专门针对跨境电商信文与实务的成熟教材。随着互联网技术的普及与跨境电商业务的快速发展，新术语不断涌现、贸易业务方式日益多样化，亟需一部跟上时代潮流、提炼我国跨境电商实务经验的教材。

本教材的编写具有三大特色：

1. 体现了新科技革命与文科融合的理念。本教材不仅扩充了运用至线下展会与数字贸易等即时性互动商务交流内容，还新增了商务短信文、新名词术语等英语信息文字传播与沟通范例。

2. 着眼于我国外贸实务的高质量发展与人才培养需求。在原有以货物贸易合同为主线的国际通用的业务规范与习语等基础上，本教材内容拓展至更广泛且综合性更强的国际服务贸易业务领域，为培养高素质外贸人才提供了支撑。

3. 彰显了全球视野下的文化自信。本教材立足于我国跨境电商实务的先进经验，以流程与信文标准化为手段，创新性地构建了以广义跨境电商为核心的系统性教材内容体系，强调突破业务专业化分割局限，着重培养学习者的全面外贸创业创新能力。

基于以上理念，本教材在编排上突破传统外贸方式及内容单一、以邮件为主的“长信文”业务沟通，补充了线上和线下方式的“即时性短信文”，并从三个部分进行内容重构：

第一部分以遵从外贸基础性函电为主，包括商务信函写作、交易前准备、交易磋商、跨境合同订立和跨境商务单据。每章均拓展了达成和履行外贸合同的综合性业务能力培养过程，帮助从业人员建立外贸整体流程的认知体系，避免因局限于特定岗位而难以提升综合能力，从而为全面外贸创业创新能力的构建奠定基础。

第二部分为跨境电商业务信文，涵盖跨境电商概述、跨境电商物流、跨境电商通关与报关、跨境电商支付、跨境电商客户沟通，新增了海外仓、跨境电商支付等内容。

第三部分注重即时商务短文，包括贸易展会和商务谈判，新增了国际商贸展会场景业务沟通、国际标准提案等提升国际贸易话语权等实务活动。

本教材旨在帮助学习者系统、完整地学习和掌握广义且全面的跨境电商业务，适用于高等院校国际贸易、国际商务、数字经济和管理等专业作为通用教材，也可以作为民办高校、高职服务经济与数字贸易专业的参考教材，同时还可作为跨境电子商务与贸易工作者的岗位培训教材和自学参考书。

本教材由中国计量大学国际经济与贸易系主任隋月红及其课程团队倾力打造，其中，隋月红副教授负责总体编写思路设计，整合了二十余年的教学讲义与课件资源并完成统纂与定稿；许可欣博士负责文字内容的中英文编写；石凯含博士结合其在国家市场监督管理总局标准创新管理司的挂职经历，编写了商务谈判中的国际标准提案部分。由于国际服务贸易涉及面广，环节众多而复杂，书中难免存在不足之处，恳请读者批评和指正。

隋月红
2025 年 3 月

CONTENTS 目录

第一章 商务信函写作
Chapter 1 Business Letter Writing

在国际贸易中，各种商务信函的写作是与国外客商沟通联系的重要部分。商务信函包括信函、电报、传真、电子邮件等书面通信方式。规范、专业的商务信函可以体现业务人员乃至公司的形象和实力，确保其与客户进行高效的沟通，促进业务的往来和发展。

学习目标

1. 熟悉商务信函的基本要素和基本内容。
2. 掌握商务信函的书写格式和写作特点。
3. 掌握商务信函的写作规范与技巧，能够熟练进行商务信函的写作。

思政目标

1. 学习规范写作，培养严谨细致的工作态度。
2. 了解不同文化，培养国际视野。
3. 强调真实准确，树立诚信意识。

第一节 商务信函的内容
Section 1 The Content of a Business Letter

商务信函由标准部分和附加部分构成，其中，标准部分是一封信函必须包括的内容，附加部分则需要在写信时根据内容进行适当的增减。

A business letter consists of a standard part and an optional part, where the standard part is the content that a letter must include, and the optional part needs to be appropriately added or removed based on the content when writing the letter.

一、标准部分
Standard part

（一）信头
Letterhead

信头包括发信人名称、地址、电话、传真、邮编等信息，一般写在信纸的右上角。在实践中，很多进出口公司都备有包括信头的信笺纸，因此写信时就不用再重复信头部分。

The letterhead includes the sender' s name, address, telephone number, fax number, postal code, and other information, usually written in the upper right corner of the letter. In practice, many import and export companies have letterhead paper, so there is no need to repeat the letterhead part when writing letters.

信头部分英文地址的写法与中文完全不同，地址按从小到大的顺序排列：第一行写门牌号码和街名；第二行写县/市、省/州、邮编、国名。写英文地址时，一般在每一行的末尾都不用标点符号，但在每一行的当中，标点符号不能省略。

The writing of the English address on the letterhead is completely different from that in Chinese. The addresses components are listed in ascending order: the first line includes the house number and street name, while the second line contains the county/city, province/state, postal code, and country name. When writing an English address, punctuation marks are generally not used at the end of each line, but punctuation marks cannot be omitted in the middle of each line.

范例

(齐头式)

F. RABBI & CO
19, SIR JEHANGIR KOTHARI BUILDING
M. A. JINNAH ROAD
KARACHI-74200, PAKISTAN
Tel: 92-21-42561722 Fax: 92-21-4526613

(二) 日期

Date

在中文书信中，日期一般写在落款的后面，但英语信函的日期要写在正文的前面。日期与信头之间的距离取决于书信的长短，如果书信较长，在信头以下 1~2 行；如果书信较短，在信头以下 2~3 行。空行的原则是把握书信各部分的布局协调。

In Chinese letters, the date typically appears after the signature, whereas in English letters, it is placed before the main body of the text. The spacing between the date and the letterhead varies depending on the length of the letter. If the letter is long, it should be 1 ~ 2 lines below the letterhead. If the letter is short, it should be 2 ~ 3 lines below the letterhead. The principle of adjusting blank lines is to grasp the layout and coordination of each part of the letter.

日期可以用数词；月份要用英语全称，不能使用缩略语；年份一概使用全称，不能简写。日期应按月、日、年（美式英语）或日、月、年（英式英语）的顺序完整写出。“日”既可用基数词（1、2、3、4 等），也可用序数词（1st、2nd、3rd、4th 等）。

Dates can use numerals. Months should be spelled out in English (abbreviations are not allowed). The full name of the year must be used and cannot be abbreviated. For example, dates should be written in full in the order of month, day, year (in American English) or day, month, year (in British English). The “day” can be either a cardinal number (1, 2, 3, 4, etc.) or an ordinal number (1st, 2nd, 3rd, 4th, etc.).

范例

2021 年 7 月 30 日的写法

July 30, 2021/July 30th, 2021 (American English)

30 July, 2021/30th July, 2021 (British English)

（三）封内地址

Inside address

在一般的社交信中，信内收信人的地址通常省略，但是在公务信函中必须包括封内地址。封内地址必须和信封上的地址完全一致，包括收信人的姓名、单位和详细地址等，一般写在左上方，在日期和称呼之间，在日期以下 3 行或更多行。

In general social letters, the recipient's address is usually omitted. However, in official letters, the inside address must be included. The inside address must be exactly the same as the address on the envelope, including the recipient's name, affiliation, and detailed address. Typically, the inside address is placed in the top left corner, between the date and the salutation, and spaced at least three lines below the date.

在写给个人的商务信函中，在姓名前要加上称谓。对男性的称谓包括 Mr.、Messrs.、Esq.。Mr. 不可只用在名字前，例如，对 Jerry Kater 的称呼是 Mr. Kater 或 Mr. Jerry Kater，而不能是 Mr. Jerry。Mr. 的复数形式 Messrs.（法语单词 Messieurs 的缩写）用于两个以上的男性，或用于两个以上的男性组成的公司或团体（如 Messrs. Brooks Brothers）。在称呼某些特殊阶层的男性（如 Judges、Magistrates）时，Esq. 有时被用来代替 Mr. 用在姓氏后（如 Davis Esq.）。如果收信人拥有特别的头衔（如 Doctor、Professor、Colonel、Sir），则用头衔代替 Mr. 或 Esq.，其官方职务写在姓氏之后。

In personal business letters, a title should be included before the recipient's name. For men, common titles include Mr., Messrs, Esq. Mr. cannot be used only before the first name. For example, Jerry Kater should be addressed as Mr. Kater or Mr. Jerry Kater, but not Mr. Jerry. The plural form of Mr. is Messrs (short for Messieurs in French), used for two or more men, or for companies/groups composed of two or more men (e. g., Messrs Brooks Brothers). For certain distinguished men (e. g., Judges, Magistrates), Esq. may replace Mr. and is placed after the last name (e. g., Davis Esq.) If the recipient holds a special title (e. g., Doctor, Professor, Colonel, Sir), use that title instead of Mr. or Esq. The official position should follow the last name.

范例

（不知道收信人时）

Advertising Manager
Kingkill Motor House Ltd.
212, D. W. Rupasinghe
Nugegoda, Srilanka

（四）称呼

Salutation

称呼是写信人对收信人的称呼用语。位置在封内地址下面2行，顶格写起，在称呼后面一般用逗号（英式英语），也可以用冒号（美式英语）。

The salutation is the language used by the writer to address the recipient. It is positioned two lines below the inside address, starting from the left margin, and is typically followed by a comma (in British English) or a colon (in American English).

范例

Dear Mr. Smith——收信人为男性（The recipient is a male individual）

Dear Mrs. Brown——收信人为已婚女士（The recipient is a married woman）

Dear Miss Jennifer——收信人为未婚女士（The recipient is an unmarried woman）

Dear Ms. Davis——收信人为女性且对方婚姻状况不明确（The recipient is female, and her marital status is unknown）

Dear Mason——收信人为熟人或朋友（The recipient is an acquaintance or a friend）

（五）正文

Body of the letter

正文一般在称呼语下面2行。正文包含写信人要传递给收信人的信息，是书信中最重要的部分，因此要求正文层次分明、简单易懂。

The body of the letter typically begins two lines below the salutation. The body of the letter contains the information that the writer wants to convey to the recipient, and is the most important part of the letter. Therefore, it is required that the main body be clear in hierarchy and simple to understand.

书信的正文可以分三段。开首段，提及对方之前的来函，对对方来信的日期、编号或查号、主题及简单内容加以综合叙述，以便了解去函的目的；阐述段，对信件的主题做出详述；结尾段，提示对收信人的要求，如希望来函或电报订货、答复询问或作必要的声明等。

The body of the letter can be divided into three paragraphs. The opening paragraph mentions the other party's previous letters, and provides a comprehensive description of the date, number or reference, subject, and brief content of the other party's letter in order to understand the purpose of the letter. The body paragraph elaborates on the topic of the letter in detail. The closing paragraph specifies required actions, such as requesting a letter or telegram to place an order, responding to enquiries, or making necessary statements.

（六）结尾敬语

Complimentary close

结尾敬语的位置在正文下面2行。结尾敬语与称呼都属于客套用语，二者在语气和风格上必须相呼应，句末用逗号。

The complimentary close should be placed two lines below the body of the letter. As a formal courtesy phrase, it must correspond with the salutation in tone and style, and end with a comma.

（七）签名
Signature

写信人必须使用钢笔在结尾敬语 4 行下签名。因为大部分签名难以辨认，所以要在签名下空 1 行打印签名人的姓名、职位，以便对方了解。英文商务信函都必须由写信人亲笔签名，没有亲笔签名的信函不具有任何法律效力。

The writer must sign in fountain pen below the complimentary close, leaving a four-line space. Since most signatures are difficult to recognize, it is necessary to leave a blank line under the signature to print the name and position of the signer for the other party to understand. English business letters must be personally signed by the author, and letters without a handwritten signature have no legal effect.

二、附加部分
Optional part

（一）经办人
Attention line

有些商务信函需要发给公司或部门，不直接发给个人。在这种情况下，为了使收信公司迅速地将信函转给经办人或经办部门办理，可以在封内地址和称呼中间加上经办人姓名。另外，在指明的收信人不在时，此类信函也允许公司的其他人查看内容。经办人姓名通常写在封内地址的下面 2 行。

In some business letter, the letter is addressed to a company or a department rather than an individual. In such cases, to ensure the letter is promptly redirected to the person responsible or department for handling, the name of the handler can be added between the inside address and the salutation. Additionally, in the absence of the specified recipient, this type of letter permits other members of the company to view its contents. The name of the handler is typically written two lines below the inside address.

（二）事由行
Subject line

事由行通常在称呼和正文之间，一般在称呼下面 2 行，在信纸的中间，也可与称呼对齐，使用 "Re:" 或 "Subject:" 字样，并加下划线或加粗或大写。事由行的作用在于使收信人准确、快速地了解信函的基本内容和目的。

The subject line is positioned between the salutation and the body of the letter, typically centered two lines below the salutation. It can also be aligned with the salutation, using the words "Re:" or "Subject:" and underlined, or bolded, or capitalized. The function of the subject line is to enable the recipient to accurately and quickly understand the core content and purpose of the letter.

范例

Dear Yuki,
Re: KH type linear ball bearings
或:
Dear Mr. Aloolakar,
Subject: Aluminium complete bottom shaft support

(三) 参考编号

Reference number

在商务信函中，参考编号不但便于日后查询信件或存档分类，还能够使信件及时送达收信人。信函的参考编号，一般由档案编号、部门代码或者有关人员的姓名的首字母构成。如果收信人在写信时提供了参考编号，回信人在复函时就应该提及该参考编号。大多数进出口企业的信笺纸的信头已经包括了参考编号部分（Our Ref. ——我方编号，即发信人编号；Your Ref. ——贵方编号，即收信人编号），写信时需要在相应的位置填上参考编号，否则就要在信头的下方添加参考编号。在实际业务操作中，也可以在回信的第一段或者事由行提及参考编号。

In business letters, reference numbers not only facilitate future queries or classification of letters, but also enable timely delivery of letters to recipients. The reference number of a letter is generally composed of the file number, department code, or the first letter of the name of the relevant personnel. If the recipient provides a reference number when writing the letter, the respondent should mention that reference number when replying. The letterhead of most import and export enterprises already includes a reference number section (Our Ref. — the sender's tracking number; Your Ref. — the recipient's provided number). The reference number needs to be filled in the corresponding position when writing a letter. Otherwise, a reference number needs to be added below the letterhead. In practical business operations, the reference number can also be mentioned in the first paragraph or subject line of the reply.

(四) 附件

Enclosure

如果在寄信的同时邮寄了商业发票、订单、合同、报价单、商品目录等，要在签名以下2行对附件做出说明。如果写信人提到两个以上的附件，要用数字标出信中所提到的附件。经常使用的形式有：Enclosure、Enclosures、Encl. 或 Enc. 等。

If commercial invoices, orders, contracts, quotations, product catalogs, etc. are mailed at the same time as the letter, an explanation of the enclosures should be provided in the following two lines of the signature. If the writer mentions two or more enclosures, use numbers to indicate the enclosures mentioned in the letter. The commonly used forms include Enclosure, Enclosures, Encl. or Enc.

（五）附言

Postscript

如果写信人在写信时忘记了某项内容，可在“抄送”以上 2 行加上 P. S. 标记，表示下面的内容是补充的。在写信时要尽量避免使用附言，因为收信人会认为写信人在写信前没有考虑清楚信件的内容。

If writers forget something while writing the letter, they can add P. S. to the two lines above “cc:” notation, indicating that the following content is supplementary. When writing a letter, try to avoid using postscript as the recipient may think that the addresser did not carefully consider the content of the letter before writing it.

（六）抄送

Carbon copy

如果信件还同时寄送给其他人，就要在附件以下 2 行加上“cc:”（Carbon Copy）的标记，后面加上收件人或公司的名称。

If the letter is also being sent to someone else at the same time, indicate this by adding “cc:” (Carbon Copy) two lines below the enclosure notation, followed by the recipient's name or company name.

范例

CNIEC SHAANXI CORP
28 Xiguan Street (**Letterhead**)
Xi'an, China 710082
Tel: 029-88623911 Fax: 029-88613616

Your Ref.: 0709182A
Our Ref.: 0709200B (**Reference Number**)

22 January, 2025 (**Date**)

Minermet S. A.
Avenue Mon-Repos 14 (**Inside Address**)
1005 Lausanne Switzerland

Attn: Miss Yuki Lee (**Attention Line**)
Dear Sirs, (**Salutation**)
Re. Shipment of 100 MT zine Ingots under your S/C No. 2708 (**Subject Line**)

(**Body of the Letter**)

We are in receipt of your letter of August 28 about the captioned goods. We take pleasure to reply here that our confirmed irrevocable L/C amounting to USD 70, 000 has been opened by Switzerland Commercial Bank this morning. Please rush the shipment of our ordered goods after you receive the L/C. It is said that Dhaka vessel will leave for our ports on or about May 28 from your end. If possible, please try your best to catch the steamer for shipment, provided this trail order makes our customers satisfied, we guarantee that our repeat order will be in large quantities.

We appreciate highly your close cooperation in this respect.

Yours faithfully, (**Complimentary Close**)
Aloolakar (**Signature**)
General manager

Encl. (**Enclosure**)
P. S. (**Postscript**)
cc: (**Carbon Copy**)

第二节 商务信函的书写格式
Section 2 Business Letter Format

一、商务信函内容的书写格式
Writing format of business letter content

(一) 缩行式
Indented form

缩行式的要领在于信头、结束语、签名和发信人姓名都靠右或偏右，而封内地址和称呼则靠左边，如果以上任一要素要分行排列时，后行要比前行缩入 2 个（或 3 个）英文字母；正文每段开始要缩入 5 个英文字母，段与段之间要空 1 行。这种讲究对称美的传统排列形式，目前只有少数英国人仍在使用。

The key to the indented format is that the letterhead, complimentary close, signature, and sender's name should all be placed to the right or slightly to the right, while the inside address and salutation should be placed to the left. If any of these elements need to be arranged in separate lines, the back line should be indented by 2 (or 3) English letters compared to the front line. Each paragraph in the main text should be indented by 5 English letters, and there should be a single line space between paragraphs. This traditional arrangement form that stresses symmetrical beauty, is currently only used by a few British people.

范例

Bidebao Import and Export Company
Room 203, Jiafa Mansion
St. Petersburg
Russia
Tel: 007-8600 Fax: 007-9600

13 March, 2014
Shanghai Yongxin Trading Co., Ltd.
8# Jilong Road, Waigaoqiao Free Trade Zone
Shanghai
China

Dear Mr. Wang,

We are pleased to receive your letter of March 12 concerning our Famous Brand Handbags. And we are grateful for your proposal to establish business relations. Will you please send us your catalog and full details of your export prices, terms of payment and shipment, together with any samples you can let us have? If the goods meet our expectations and your prices are competitive, we would expect to place a regular order. We should also like to know what price you offer on Famous Brand Handbags.

We are looking forward to your early reply.

Yours faithfully,
Bidebao Import and Export Company
Nalesjin

（二）全齐头式

Full block form

全齐头式是商务信函中最为常用的格式，全部内容包括日期、结尾敬语、签名，都从左侧顶格开始。段落开头不空格，各段之间空 1～2 行。

The full block form is the most commonly used format in business letter, which includes the date, complimentary close, and signature, all starting from the top left grid. At the beginning of each paragraph, there should be no indentation, and there should be 1～2 blank lines between each paragraph.

范例

Shanghai Yongxin Trading Co., Ltd.
8# Jilong Road, Waigaoqiao Free Trade Zone
Shanghai
China

12 March 2014
Bidebao Import and Export Company
Room 203, Jiafa Mansion, St. Petersburg, Russia
Tel: 007-8600 Fax: 007-9600

Dear Mr. Nalesjin,
We obtained your name and address through international e-commerce platforms in March 2014, and we learned that you are interested in Famous Brand Handbags. Now we are writing to you to hope to establish business relations with you. We are the leading exporter with a long-standing and high reputation, specializing in all kinds of luggage. We are confident that with our experience in this line for more than 15 years, and we can give our customers complete satisfaction.

In order to give you a general idea of the Famous Brand Handbags, we are sending you our latest catalogue for your reference. For our financial standing, you may refer to Bank of China, Shanghai Branch.

Please let us know immediately if you are interested in our products. We will send you our price list and sample to you as soon as we receive your specific enquiry. We look forward to your early reply.

Yours faithfully,
Shanghai Yongxin Trading Co., Ltd.
Guoxin Wang

（三）改良齐头式

Modified block form

改良齐头式曾经是商务函电广泛使用的一种格式，但随着时间的推移，改良齐头式被认为过时和不够专业。与全齐头式不同，改良齐头式中的事由行居中，信头、日期、结尾敬语和签名都从中间开始，其余部分从左边开始。

The modified block form was once a widely used format in business letter, but over time, it has been considered outdated and unprofessional. Unlike the full block form, the subject line in the modified block form is centered, with the letterhead, date, complimentary close, and signature starting from the middle, and the rest starting from the left.

范例

Shanghai Yongxin Trading Co., Ltd.
8# Jilong Road, Waigaoqiao Free Trade Zone
Shanghai
China

28 March, 2014
Bidebao Import and Export Company
Room 203, Jiafa Mansion, St. Petersburg, Russia
Tel: 007-8600 Fax: 007-9600

Dear Mr. Nalesjin,
We have received your counter-offer of March 22. Although your counter-offer is obviously on the low side, after careful consideration of your request for the price, we will accept the order at the price USD 34/pe. We have faxed you the specimen sales confirmation No. CT0001054 in duplicate for your checking the terms and conditions. Please sign and return one copy to us for our file. Now you are requested to establish a L/C in our favor covering the above mentioned goods as soon as possible. We would like to remind you that the stipulations in the relevant L/C should strictly conform to the terms stated in our sales confirmation so as to avoid subsequent amendments.
We appreciate your close cooperation and look forward to receiving your further orders.

Yours faithfully,
Shanghai Yongxin Trading Co., Ltd.
Guoxin Wang

二、信封格式
Addressing envelopes

信封的内容包括：
（1）发信人的名称、地址。
（2）收信人的名称、地址。
（3）邮递指示。
（4）附记事项。

The contents of the envelope include：

(1) The sender's name and address.

(2) The recipient's name and address.

(3) Mailing direction.

(4) Additional notes.

其中，附记事项可能为：机密、绝密、私人亲启、亲启、急件、印刷品。

Among them, the additional notes may be：Confidential, Top Confidential, Private, Personal, Urgent, Printed Matter.

信封上的收信人名称、地址必须正确，以免误递或无法投递，并且必须与封内地址完全一致。收信人的名称、地址的排列行数如果不超过 4 行，则每行之间宜采用双行间隔，4 行以上则采用单行间隔，发信人/收信人名称、地址每行的起首排列有齐头式，也有缩进式。

The recipient's name and address on the envelope must be correct to avoid accidental delivery or inability to deliver, and must be exactly the same as the address inside the envelope. If the number of lines arranged for the recipient's name and address does not exceed 4, double line spacing should be used between each line, and single line spacing should be used for lines above 4. The starting arrangement of each line for the sender/recipient's name and address can be either block form or indented form.

范例

(全齐头式)

John Hill
Harper Collins Publishers (New Zealand) Ltd.
31 View Road, Auckland
New Zealand　　　　　　　　Par avion/By Air

　　　　　　　　Cao Yammer
　　　　　　　　48 Yenta Road (N)
　　　　　　　　Xi'an City 710054
　　　　　　　　Shaanxi Province
Personal　　　　　　　　People's Republic of China

第三节 Section 3 商务信函的书写原则 Principles of Writing Business Letters

商务信函、传真、电子邮件是我们在从事外经贸活动时对外联络的主要方式。一封内容清楚、简洁，格式正确、完整的信函不仅能给客户留下良好的印象，而且将提高工作效率。所以在写作商务信函时，应运用恰当的格式，遵守其特有的写作原则。

Business letters, faxes, and emails are our main ways of external communication when engaging in foreign trade and economic activities. A clear, concise, formatted, and complete letter can not only leave a good impression on customers, but also improve work efficiency. Therefore, when writing business letters, appropriate formatting should be used and unique writing principles should be followed.

一、体谅
Consideration

写信时要设身处地替对方着想，考虑对方的需求，而不是从自身的角度看问题，以“我”为主导地位。要学会灵活、自然地运用第二人称代词“you”和“your”，使对方感到被重视。第一人称代词（I、we、our、us）的使用应该恰如其分，避免招致对方的反感。

When writing a letter, one should put oneself in the other person's shoes and consider his needs, rather than looking at the problem from one's own perspective and taking the "I" as the dominant position. Use second person pronouns such as "you" and "your" flexibly and naturally, making the other person feel valued. The use of first person pronouns (I, we, our, us) should be appropriate to avoid arousing the other person's uncomfortable.

二、礼貌
Courtesy

在信函写作中，不但要在语言、态度上礼貌、谦虚，而且要在行为上表现出自己的涵养和素质，例如及时回复对方的信件。收到信件时，即使是当时处理不了，也要先做一个简单的回复，告知对方信件已经收到，对客户表示最起码的尊重和重视。

In letter writing, one should not only be polite and humble in language and attitude, but also demonstrate cultivation and quality in behavior, such as responding to the other party's letters in a timely manner. When receiving a letter, even if it cannot be processed at the time, a simple reply should be made first to inform the other party that the letter has been received, showing basic respect and courtesy to the customer.

三、完整
Completeness

商务信函应包括一切必要的信息。尽量不要在商务信函中使用附言，否则会让对方感觉写信人做事不够认真、态度不够真诚。另外，在信函写作中，每个段落都要围绕一个主题，段落中的每个句子都要与主题相关，做到条理清楚、内容完整。

Business letters should include all necessary information. Try not to use postscript in business letters, otherwise it will make the other party feel that the addresser is not serious enough and his attitude is not sincere enough. In addition, in letter writing, each paragraph should focus on a single theme, and each sentence in the paragraph should be related to the theme, achieving clear organization and complete content.

四、清楚
Clarity

信函中的语言表述要能够清楚表达写信人的观点，可能引起歧义的表达会使对方产生误解。信函内容要结构清晰，层次分明。例如“As to the steamers sailing from Hong Kong to San Francisco, we have bimonthly direct services.”中的“bimonthly”既可以理解为“一个月两次”，又可以理解为“两个月一次”。

The language used in letters should clearly convey the writer's viewpoint, as ambiguous expressions may cause misunderstandings for the other party. The content of the letter should have a clear structure and distinct hierarchy. For example: As to the steamers sailing from Hong Kong to San Francisco, we have bimonthly direct services. The word "bimonthly" in the sentence can be understood as either "twice a month" or "once every two months".

五、简洁
Conciseness

在力求商务信函完整、清楚的同时要做到简洁，也就是使用最简洁的语句表达最完整的意思。其原则是：能使用单词的不使用短语，能使用短语的不使用句子，能用短句的不用长句。同时，避免不必要的重复。但是，简洁的原则是以不影响对内容的理解为前提，清楚始终是商务书信的首要要求。

While striving for both completeness and clarity in business letters, concise is equally important — using the most concise language to express the most complete meaning. Follow these principles: use a word instead of a phrase when possible, use a phrase instead of a full sentence when possible, and prefer short sentences over long ones. Avoid unnecessary repetition at the same time. However, the principle of conciseness is based on the premise of not affecting the understanding of the content, and clarity is always the primary requirement of business letters.

范例

We acknowledge receipt of you letter dated September 20. 可改为：We appreciate your letter dated September 20.

六、具体
Concreteness

在信函写作中，必须使用意义明确的表达，以使信函中所涉及的对象具体、明确，避免使用笼统的词语。

In letter writing, it is necessary to use clear and meaningful expressions to make the objects involved in the letter specific and clear, and avoid using vague words.

范例

(a) We wish to confirm our quotations yesterday.

(b) Please make immediate shipment of our order to Bombay.

七、准确
Correctness

在信函写作中，语法、标点及拼写必须准确无误，同时需使用规范的语言、恰当的叙述和准确的贸易术语。在给商务信函签名时，应检查其内容是否准确，因为即使是个别细微的失误，也可能会损害写信者的可信度，甚至引发对其他信息的质疑。

In letter writing, grammar, punctuation, and spelling must be correct, while standard language, appropriate narration, and accurate trade terms are equally essential. When signing business letters, the correctness of their content should be checked, as minor errors in the letter may undermine the writer's credibility and cast doubt on other information.

范例

如果以“We require short delivery for our order.”表达“要求尽早交货”，肯定会使对方不知所云，因为 short delivery 不是“快点交货”的意思，而是“短交货”的意思。

课后练习

I. 选词填空。

Fill in the blanks with the appropriate words.

(consideration; courtesy; completeness; clarity; conciseness; concreteness; correctness inside address; subject line; enclosure)

1. In business letter, it is important to put yourself in the recipient's shoes and focus on their needs. This principle is known as ____________.

2. To ensure that the recipient understands your message without confusion, you should always aim for ____________ in your writing.

3. When writing a business letter, including all necessary information and avoiding the use of postscripts demonstrates ____________.

4. The line that indicates the main topic of a business letter, usually placed between the salutation and the body, is called the ____________.

5. To maintain professionalism and avoid misunderstandings, always check your letter for grammatical errors and proper use of trade terms. This is known as ensuring ____________.

6. Using precise and specific language instead of vague terms helps achieve ____________ in business writing.

7. The address of the recipient, which must be included in a business letter and should match the address on the envelope, is referred to as the ____________.

8. When writing a business letter, try to express complete ideas using the fewest possible words. This principle is called ____________.

9. If you are sending additional documents along with your letter, you should mention them in the ____________ section below your signature.

10. Responding to a client's letter promptly and politely demonstrates good ____________ and helps build a positive relationship.

Ⅱ. 写作题。

Writing.

You are the manager of a company that specializes in exporting handmade crafts. Write a business letter to a potential overseas client introducing your company's products and services. Include the following elements in your letter:

1. A formal letterhead with your company's name, address, and contact information;
2. An appropriate inside address and salutation;
3. A clear subject line indicating the purpose of your letter;
4. A body that includes an introduction to your company, a description of your products, and an invitation for the client to place an order or request a catalog;
5. A polite and professional closing;
6. Your signature and printed name;
7. A mention of any enclosures (e. g., product catalog).

Ensure that your letter follows the principles of consideration, courtesy, completeness, clarity, conciseness, concreteness, and correctness.

第二章 Chapter 2 交易前准备 Transaction Preparation

在开展任何一项跨境贸易之前，交易准备阶段必不可少。充分且全面的交易准备工作，能够极大地提高获取跨境贸易订单的概率，对建立长久的跨境商务关系和降低信息不完全等干扰因素造成的商业风险具有重要意义。本章内容包括跨境市场调研、跨境客户开发、跨境资信调查、跨境业务联系四部分，通过对跨境电商前的交易准备流程的梳理，帮助学生了解跨境市场调研与客户开发的途径与方法，掌握线上线下贸易活动的沟通技巧与信函写作，实现更高效的跨境贸易活动，促进跨境贸易的成功开展。

学习目标

1. 熟悉跨境市场调研的主要内容与方法。
2. 熟悉跨境客户开发的主要途径。
3. 了解贸易展会等线下贸易活动的沟通技巧。
4. 掌握跨境资信调查和跨境业务联系建立的主要途径与信函写作方法。

思政目标

1. 重视市场调研，培养实事求是的精神。
2. 学习开发技巧，培养沟通能力。
3. 学会识别风险，树立风险防范意识。

第一节 Section 1 跨境市场调研 Cross border Market Research

一、跨境市场调研的内容

Content of cross-border market research

跨境市场调研主要包括：国际市场环境调研、国际市场商品情况调研、国际市场营销情况调研、国外客户情况调研等。

Cross-border market research mainly includes: international market environment research, international market commodity situation research, international marketing situation research, foreign customers situation research, etc.

（一）国际市场环境调研

International market environment research

企业开展国际商务活动，将产品打入国际市场，需先了解商务市场环境，做到知己知彼、百战不殆。企业对国际市场环境调研的主要内容如下：

（1）国外经济环境，包括一国的经济结构、经济发展水平、就业、收入分配等。

（2）国外政治和法律环境，包括政府机构的重要经济政策，政府对贸易实行的鼓励政策、限制措施，特别是有关外贸方面的法律法规，如关税、配额、国内税收、外汇限制、卫生检疫安全条例等。

（3）国外文化环境，包括使用的语言、教育水平、风俗习惯、价值观念等。

（4）其他，包括国外人口、交通、地理等情况。

To engage in international business activities and enter the international market with products, enterprises need to first understand the business market environment, achieve self-awareness and market insight, and adopt a strategic approach. The main content of enterprise research on the international market environment as follows:

(1) The foreign economic environment, including a country's economic structure, level of economic development, employment, income distribution, etc.

(2) The foreign political and legal environment, including important economic policies of government agencies, encouragement policies and restrictive measures implemented by the government on trade, especially laws and regulations related to foreign trade, such as tariffs, quotas, domestic taxation, foreign exchange restrictions, health and quarantine safety regulations, etc.

(3) Foreign cultural environment, including language used, educational level, customs, values, etc.

(4) Other factors, including foreign population, transportation, geography, etc.

（二）国际市场商品情况调研

International market commodity situation research

企业要把产品打入国际市场或从国际市场进口产品，除需了解国外市场环境外，还需了解国外市场商品情况，主要有：

（1）国外市场商品的供给情况，包括商品供应的渠道、来源，国外生产厂家、生产能力、数量及库存情况等。

（2）国外市场商品的需求情况，包括国外市场对商品需求的品种、数量、质量要求等。

（3）国际市场商品的价格情况，包括国际市场商品的价格、价格与供求变动的关系等。

For enterprises to export products or import products from the international market, in addition to understanding the foreign market environment, they also need to understand the foreign market commodity situation, mainly including:

(1) The supply situation of goods in foreign markets, including the channels and sources of supply, foreign manufacturers, production capacity, quantity, and inventory situation, etc.

(2) The demand for goods in foreign markets, including the variety, quantity, quality requirements, etc.

(3) The price situation of goods in the international market, including the prices of goods in the international market, the relationship between prices and supply and demand changes, etc.

(三) 国际市场营销情况调研

International marketing situation research

国际市场营销情况调研是对国际市场营销组合情况的调研，除上述已经提到的商品及价格外，一般还应包括：

(1) 商品销售渠道，包括销售网络建立、批发商和零售商的经营能力、经营利润、消费者对他们的印象、售后服务等。

(2) 广告宣传，包括消费者购买动机、广告内容、广告时间、方式、效果等。

(3) 竞争分析，包括竞争者产品质量、价格、政策、广告、分配路线、占有率等。

International marketing situation research is a study of the international marketing mix, which should generally include, in addition to the products and prices mentioned above:

(1) Product sales channels, including the establishment of sales networks, the operational capabilities of wholesalers and retailers, operating profits, consumer impressions of them, after-sales service, etc.

(2) Advertising and promotion, including consumer purchasing motivations, advertising contents, advertising time, methods, effects, etc.

(3) Competitive analysis, including competitor product quality, price, policy, advertising, distribution routes, market share, etc.

(四) 国外客户情况调研

Foreign customers situation research

每个商品都有自己的销售（进货）渠道。销售（进货）渠道是由不同客户所组成的。企业进出口商品必须选择合适的销售（进货）渠道与客户，做好国外客户的调查研究。

(1) 委托国内外咨询公司对客户进行资信调查。

(2) 委托中国银行及其驻外分支机构对客户进行资信调查。

(3) 通过我国外贸公司驻外分支机构或商务参赞、代表处对客户进行资信调查。

(4) 利用交易会、洽谈会、客户来华谈判、派出国代表团、推销小组等对客户进行资信调查。

通过上述调查，企业可有针对性地选择客户进行交易。此外，企业在进行国外市场调查的同时，也应注意做好国内货源及需求方面的调查。

Each product has its own sales (procurement) channel. The sales (procurement) channel is composed of different customers. Enterprises must choose appropriate sales (procurement) channels and customers for their import and export goods, and conduct research on foreign customers.

(1) Entrust domestic and foreign consulting firms to conduct credit investigations on clients.

(2) Entrust Bank of China and its overseas branches to conduct a credit investigation on customers.

(3) Conduct credit investigations on customers through the overseas branches of China's foreign trade companies or commercial counselors or representative offices.

(4) Conduct credit investigations on customers through trade fairs, negotiation meetings,

customer negotiations in China, sending overseas delegations, and sales teams.

Through the above investigations, enterprises can selectively choose customers for transactions. In addition, while conducting overseas market research, enterprises should also pay attention to conducting research on domestic supply and demand.

二、寻找和了解目标市场的途径
Ways to find and understand the target market

（一）直接调研的途径
Direct research approach

1. 直接到实地考察当地市场
Directly conduct on-site inspections of the local market

为了了解市场信息，调研单位可以在条件许可时直接前往目标国家当地市场进行考察，掌握当地市场的供给和需求情况。跨境电商卖家也可以通过举办交易会、展览会、技术交流会和学术讨论会等，倾听客户网络购物的需求。

In order to understand market information, research units can directly visit the local market of the target country for investigation when conditions permit, and grasp the supply and demand situation of the local market. Cross-border e-commerce sellers can also listen to customers' online shopping needs by holding trade fairs, exhibitions, technical exchange meetings, and academic discussions.

2. 通过搜索引擎寻找目标客户与市场信息
Search for target customers and market information through search engines

由于条件的限制，大部分跨境电商企业无法做到出国考察市场。这时，企业可借助搜索引擎、网络及其分析工具，从而全面掌握销售市场的发展情况。搜索引擎主要分为三种，分别是全文搜索引擎（Google、Fast/AllTheWeb、AltaVista、Inktomi、Teoma、WiseNut 和百度等）、目录索引类引擎（Yahoo、DMOZ、LookSmart、About、新浪和网易等）以及利用网络分析工具进行的元搜索引擎。下面重点介绍 Google 搜索引擎和网络分析工具。

（1）Google 搜索引擎。Google 是全球最大的搜索引擎，跨境电商市场开发人员可以充分利用这一工具进行数据分析。现以全棉色织面料产品为例，全棉色织面料可制作衬衫等产品，若以衬衫 shirt 作为关键词，在 www. google. com 进行搜索，会发现很多在 Google 上进行推广的生产衬衫的公司，而这些公司就是待开发的潜在客户。网站上这些生产衬衫的公司出于推广的需要，往往附有详细的联系方式，沟通非常方便。建立联系后，可进一步了解其对全棉色织面料产品的质量、交期和结算方式等的具体要求。这种方式可使业务员在足不出户的情况下，也可以获得目标国市场对产品的需求状况，沟通能力较强的业务员甚至可以轻松获得订单。

（2）网络分析工具。跨境电商卖家可以借助网络分析工具开展针对性的数据搜索与分析：①利用 Google Trends 跨境电子商务工具分析品类的周期性特点，把握产品开发先机；②借助 Keyword Spy 工具可发现品类搜索热度和品类关键词；③借助 Alea 可选择某品类中以该市场作为主要目标市场的竞争对手网站，作为对目标市场产品品类分析和选择的参考；

④借助 Terapeak 工具可全面分析 eBay 和 Amazon 平台账号。此外，调查者还可以访问竞争者的网站，认真阅读竞争者的网站风格、内容和主要特色，并通过专业分析工具挖掘有用的商业信息。

Due to limitations in conditions, most cross-border e-commerce enterprises are unable to conduct market research abroad. At this point, enterprises can use search engines, the Internet and its analysis tools, to comprehensively grasp the development of the sales market. There are three main types of search engines, namely full-text search engines (Google, Fast/AllTheWeb, AltaVista, Inktomi, Teoma, WiseNut, and Baidu, etc.), directory indexing engines (Yahoo, DMOZ, LookSmart, About, Sina, and NetEase, etc.), and meta-search engines using network analysis tools. The following section focuses on the Google search engine and network analysis tools.

(1) Google search engine. Google is the world's largest search engine, and cross-border e-commerce market developers can fully utilize this tool for data segmentation and analysis. Taking all-cotton color-woven fabric products as an example, all-cotton color-woven fabric can be used to make shirts and other products. If you use "shirt" as a keyword and search on www. google. com, you will find many companies promoting shirt production on Google, and these companies are potential customers waiting to be developed. The companies that produce shirts on the website often provide detailed contact information for promotional purposes, making communication very convenient. After establishing contact, one can further understand their requirements for the quality, delivery time, and settlement method of all-cotton color-woven fabric products. This method allows salespeople to obtain the demand for products in the target country's market without leaving their homes, and salespeople with strong communication skills can even easily obtain orders.

(2) Network analysis tools. Cross-border e-commerce sellers can use network analysis tools to conduct targeted data search and analysis: ① Use Google Trends cross-border e-commerce tools to analyze the cyclical characteristics of categories and seize product development opportunities; ② By using the Keyword Spy, they can discover the popularity of category search and category keywords; ③ Alea can be used to select competitor websites in a certain category with that market as the main target market, as a reference for analyzing and selecting product categories in the target market; ④ The Terapeak enables comprehensive analysis of eBay and Amazon platform accounts. In addition, investigators can also visit competitor websites, carefully read their website style, content, and main features, and use professional analysis tools to mine useful business information.

需要注意的是，跨境电商企业在利用搜索引擎前，必须先做好搜索前的定位工作，限定搜索范围。比如，事先应确定需要分析的目标客户所属的国家与地区，锁定商品潜在客户的类型，从而确定最有效率的关键词。企业可以采用多种不同的搜索引擎来对比搜索结果，以免造成客户信息的流失。因为每个搜索网站每天都会收录其他网站更新的信息，多个搜索引擎并用可以发现最新的商机。

It should be noted that cross-border e-commerce enterprises must first do a good job of pre-search positioning and limit the search scope before using search engines. For example, it is necessary to determine the country and region of the target customers to be analyzed in advance, identify the types of potential customers for the product, and thus determine the most efficient keywords. Enterprises can use various search engines to compare search results and avoid the loss of customer information. Because each search website collects updated information from other websites every day, multiple search engines working together can discover the latest business opportunities.

3. 利用跨境电商平台的数据分析

Utilize data analysis from cross-border e-commerce platforms

跨境电商平台是以全球交易数据为依据的，是收集国际市场行情资料的主要渠道。调查者可以通过观察跨境电商平台的买家界面及通过关键词搜索，来了解网络平台消费的新潮流，从而收集到有助于选品的信息。此外，调查者还可以通过全球速卖通后台数据对拟售产品进行行业分析，了解在统计时间内的几个重要参考指标：边客①数占比、浏览量占比、支付金额占比、成变订单②占比和供需指数等。

Cross-border e-commerce platforms are based on global transaction data and are the main channel for collecting information on international market trends. Investigators can learn about new trends in online platform consumption by observing the buyer interfaces of cross-border e-commerce platforms and searching for keywords, thereby collecting information that is helpful for product selection. In addition, investigators can also conduct industry analysis on proposed products through AliExpress backend data to understand several important reference indicators during the statistical period: the proportion of side customers, browsing volume, payment amount, variable orders, and supply and demand index.

4. 通过相关消费网站了解国外消费者的消费习惯

Understand the consumption habits of foreign consumers through relevant consumer websites

例如，为了了解美国消费者的消费习惯，可以通过浏览美国消费者常用的综合性购物网站来了解当地消费者的消费潮流与趋势。美国消费者常用的综合性购物网站如下：

（1）cn. shopbop. com（Shopbop 是美国一个专门针对女性的时尚购物网站）；

（2）www. macys. com（梅西百货是美国著名的高档百货公司，在美国有很高的知名度）；

（3）www. youtube. com（YouTube 是全世界访问量最大的视频网站之一，可供网民上载、观看、分享影片或短片）；

（4）www. amazon. com（亚马逊是全球知名的大型综合性购物网站）；

（5）www. toysrus. com（Toys “R” Us 是全球领先的玩具及婴幼儿用品专门零售商，总部位于美国新泽西州的韦恩，为顾客搜罗款式繁多的特色玩具和婴儿产品）；

（6）www. ebay. com（eBay 是一个全球性的线上拍卖及购物网站，其主营业务有网上拍卖、电子商务和购物商场等）；

（7）www. bluefly. com（Bluefly 世界上最大的折扣时尚电子商务网站，各大品牌均有销

---

① “边客”通常指的是非核心目标客户群体，即那些偶然浏览或购买，但并非平台或商家的主要目标受众的消费者。——编者注

② “成变订单”通常是指成交转化订单，即由浏览、加购等行为最终转化为实际支付的订单。——编者注

售，折扣较大）。

For example, in order to understand the consumption habits of American consumers, one can browse comprehensive shopping websites commonly used by American consumers to understand the consumption trends and tendency of local consumers. The commonly used comprehensive shopping websites for American consumers are as follows:

(1) cn. shopbop. com (Shopbop is a fashion shopping website specifically targeting women in the United States);

(2) www. macys. com (Macy's Department Store is a well-known high-end department store in the United States with high popularity);

(3) www. youtube. com (YouTube is one of the most visited video websites in the world, allowing netizens to upload, watch, and share videos or short videos);

(4) www. amazon. com (Amazon is a globally renowned large comprehensive shopping website);

(5) www. toysrus. com (Toys "R" Us is a leading global retailer specializing in toys and baby products, headquartered in Wayne, New Jersey, USA, searching for a wide range of unique toys and baby products for customers);

(6) www. ebay. com (eBay is a global online auction and shopping website that specializes in online auctions, e-commerce, and shopping malls);

(7) www. bluefly. com (Bluefly is the world's largest discount fashion e-commerce website, sold by major brands with high discounts).

5. 利用网络在线调查收集客户意见

Utilize online surveys to collect customer feedback

网络在线调查法是通过网络站点发布电子问卷，利用计算机及统计分析软件进行整理并分析数据，它具有成本低、速度快、调查范围广等传统调查方法无可比拟的优势。通常是由跨境电商市场分析人员事先设计好问卷，并通过以下方式收集市场的反馈意见：一种是通过邮件将调查问卷发给一些特定的网上用户，被访问者回答完毕回复邮件即可，其优点是专业针对性强、成本低，但回收率低，而且容易引起被访问者的反感；另一种是由专业的调查公司或有选择地在调查项目相关的专业网站下进行，例如在一个生活百货超市的网站中建立一个消费者需求调查站点等，以保证专业性和较高的访问率，这种调研渠道特别适合于一般消费品和服务的网上市场调研。

The online survey method is to distribute electronic questionnaires through online sites, using computers and statistical analysis software to process and analyze data. Compared to traditional survey methods, it has unparalleled advantages, such as lower costs, faster execution, and broader coverage. Usually, cross-border e-commerce market analysts design questionnaires in advance and collect market feedback through the following methods. One is to send the survey questionnaire to specific online users by email, and the respondents can reply to the email after answering. Its advantages are high professional targeting, low cost, but low response rate, and easy to arouse the respondents' aversion. The other is conducted by professional survey companies or selectively on professional websites related to survey projects, such as establishing a consumer demand survey site on the website of a daily necessities supermarket, to ensure professionalism and high access rates. This survey channel is particularly suitable for online market research of general consumer goods and services.

（二）间接调研的途径

Indirect research approach

间接调研，是指调查与用户有关的二手资料来间接获取与调查相关的信息。其中，互联网可以帮助调研者迅速收集遍布全球的二手调研资料。跨境电商市场间接调研的途径包括以下几个方面。

The indirect research refers to the investigation of secondary data related to users to indirectly obtain information related to the investigation. Among them, the Internet can help researchers quickly collect secondary research data all over the world. The indirect research approaches for cross-border e-commerce market include the following aspects.

1. 通过网络搜索引擎了解竞争者信息

Understand competitor information through network search engines

调研者可以从有关新闻中获取竞争者的信息，利用所有的相关关键词和喜爱的搜索引擎搜索竞争者信息。寻找全球性竞争对手信息的最好方法是在全球八大导航网站中查找——Yahoo、AltaVista、InfoSeek、Excite、HotBot、WebCrawler、Lycos 和 PlanetSeareh。

Researchers can obtain information about competitors from relevant news and use all relevant keywords and favorite search engines to search for competitor information. The best way to find information about global competitors is to search on the top eight navigation websites worldwide — Yahoo, AltaVista, InfoSeek, Excite, HotBot, WebCrawler, Lycos, and PlanetSeareh.

2. 通过政府及民间组织了解客户信息及本行业国际市场信息

Understand customer information and international market information of the industry through government and civil organizations

调研者可以通过有关国家的商会、银行、驻外机构、咨询公司和各国民间贸易组织来了解客户资信、销售渠道和经营范围等。也可以通过政府相关机构及民间机构发布的信息，了解相关信息。

Researchers can learn about customer credit, sales channels, and business scope through chambers of commerce, banks, overseas agencies, consulting firms, and civil trade organizations in relevant countries. Relevant information can also be obtained through information released by government agencies and private organizations.

3. 通过第三方机构了解国外跨境电商行业发展现状及趋势信息

Understand the current development status and trends of foreign cross-border e-commerce industry through third-party organizations

调研者可以在互联网上找到各种国际第三方机构发布的行业调研报告、贸易杂志和数据库等，可以通过这些来了解行业发展的动态信息。这些服务有很多是免费的，即使是付费的，一般来讲，购买二手数据也比收集一手数据更快、更便宜。例如，可以从艾瑞咨询、eMarketer 等机构发布的数据中了解跨境电商主流国家（如美国）的市场行情及发展趋势。

Investigators can access industry research reports, trade magazines and databases published by various international third-party institutions on the Internet, using these resources to learn about the dynamic information of industry development. Many of these services are free, and even if they are paid for, generally speaking, purchasing secondary data is faster and cheaper than collecting primary data. For example, the market conditions and development trends of mainstream cross-border e-commerce countries (such as the United States) can be understood from data released by institutions such as iResearch Consulting and eMarketer.

第二节 跨境客户开发
Section 2 Cross-border Customer Development

一、跨境客户开发的线上途径
Online channels for cross-border customer development

（一）借助跨境电商平台开发客户
Utilize cross-border e-commerce platforms to develop customers

跨境电商平台为全球数以百万计的买家和供应商提供了一个公平交易的场所，但国际客户开发不是一个简单的过程。在生产技术越来越发达的今天，跨境电商平台卖家间的竞争已经变成以满足客户需要而安排开发、生产和营销的竞争。只有具备有效的客户关系管理才能更好地发现客户和服务客户，建立长期稳定的客户群。当跨境电商企业完成目标市场选择及商品选择后，接下来一项非常重要的工作就是如何在维护老客户的同时，将平台的大量潜在客户变为企业的真实客户。为此，跨境电商企业需要做好以下几项工作。

Cross-border e-commerce platforms provide a fair-trading ground for millions of buyers and suppliers worldwide, but international customer development is not a simple process. In today's increasingly advanced production technology, the competition among sellers on cross-border e-commerce platforms has become a competition that arranges development, production, and marketing to meet customer needs. Only with effective customer relationship management can we better identify and serve customers, and establish a long-term stable customer base. After cross-border e-commerce enterprises complete the selection of target markets and products, the next very important task is how to maintain old customers while turning a large number of potential customers on the platform into real customers for the enterprise. Therefore, cross-border e-commerce enterprises need to do the following work well.

1. 建立规范的客户关系管理流程，提高客户的满意度

Establish a standardized customer relationship management process to improve customers' satisfaction

企业的每个部门都要建立以客户为中心的理念，要在平台上建立一个系统、规范的客户关系管理流程，让每个客户的需求都能通过这个流程得到妥善的处理。同时，让服务于同一位客户的企业各个部门和人员协同合作，提高服务的有效度和针对性，满足客户的表面需求和潜在需求，以提高现有客户的忠诚度，同时通过获取客户的好评与“点赞”获取更多的流量，并通过“马太效应”吸引更多的新客户。

Every department within an enterprise should establish a customer-centric concept and establish a systematic and standardized customer relationship management process on the platform, so that the needs of each customer can be properly handled through this process. At the same time, collaborate with various departments and personnel of the enterprise serving the same customer to improve the effectiveness and targeting of services, meet the surface and potential needs of customers, and enhance the loyalty of existing customers. At the same time, obtain more traffic by receiving customer reviews and likes, and attract more new customers through the “Matthew Effect”.

2. 加强与客户的沟通与交流，提高客户的忠诚度

Strengthen communication and exchange with customers to improve their loyalty

跨境电商交易主体分属不同关境，双方的交流与沟通不可避免地会受到语言、地域、气候、价值观念、思维方式和风俗习惯等因素的影响。因此，良好、有效的沟通是能够增加跨境电子商务利润的强大商业驱动力，也是维护老客户与开发新客户的重要因素。为此，跨境电商卖家要使用数据挖掘和数据库分析技术，了解客户行为、客户历史和客户需要，分析客户的观念以及客户的忠诚度，根据分析的结果，按照其地区和交易习惯为其量身打造相关的沟通技巧和营销策略。

Cross-border e-commerce transaction entities belong to different customs, and communication between the two parties is inevitably influenced by factors such as languages, regions, climates, values, ways of thinking, and customs. Therefore, good and effective communication is a powerful business driver that can increase cross-border e-commerce profits, and is also an important factor in maintaining old customers and developing new ones. Therefore, cross-border e-commerce sellers need to use data mining and database analysis techniques to understand customer behavior, customer history, and customer needs, analyze customer concepts and loyalty, and tailor relevant communication skills and marketing strategies according to their region and transaction habits based on the analysis results.

3. 加强平台信息安全管理，提高客户的安全感

Strengthen platform information security management and enhance customers' security

跨境电子商务平台进行交易的双方并不见面，是通过网络进行沟通的，但网络在推动经济发展的同时也给经济安全带来了新的挑战，网络犯罪的案件也在逐渐增多。保证跨境电商平台交易双方的信息安全非常重要。因此，跨境电商企业一方面需要对现有的询价信息进行分析，判断哪些是潜在的客户，哪些是竞争对手在刺探价格；另一方面，要随时对自己的信息进行更新，保证自己信息的有效性、真实性和完整性，这样才能吸引更多的买家进行询价，进而带来潜在的客户。此外，作为第三方的跨境电商平台，通过有效的安全技术措施，保障电子商务信息的安全、真实和有效非常关键，这是赢得客户信任的前提。

The two parties conducting transactions on cross-border e-commerce platforms do not meet and communicate through the Internet. However, while the Internet promotes economic development, it also brings new challenges to economic security, and cases of cybercrime are gradually increasing. Ensuring the information security of both parties involved in cross-border e-commerce platform transactions is very important. Therefore, on the one hand cross-border e-commerce enterprises need to analyze existing enquiry information to determine which are potential customers and which competitors are probing prices. On the other hand, it is important to constantly update their information to ensure its validity, authenticity, and completeness, in order to attract more buyers to enquire and attract potential customers. In addition, as a third-party cross-border e-commerce platform, it is crucial to ensure the security, authenticity, and effectiveness of e-commerce information through effective security technology measures, which is a prerequisite for winning customer trust.

（二）借助网上商务信息发布开发客户

Utilize online business information release to develop customers

网上商务信息是指通过计算机网络传递的商务信息，包括文字、数据、表格、图形、影像、声音，以及内容能够被人或计算机察知的符号系统。在跨境电商市场调研活动中，虽然网络系统提供了许多检索方法，但全球范围内的各行各业的海量信息，常常会把企业营销人员淹没在信息海洋中。因此，跨境电商市场开发人员除了可以从前面所讲述的各种渠道获取调研信息外，还可以通过合适的渠道主动发布相关重点商务信息，在实现营销推广的同时，也可以通过观察被调查者网上点击率、征求客户意见等互动形式，收集市场对待售商品或试销商品的评价信息，从而帮助其制订进一步的营销方案。

跨境电商市场调研者发布网上商务信息的途径如下。

Online business information refers to business information transmitted through computer networks, including text, data, tables, graphics, images, sound, and symbol systems whose content can be perceived by people or computers. In cross-border e-commerce market research activities, although network systems provide many search methods, the massive amount of information from various industries worldwide often submerges enterprise marketers in the ocean of information. Therefore, cross-border e-commerce market developers can not only obtain research information from various channels mentioned earlier, but also actively release relevant key business information through appropriate channels. While achieving marketing promotion, they can also collect market evaluation information on products for sale or trial sale through interactive forms such as observing the online click-through rate of respondents and soliciting customer opinions, thereby helping them formulate further marketing plans.

The channels for cross-border e-commerce market researchers to release online business information are as follows.

1. 电子邮件群发软件

Email group-sending software

电子邮件群发软件可以在很短的时间内将商业推广信息及商业广告发送到数千万客户的电子邮箱中。它的广告宣传效果完全可以与花费很多资金的广告相媲美，而成本却低许多。目前，市场上有相当多的邮件群发软件，它们已逐渐成为企业在互联网上进行网络建设和形象宣传的平台。比较知名的有 U-MAIL 邮件营销平台，它拥有国内外众多优质 IP 发送资源，可以结合灵活智能的矩阵投递系统，自动投递邮件，用户无须自己更换 IP 和发件箱。当然，电子邮件群发软件的使用必须合法、合规。

Email group-sending software can quickly send commercial promotional information and advertisements to the email addresses of millions of customers. Its advertising effectiveness is comparable to advertising that costs a lot of money, but the cost is significantly lower. At present, there are quite a number of email group-sending softwares on the market, which have gradually become a platform for enterprises to carry out network construction and image promotion on the Internet. A well-known email marketing platform is U-MAIL, which has numerous high-quality IP sending resources both domestically and internationally. It can be combined with a flexible and intelligent matrix delivery system to automatically deliver emails, eliminating the need for users to change their IP and outboxes. Of course, the use of email group-sending software must comply with laws and regulations.

2. 企业网站

Enterprise website

企业网站相当于是一个企业的网络名片，不但可以良好地宣传企业的形象，同时还可以辅助企业的销售，最重要的是，将有价值的信息及时发布在自己的网站上，可以充分发挥网站的功能，例如新产品信息、优惠促销信息等，从而直接帮助企业实现产品的销售。因此，企业网站的作用就是展示企业形象、加强客户服务、完善网络业务，以及与潜在客户建立商业联系。

A enterprise website is like a network business card of a enterprise, which can not only promote the enterprise's image well, but also assist in its sales. Most importantly, timely releasing valuable information on one's own website can fully utilize the website's functions, such as new product information, promotional information, etc., thereby directly helping the enterprise achieve product sales. Therefore, the role of a enterprise website is to showcase the enterprise's image, enhance customer service, improve online business, and establish business connections with potential customers.

3. 第三方网站或跨境电商平台

Third-party websites or cross-border e-commerce platforms

随着网络的发展，出现了以提供网络资讯为营利手段的网站或第三方平台，这些网站（平台）由于整合了相关领域的多数企业，并为这些企业提供了相关领域的供求信息，具有一定的针对性和高效性，因而往往知名度比较高，所以，在此类网站（平台）上发布商务信息的企业也比较多，如付费的阿里巴巴平台就是一个较好的对外发布信息渠道平台。

With the development of the Internet, websites or third-party platforms have emerged that profit by providing online information. These websites (platforms) integrate most enterprises within specific industries and provide them with supply and demand information in related fields, which have a certain degree of specificity and efficiency. Therefore, they are often well-known. As a result, there are also many enterprises releasing business information on such websites (platforms). The paid Alibaba platform is a good channel for external information dissemination.

4. 社交媒体

Social media

社交媒体，是指允许人们自主编写、自由共享、互相评论及沟通的网站或技术，是人们用来分享彼此之间的观点、思想、经验及见解的工具和平台。使用社会化媒体发布商务信息是信息时代衍生的新型网络营销渠道。目前主要包括微博、论坛、LinkedIn 营销和 Facebook 营销等。

Social media refer to websites or technologies that allow people to independently write, freely share, comment on, and communicate with each other. It is a tool and platform used by people to share their views, ideas, experiences, and insights with each other. The use of social media to release business information is a new type of online marketing channel derived from the information age. At present, it mainly includes Weibo, forum, LinkedIn marketing, and Facebook marketing.

二、跨境客户开发的线下途径

Offline approaches for cross-border customer development

（一）他人介绍

Introduction by others

企业通过以下渠道获取客户：我国驻外使领馆的商务参赞、代办处或外国驻华使领馆的商务参赞、代办处，国内外各种商会、银行，以及已有业务往来的合作企业推介。

The enterprise acquires customers through the commercial counselors and representative offices of Chinese embassies/consulates abroad, foreign embassies/consulates in China, various domestic and foreign chambers of commerce, banks, and referrals from partner enterprises with business relationships.

（二）参加展会

Participate in exhibitions

1. 获取展会相关信息

Obtain exhibitions related information

企业可以通过在国内外参加或举办各种交易会、展览会的方式找到客户。

Enterprises can find customers through participating in or holding various trade fairs and exhibitions both domestically and internationally.

2. 展会即时沟通与范例

Exhibition instant communication and examples

范例1

Mr. White meets Mr. Zhang at the trade fair. (A: Mr. White; B: Mr. Zhang)

A: Good morning. My name is Alan White. Here's my card.

B: Thank you. My name is Zhang, and here's my card.

A: Nice to meet you, Mr. Zhang.

B: Nice to meet you, too. Would you like something to drink, coffee or tea?

A: A cup of tea, please. I like Chinese green tea.

B: This is Longjing tea, the famous green tea produced in Hangzhou.

A: Oh, I've heard about it. Thank you.

B: Is this your first visit to the fair?

A: That's right. And also my first visit to China. The purpose of my visit to the fair is to establish business relations with some Chinese companies in our business line.

B: I'm so delighted to have made your acquaintance, Mr. White. May I know the main products you trade in?

A: We mainly deal in glassware. We've been in this line for almost twenty years. In the past we used to import products from some European countries. Now I wish to buy from China. I heard your company is a top exporter that handles glassware and do business with all countries, big or small, on equal terms.

B: It's very nice of you to say so. In fact, it is our desire to trade with all countries in the world, big or small.

A: You said it.

B: And our foreign trade policy is to do business with merchants of all countries on the basis of equality and mutual benefit.

A: I quite believe so. I'm sure when trading with you, I can expect a fair play.

B: That's just what I was going to say. We always honor contracts and keep our promises.

A: I think I can rely on your cooperation in future dealings, can't I?

B: Absolutely. We'll do our best to cooperate with you.

范例2

A dialogue between a sales representative of a golf manufacturing company, Golf Pro, and a potential customer at an international golf fair. (A: Mr. Hubert; B: Mr. Usuki)

A: Good morning.

B: Good morning.

A: Can I help you?

B: Er, thank you, but I'm just looking at the moment.

A: Yes, please do. Have you come a cross our products before?

B: I think I have heard of them.

A: We're relatively new but Golf Pro is acquiring a reputation very quickly. We have become one of the world leaders in metal woods.

B: Really? Well, actually I'm quite interested in metal woods. Could you tell me what the prices are for this range?

A: Of course. The prices start at £ 90, and they go up to £ 149.

B: Did you say £ 149?

A: That's right. I wonder if you would be interested in our new range of ladies' clubs as well.

B: Well, possibly. Could you give me the prices, please?

A: Yes. The range is called Golf Pro Lady and a full set of nine irons comes to £ 465. A set of the three woods is £ 240 and putters are £ 46 each.

B: Sorry, that was £ 46 each, wasn't it?

A: Yes, 46 each.

B: Right, thank you. Could you give me some information about your top of the range clubs as well?

A: Of course. That's our Golf Pro X. This is really state-of-the-art when it comes to professional clubs. A set of nine irons comes to £ 835. Very reasonable, I think you'll agree.

B: Mmm, not bad.

A: Would you like to try one out in the practice area?

B: Er, no, thank you. I'm afraid I don't have time at the moment. But I would like to read some more about your products.

A: Of course. Here are some of our latest brochures with up-to-date information on all the ranges, and also my card.

B: Thank you.

A: Please contact me, if you need any more information.

第三节 跨境资信调查
Section 3 Cross-border Credit Investigation

一、概述
Overview

可通过以下方式对准备建立业务联系的公司进行资信调查：

（1）对方提供的证明；

（2）银行验证；

（3）行业协会资源；

（4）咨询机构报告；

（5）自主调研分析。

Credit investigations can be conducted on companies preparing to establish business contacts through the following methods:

(1) proof provided by the other party;

(2) bank verification;

(3) industry association resources;

(4) consulting agency reports;

(5) independent search and analysis.

判断依据主要有以下几个方面：

（1）企业概况。包括公司名称、地址、电话、传真、邮编、企业性质、业务范围、员工总数。应弄清厂商企业的中英文名称、详细地址，防止出现差错。

（2）历史背景。包括成立日期、注册机关、注册资金及号码、历史沿革、股东/股份、上级主管部门。资信情况包括企业的资金和信用两个方面。资金是指企业的注册资金、财产以及资产负债情况等；信用是指企业的经营作风、履约信誉等。

（3）管理人员。包括企业最高权力机构、法定代表人、董事长、总经理、副总经理等的姓名、教育背景、工作经历、组织机构。

（4）财务状况。包括资产负债表、损益表、财务比率分析。

（5）银行往来。包括企业开户银行及账号。按规定，企业资金往来账户只能有一个开户行和一个账号，如果是进出口企业，则还另有一个外币账户和账号。

（6）经营范围。主要是指企业生产或经营的商品、经营的性质，是代理商、生产商，还是零售批发商等。

（7）经营能力。包括每年的营业额、销售渠道、经营方式以及在当地和国际市场上的贸易关系等。

The main criteria for judgment are as follows:

(1) Overview of the enterprise. It includes company name, address, phone number, fax number, postal code, nature of the enterprise, scope of business, and total number of employees. It is necessary to clarify the Chinese and English names and detailed addresses of manufacturers and enterprises to prevent errors.

(2) Historical background. It includes establishment date, registration authority, registered capital and number, historical evolution, shareholders/shares, and superior supervisory department. The credit situation includes two aspects: the company's funds and credit. Funds refer to the registered capital, assets, and liabilities of an enterprise. Credit refers to the business style, performance reputation, etc. of an enterprise.

(3) Management personnel. It includes the names, educational background, work experience, and organizational structure of the highest authority, legal representative, chairman, general

manager, deputy general manager, etc. of the enterprise.

(4) Financial condition. It includes balance sheet, income statement, and financial ratio analysis.

(5) Bank transactions. It includes the bank and account number of the enterprise's account opening. According to regulations, a company's fund transaction account can only have one opening bank and one account. If it is an import and export enterprise, there is also a foreign currency account and one account.

(6) Business scope. It mainly refers to the nature of the goods and operations produced or operated by the enterprise, whether it is an agent, manufacturer, or retail wholesaler.

(7) Business capability. It includes annual revenue, sales channels, operating methods, and trade relations in local and international markets.

二、跨境资信调查信文
Cross-border credit investigation letter

(一) 资信调查信文的主要内容
The main content of the credit investigation letter

如果是询问客户情况，则需表达以下内容：

(1) 事由；

(2) 表明咨询的意愿；

(3) 表示感谢并向对方保证保密。

If enquiring about the customer's situation, the following should be expressed:

(1) purpose of the enquiry;

(2) willingness to provide consultation;

(3) appreciation with confidentiality assurance.

如果是回复资信调查，则应包含以下内容：

(1) 提供咨询并给出建议；

(2) 强调信息的保密性。

If it is a response to a credit investigation, it should include the following content:

(1) providing consultation and suggestions;

(2) emphasizing the confidentiality of information.

(二) 信文与范例
Letters and examples

范例1

(Writing letters of Credit Enquiry of a new customer)

Dear Sirs,

We have received an order for USD 56,500 worth of goods from Atlantic Electronic Co. Ltd., U. S. A. They have given us your bank as a reference. We wish to know if they are good for this amount and in every way trustworthy and reliable. We shall be most grateful for any information you give us.

We should, of course, treat as strictly confidential any advice you give us and be only too pleased to perform a similar service for you should the opportunity ever arise. We enclose a stamped and addressed envelope for your reply.

Yours faithfully,

×××

范例2

(Favorable reply from a firm)

Dear Sirs,

We are pleased to state that the company you referred to in your letter of November 12, 2007 is a small but well-known company and has enjoyed high reputation that has been in this line in our city for nearly forty years.

We have been doing business with the company for many years and have found that they are very reliable and their financial status is sound. Although they have not taken advantage of our cash discounts as a rule, they have always paid their accounts promptly on the net dates. The credit we often allow has been well above the amount you mention in your letter.

Though the information is given to the best of our knowledge, we hope it will be helpful and trust you will treat it as confidential.

Yours faithfully,

×××

范例3

(Unfavorable reply)

Dear Sirs,

We have completed our investigations about the company mentioned in your letter of November 12 and regret that we must advise you to regard their request for credit with caution.

About two years ago the company experienced a serious difficulty in finance and an action was brought against it by one of its suppliers for recovery of sums due, though payment was later recovered in full.

Our investigations reveal nothing but to suggest that the company's difficulty was due to bad management, particularly overtrading. Consequently, most of the company's suppliers either give only very short credit for limited sums or make deliveries on a cash basis.

We trust that the information we give is of course supplied in the strictest confidence and we won't hold any responsibility on our part.

Yours faithfully,

×××

第四节 跨境业务联系
Section 4 Cross-border Business Contact

一、概述
Overview

可以说，没有客户，就没有业务，与潜在客户建立业务关系不仅对于新成立的公司很重要，对于那些想要扩大业务范围、增加营业额的公司来说，同样很重要。

It can be said that without customers, there is no business. Establishing business relationships with potential customers is not only important for newly established companies, but also for those who want to expand their business scope and increase revenue.

如果一家新公司，想要在国外打开市场，买入或者卖出产品，那么，该公司首先必须做的就是要明白与谁做业务，通常，这类信息可以通过以下渠道获得：

（1）通过写信交流；

（2）参加出口商品交易会；

（3）出席国内外举办的展览会；

（4）互派贸易代表团。

If a new company, wants to open up markets abroad, buy or sell products, then the first thing it must do is understand who it do business with. Usually, this type of information can be obtained through the following channels:

(1) communicate through writing letters;

(2) participate in export commodity trade fairs;

(3) attend exhibitions held domestically and internationally;

(4) exchange trade delegations.

上述所有途径中，写信使用得最为广泛。通过写信，可以从银行、杂志、报纸电视广告、业务关系介绍、市场调查、商务参展、商会、商务参展、中间人、自我介绍等来获取所需要的信息。

Among all the above channels, letter writing is the most widely used. By writing a letter, one can obtain all the necessary information from banks, magazines, newspapers and television advertisements, business relationship introductions, market research, business exhibitions, chambers of commerce, business exhibitions, intermediaries, self-introductions, and so on.

从上述任何渠道获得想要得到的公司名称和地址之后，就开始着手写信与之联系。这类信是第一次寄出去的信，可称为“初次询盘”。通常这类信函最初告诉阅信人他的基本信息，主要包括下列内容：

（1）信息来源；

（2）意向；

（3）经营范围和子公司、分公司，如有的话；

（4）公司的财务和诚信情况。

After obtaining the desired company name and address from any of the above channels, start writing letters to contact them. This type of letter is the first time it has been sent out, also known as a “first enquiry”. Usually, this type of letter initially tells the reader his basic information, which mainly includes the following content:

(1) information sources;

(2) intention;

(3) business scope and subsidiaries, branches, if any;

(4) the financial and credit situation of the company.

如果想要进口买入，可以要求看样品、价格单等。写信人可以简明扼要地说明想要购买何物。

If the writer want to import and buy, he can request to see samples, price lists, etc. The writer can succinctly explain what he want to buy.

收到这类信函后要立即回信，不能延误，并写得有礼貌，以便给对方留下一个良好的印象。这就是外贸业务信函最重要的功能。

After receiving such letters, the recipient should reply immediately without delay and write politely to leave a good impression on the other party. This is the most important function of foreign trade business letters.

对于外贸公司来说业务往来非常重要，因此，交易商不仅要尽力巩固与已有客户的业务关系，也要不断寻求新的客户。

For foreign trade companies, business dealings are very important. Therefore, traders should not only try their best to consolidate their business relationships with existing customers, but also constantly seek new customers.

二、信文与范例

Letters and examples

范例1

(Wishing to establish relations)

Dear Mr. J B Lewis,

We have got to know your name and address from the advertisement in “China Foreign Trade Centre”. As an import and export company specializing in Annatto Furniture, we are keen to expand our foreign trade. As yet, we have no business contracts in Iran, and would be pleased to consider any business proposals you may have. Enclosed please find our latest illustrated catalogue, price list and terms and conditions of sales. We would be pleased to deal with any specific enquiries you may have concerning any of our products.

Should you require any further details about our company, please do not hesitate to contact us. We look forward to hearing from you in the near future.

Yours sincerely,

×××

范例2

(Importer writes to exporter)

Dear Sirs,

We were much impressed by the captioned goods displayed at the Chinese Economic and Trade Exhibition held in Saudi Arabia last July, and we have been told that you export these products.

As one of our potential customers intends to purchase a number of Computer Parts, we would be therefore grateful if you could send us a proforma invoice for computer motherboards, memory sticks, keyboards and mice (400 pieces each) at your rock-bottom price, including our commission. On replying, please state the earliest possible date of delivery.

We look forward to hearing from you as soon as possible.

Yours sincerely,

×××

范例3

(Exporter writes to importer)

Dear Sirs,

We have come to know the name of your firm from the advertisement in "China Foreign Trade Centre" and have the pleasure of addressing this letter to you in the hope of establishing business relations with you.

We specialize in the export of Chinese light industrial products that have enjoyed great popularity in the world markets. Enclosed you will find a copy of our catalogue for your reference and hope that you would contact us if any items were of interest to you.

Yours faithfully,

×××

第五节 Section 5 重点短语与句型 Key Phrases and Sentence Patterns

一、常用单词与短语
Common words and phrases

1. cross-border e-commerce 跨境电子商务
2. cross-border market research 跨境市场调研
3. international market environment 国际市场环境
4. supply and demand of goods in foreign markets 国外市场商品供需
5. digital trade 数字贸易
6. digital products 数字产品
7. digital services 数字化服务
8. Global Public Digital Trade Platform 全球公共数字贸易平台
9. the Belt and Road Initiative “一带一路”倡议
10. Silk Road Economic Belt 丝绸之路经济带
11. Digital Silk Road 数字丝绸之路
12. connectivity over land, maritime, air and cyberspace “陆海天网”四位一体
13. production place 产地
14. item No. 产品编号
15. products guide 产品指南
16. product categories 产品类别
17. product introduction 产品介绍
18. guide for paving & sticking of products 产品铺贴指导
19. international marketing situation 国际市场营销情况
20. channel of goods distribution 商品销售渠道
21. market competitiveness analysis 市场竞争力分析
22. chairman/president/director 董事长,总裁
23. managing director/general manager 总经理
24. executive vice president 执行副总裁
25. chief executive officer(CEO) 首席执行官
26. chemical 化工
27. textiles 纺织品
28. cereals, oil & foodstuffs 粮油食品
29. native produce & animal by-products 土特产
30. instrument 仪器
31. light industrial products 轻工业产品

32. non-ferrous metal　有色金属
33. metals & minerals　五金矿产
34. arts & crafts　工艺品
35. machinery　机械
36. medicines & health products　医药保健品
37. electronic products　电子产品
38. complete-plant　成套设备
39. corporation　[美]公司，有限责任公司；大中型贸易公司
40. incorporated　[美]股份有限公司，可写作 Inc.
41. firm　商号(泛指)
42. company　公司,大多用作专有名词的一部分或与划分公司类别的词一起用
43. to establish/enter into/set up business relationship　建立业务关系
44. to continue business relationship　继续业务关系
45. to maintain business relationship　保持业务关系
46. to improve business relationship　改善业务关系
47. to promote business relationship　促进业务关系
48. to speed up business relationship　加快业务关系的发展
49. to enlarge/widen/business relationship　扩大业务关系
50. to restore/resume/business relationship　恢复业务关系
51. to interrupt business relationship　中断业务关系
52. to cement business relationship　巩固业务关系
53. Commercial Counselor's Office　商务参赞处
54. chambers of commerce both at home and abroad　国内外商会
55. open up　开发
56. build up　建立
57. financial position　财务状况
58. without any delay　赶快，立刻，毫不迟延
59. lay the foundations　打地基
60. owe one's name and address to　承蒙……告知贵公司的名称和地址
61. be in the market for　想要购买
62. avail oneself of　利用
63. approach　接洽，与……接洽
64. leading　最主要的
65. enjoy excellent reputation　享有盛誉
66. mutual benefits　互利互惠
67. by joint efforts　共同努力
68. favorable　有利的，赞成的，有帮助的
69. enter into business relations with　与……建立贸易联系

70. terms of payment　支付方式，付款条件
71. time of delivery　装船期，交货期
72. appreciate　感谢，感激；理解，体会
73. contact　与……联系，与……接触；联系，交往
74. place an order　订货
75. business directory　企业名录
76. catalogue　目录
77. latest catalogue　最新目录
78. standing　资信情况，信誉；固定的，永久的
79. standing cost　长期成本，固定成本
80. standing orders　长期订单
81. standing director　常务董事
82. come under the scope of our trade activities　属于经营范围
83. be in a position to　能够(指处于能够做某事的地位)
84. joint venture　合资企业；联合经营
85. specializing in　专门从事
86. be of interest to　对……是有意义的；对……有趣
87. upon receipt of　一收到……即
88. product lines　生产线；产品线；产品目录
89. a general idea of…　……的大意；……的梗概
90. available for…　适用，宜于；有效；可用于……的；对……有效的
91. be now available from stock　现在有存货
92. take the matter further　进一步探讨这个问题

二、常用句型
Common sentence patterns

1. Here is my business/name card. These are the samples of our newly developed products. Please have a look.

这是我的名片，这些是我们新研发的产品，请看一下。

2. If you want to buy a large quantity, we will give you a discount.

如果您大量购买，我们将给您一些折扣。

3. We have come to this show in order to let more people know about our new products as well as our country.

为了让更多的人了解我们的新产品和我们的国家，我们来参加这个展会。

4. After seeing the demonstration, you'll know how to use our product.

看完产品演示之后，您就知道该怎样使用我们的产品了。

5. You can find our telephone number and email address in the brochure I give you or from the business directory. We hope we'll keep in touch.

您可从我给您的小册子上或企业名目上找到我们的电话和电子邮箱地址。希望我们能保持联络。

6. Where can I get some useful information about trade fairs?

我从哪里能获得商展的有用信息呢?

7. What's the capacity of your exhibition hall?

你们展厅的容量如何?

8. In order to let more foreign friends know about our products and to enlarge our market as well, we'd like to take part in some international trade shows.

为了让更多的外国朋友了解我们的产品，同时扩大我们产品的销路，我们很想参加一些国际商展。

9. You can get the main exhibitions schedule for this year and next year from the chamber of commerce.

您可以通过商会的小册子了解今年和明年的主要商展计划。

10. Please accept our thanks for the trouble you have taken.

有劳贵方，不胜感激。

11. We are obliged to thank you for your kind attention in this matter.

不胜感激贵方对此事的关照。

12. We tender you our sincere thanks for your generous treatment of us in this affair.

对贵方在此事中的慷慨之举，深表感激。

13. Allow us to thank you for the kindness extended to us.

对贵方的盛情，不胜感激。

14. We thank you for the special care you have given to the matter.

贵方对此悉心关照，不胜感激。

15. We should be grateful for your trial order.

如承试订货，则不胜感激。

16. We should be grateful for your furnishing us details of your requirements.

如承赐示具体要求，则不胜感激。

17. It will be greatly appreciated if you will kindly send us your samples.

如承惠予样品，则不胜感激。

18. We shall appreciate it very much if you will give our bid your favorable consideration.

如承优惠考虑报价，则不胜感激。

19. We are greatly obliged for your bulk order just received.

收到贵方大宗订货，不胜感激。

20. We assure you of our best services at all times.

我方保证随时向贵方提供最佳服务。

21. If there is anything we can do to help you, we shall be more than pleased to do so.

贵公司若有所需求，我公司定尽力效劳。

22. It would give us a great pleasure to render you a similar service should an opportunity occur.

我方如有机会同样效劳贵方，将深感荣幸。

23. We spare no efforts in endeavoring to be of service to you.

我方将不遗余力为贵方效劳。

24. We shall be very glad to handle for you at very low commission charges.

我方将很高兴与贵方合作，收费低廉。

25. We have always been able to supply these firms with their monthly requirements without interruption.

我方始终能供应这些公司每月所需量，不会间断。

26. We take this opportunity to re-emphasize that we shall, at all times, do everything possible to give you whatever information you desire.

我们借此机会再次强调，定会尽力随时提供贵方所需的信息。

27. We are always in a position to quote you the most advantageous prices for higher quality merchandise.

我们始终能向贵方提供品质最佳的产品，报价最为优惠。

28. It places our dealers in a highly competitive position and also enable them to enjoy a maximum profit.

这样可以使我方经营者具有很强的竞争力，还可获得最大的利润。

29. We solicit a continuance of your confidence and support.

恳请贵方继续给予信任，大力支持。

30. They mainly trade with Japanese firms.

他们主要和日本商行进行贸易活动。

31. For the past five years, we have done a lot of trade with your country.

在过去的五年中，我们与贵国进行了大量的贸易活动。

32. Our trade is conducted on the basis of equality.

我们是在平等的基础上进行贸易活动的。

33. There has been a slowdown in the wool trade with you.

和你们的羊毛贸易已有所减少。

34. Our foreign trade is continuously expanding.

我们的对外贸易不断发展。

35. Trade in leather has gone up (down) 3%.

皮革贸易上升（下降）了3%。

36. Trade in general is improving.

贸易情况正在好转。

37. Our company mainly trades in arts and crafts.

我们公司主要经营手工艺品。

38. They are well-known in trade circles.

他们在贸易界很有名望。

39. We trade with people in all countries on the basis of equality and mutual benefit.

我们在平等互利的基础上和各国人民进行贸易活动。

40. To respect the local custom of the buying country is one important aspect of China foreign policy.

尊重买方国家的风俗习惯是我国贸易政策的一个重要方面。

41. Our purpose is to explore the possibilities of developing trade with you.

我们的目的是和你们探讨一下发展贸易的可能性。

42. We want to develop direct contact with European buyers for ourselves.

我们想同欧洲买主建立起直接的联系。

43. We see that your firm specializes in Light Industrial Goods, and we are willing to establish business relationship with you.

得知贵公司专门经营轻工业产品，我们愿意与贵公司建立业务关系。

44. We are one of the largest importers of Electric Goods in this city, and we wish to establish business relationship with you.

我们是此地最大的电器产品进口商之一，愿意与你们建立业务关系。

45. We are willing to enter into business relationship with your company on the basis of equality and mutual benefit.

我们愿在平等互利的基础上与贵公司建立业务关系。

46. Our two countries have had trade relations for ten years.

我们两国之间已经有了 10 年的贸易关系。

47. We've never had any difficulties with our Chinese partners, and we'd like to make as many new contacts as we can.

和中国合作方共事从来没遇到过什么困难，希望今后我们之间尽可能多地建立新的关系。

48. We have made a very good start in our business with Japan.

我们和日本在业务上有了良好的开端。

49. Our company is thinking of expanding its trade relationship with China.

我公司想扩大与中国的贸易关系。

50. As is known, we set great store by the trade relationship with the third world countries

众所周知，我们十分重视同第三世界国家的贸易关系。

51. We look forward to reactivating our business relationship.

我们盼望我们的业务关系重新活跃起来。

52. We shall welcome a chance to renew our friendly relationship.

很高兴能有机会来恢复我们的友好关系。

53. We'll try our best to widen our business relationship with you.

我们将尽力扩大同你们的业务关系。

54. We're writing you in order to establish business relationship.

我们写此信是为了与贵方建立业务关系。

55. The arrangement will contribute to cement our pleasant relationship.

此项安排将有助于巩固我们的良好关系。

56. We're willing to restore our business relationship.

我们希望能恢复业务关系。

57. It will be advantageous if steps are taken to resume our business relationship on the basis of mutual benefit.

如果我们采取措施在互利的基础上恢复业务关系，那么对我们都是有利的。

58. The depressed market results in he stagnation of trade.

市场萧条导致贸易停滞。

59. We have been doing quite well in our business, and we are willing to open an account with you.

我们的生意一直做得不错，希望能与你们建立账户往来关系。

60. When could you introduce me to your sister company?

什么时候能将我们介绍给你们的兄弟公司？

61. Would you please introduce us to some relatively reliable exporters of Chinese handicrafts?

请向我们推荐一些比较可靠的中国手工艺品出口商，可以吗？

62. If you are interested in dealing with us in other products of our company, please inform us of your requirements as well as your banker's name and address.

如果你们有意经营我公司的其他产品，请告知你方要求及往来银行的名称和地址。

63. Because of the rapid development of our business in Asia, we think it's necessary to open a branch at the following address.

鉴于我们在亚洲地区业务的迅速发展，有必要在下列地点设立分公司。

64. We've often expressed our interest in investing in China.

我们一直对在中国投资很感兴趣。

65. Our abundant resources and stable policy provide foreigners with the advantages they invest here.

我们丰富的资源和稳定的政策为外商投资提供了有利条件。

66. Thank you for your manner of business cooperation.

我们对你们的合作态度非常满意。

67. We have been working on expanding our scope of cooperation with China.

我们一直努力设法扩大与中国的合作范围。

68. We believe in long-term cooperation with China because we view the future as bright.

我们相信与中国长期合作的前途是光明的。

69. We own your name to the First Commercial Bank at your end, through whom we understand that you are well experienced in the export of engineering equipment with services.

经贵地第一商业银行介绍，得知贵公司在经营工程设备的出口业务及售后服务等方面有丰富的经验。

70. We avail ourselves of this opportunity to write to you and see if we can establish business relations with you.

我们利用此次机会写信给贵方，看看是否能够与贵方建立业务关系。

71. We are favorable to your terms and conditions of this transaction.
我们同意你方的交易条款与条件。

72. We are writing with a desire to enter into direct business relations with you.
为了与贵公司建立业务关系，特致函联系。

73. For further details, please contact our local office.
详情请向我们当地的分支机构探询。

74. We have been in contact with that firm for nearly two years.
我们与那家公司有近两年的交往。

75. We are permitted to mention the Bank of America, Washington, as a reference.
我们已征得华盛顿的美国银行同意，把它作为我们的咨询银行。

76. Quotations and samples will be sent upon receipt of your specific enquiries.
一经收到贵公司的具体询价，我们将送上样品及其报价。

课后练习

Ⅰ. 选词填空。

Fill in the blanks with the appropriate words.

(indicate; captioned; prompt; packed; current; assure; refer; conclude; enable; supply)

1. Please let us know if you can supply us with 200 cases of Luncheon Meat for ____________ shipment.

2. We have sent an enquiry to your Shanghai Branch for the ____________ of 10 metric tons of Frozen Rabbit Meat.

3. We are interested in the ____________ goods, and shall be obliged if you send us quotations on CIF Liverpool basis, including 3% commission for us.

4. When airmailing the samples, please ____________ the reference number of this letter on the package.

5. We require the goods to be ____________ in gunny bags of about 50 kilos net each.

6. If the following items are available in your ____________ stock, please quote your lowest price with full details of specifications and origin.

7. We wish to ____________ to our Quotation Sheet No. 234 dated March 14 for Walnut meat.

8. Your early reply will ____________ us to arrange supply from stock.

9. We hope to ____________ the business to our mutual benefit.

10. We ____________ you of our readiness to serve you in this end all future business.

Ⅱ. 将下列句子翻译为中文。

Translate the following sentences into Chinese.

1. We look forward to your favorable and prompt reply.

2. We are state-owned corporation specializing in the export of table-cloth.

3. We are convinced that with joint efforts business between us will be developed to our mutual benefit.

4. It will be greatly appreciated if you will give us your cooperation.

5. As requested, we are airmailing to you, under separate cover, a sample each of Art. No. 1254 and 1261 for your reference.

6. We can assure you that all your orders will receive our immediate attention.

7. This type of letter is an outgoing letter and may be called a "First Enquiry".

8. We are the largest food trading company in Japan, and have offices or representatives in all major cities and towns in Japan.

9. Your letter of November addressed to our sister corporation in Shanghai has been transferred to us for attention.

10. As the items falls within the scope of our business activities, we shall be pleased to enter into direct business relations with you.

Ⅲ. 将下列句子翻译为英文。

Translate the following sentences into English.

1. 我们向你们报最优惠价，按此价我们已与其他客户做了大批生意。

2. 这是我的名片以及我们公司的产品价格表，供您参考。不知是否有您感兴趣的商品？

3. 我们一直在提高产品的设计水平，以满足世界市场的要求。

4. 我认为它会在贵国市场上畅销。

5. 感谢贵方的询价，但是很抱歉，我们已经是最低报价了。

Ⅳ. 按照以下内容写一封跨境电商信文。

Write a letter with the following contents.

通过杭州数字贸易博览会的会面，得知贵公司专营太阳能电池业务，并正在尽力发展这种商品的跨境电子商务与贸易活动。考虑到当地清洁能源消费越来越受欢迎，我们有兴趣引进中国制造的太阳能电池，现希望与贵公司建立业务关系。

第三章 交易磋商
Chapter 3 Transaction Negotiation

交易磋商是国际贸易的重要环节之一，能否顺利签订商品的国际交易合同，主要取决于交易双方对交易条件磋商的结果。交易磋商可以是口头的（面谈或电话），也可以是书面的（传真或信函）。交易磋商的过程可分成询盘、报盘、还盘和接受四个环节，其中报盘和接受是必不可少的，是达成交易所必需的法律步骤。

学习目标

1. 理解交易磋商的基本概念、流程和重要性。
2. 熟悉交易磋商的各个环节。
3. 掌握询盘、报盘、还盘和接受的函电写作技巧。
4. 培养运用所学知识进行交易磋商的实际操作能力。

思政目标

1. 学习交易磋商环节，培养沟通与协商能力。
2. 增强法律意识，确保合法合规。
3. 培养诚信交易观念，树立诚信意识。

第一节 询盘
Section 1 Enquiry

一、询盘的含义
The meaning of enquiry

询盘，是指准备购买或出售某种商品的人向潜在的供货人或买主探询该商品的成交条件或交易的可能性的业务行为，它不具有法律上的约束力。

Enquiry, refers to the business behavior of a person preparing to purchase or sell a certain commodity to explore the transaction conditions or possibilities of the commodity with potential suppliers or buyers. It does not have legally binding force.

询盘的内容可涉及价格、规格、品质、数量、包装、装运以及索取样品等，而多数只是询问价格。

The content of an enquiry may involve price, specifications, quality, quantity, packaging, shipping, and requesting samples, but most of them only enquire about the price.

询盘不是每笔交易必经的程序，如交易双方彼此都了解情况，不需要向对方探询成交条件或交易的可能性，则不必使用询盘，可直接向对方报盘。

Enquiry is not a necessary procedure for every transaction. If both parties understand each other's situation and do not need to enquire about the transaction conditions or possibilities, there is no need to use enquiry. One can directly send an offer to the other party.

在实际业务中，询盘只是探询买或卖的可能性，所以不具备法律上的约束力，询盘的一方对能否达成协议不负有任何责任。由于询盘不具有法律效力，所以可作为与对方的试探性接触，询盘人可以同时向若干交易对象发出询盘。但合同订立后，询盘的内容就会成为磋商文件中不可分割的部分，若发生争议，也可作为处理争议的依据。

In practical business, enquiries only explore the possibility of buying or selling, so they do not have legally binding force. The party making the enquiry is not responsible for whether an agreement can be reached. As enquiries do not have legal effect, they can be used as exploratory contacts with the other party, and the enquirer can simultaneously send enquiries to several trading partners. But after the contract is signed, the content of the enquiry becomes an integral part of the negotiation document, and in the event of a dispute, it can also serve as a basis for resolving the dispute.

二、询盘的内容
The content of enquiry

询盘可采用口头或书面形式，包括一般询盘和具体询盘。

Enquiries can be made in oral or written form, including general enquiries and specific enquiries.

（一）一般询盘
General enquiry

一般询盘主要包括商品的一般信息：

（1）目录；

（2）价目表或报价单；

（3）样品；

（4）图片。

A general enquiry mainly includes general information about the product:

(1) a catalogue;

(2) a price list or quotation sheets;

(3) samples;

(4) illustrated photo prints.

（二）具体询盘
Specific enquiry

具体询盘主要包括具体交易信息：

（1）商品名称；

（2）规格；

（3）数量；

(4) 单价;
(5) 装船期;
(6) 付款方式。

A specific enquiry mainly includes specific transaction information:
(1) name of the product;
(2) specifications;
(3) quantity;
(4) unit price;
(5) time of shipment;
(6) terms of payment.

完整的询盘函一般包含:
(1) 获取该公司名称及地址的方式或途径;
(2) 对本公司进行介绍以便对方了解业务;
(3) 说明去信目的及期望;
(4) 详细询问各项交易条款，如价格、装运期、付款方式等;
(5) 表明良好愿望，期待早日收到回复。

A complete enquiry letter generally includes:
(1) ways or means to obtain the company's name and address;
(2) an introduction of your company to help the other party understand your business;
(3) an explanation of the letter's purpose and expectations;
(4) detailed questions about various transaction terms, such as price, shipping period, payment method, etc;
(5) expressing good wishes and looking forward to receiving a response soon.

三、信文与范例
Letters and examples

范例1

Dear sirs,

We are pleased to tell you that we are interested in hand-made gloves in a variety of genuine leather. Recently there is a growing demand here for gloves of high quality at our end. Although sales are not particularly high, good price can be obtained.

We wish you would send us a copy of your illustrated catalogue of the gloves we wish to buy, together with detail of your price and terms of payment. We should find it most helpful if you could also send us samples of the various leather, of which the gloves are made.

Yours faithfully,

×××

范例2

Dear sirs,

We learned from our common business partner JIAFU Ltd. that your company is one of the major exporters of cashmere products in Australia.

We are a leading dealer in high-quality textiles in China and are very much interested in importing your goods especially men's cashmere sweater.

We would appreciate your sending us catalogues, sample books or even samples if possible. Please give us detailed information on CIF① Dalian Prices, terms of payment and discount you would allow on purchases of quantities of no less than 10,000 pieces.

We hope this will be a good start for a long and profitable business relation.

Yours faithfully,

×××

第二节 报盘
Section 2 Offer

一、报盘的含义和内容
The meaning and content of offer

报盘（又称发盘），在法律上又称“要约”，是指买方或卖方向对方提出的各项交易条件。报盘通常是一方收到对方的询盘之后所提出的，但也可不经过对方询盘而主动向对方提出。报盘有实盘和虚盘之分。实盘是报盘人在规定的期限内对所提条件的肯定表示，报盘人在有效期内不得随意改变和撤回报盘内容，报盘一经买方接受买卖立即敲定，双方就有了具有法律约束力的合同关系。虚盘是报盘人所作的非承诺性表示，附有保留条件，如“以我方最后确认为准”等。

An offer, also known as a "tender offer" in legal terms, refers to various transaction conditions proposed by the buyer or seller to the other party. An offer is usually made by one party after receiving an enquiry from the other party, but it can also be made proactively to the other party without going through the other party's enquiry. There are two types of offers: firm offers and non-firm offers. The firm offer is the affirmative expression of the conditions proposed by the offeror within the prescribed period. The offeror shall not arbitrarily change or withdraw the content of the offer within the validity period. Once the offer is accepted by the buyer, the sale is immediately finalized, and both parties have a legally binding contractual relationship. The non-firm offer is a non-commitment

① CIF，即 cost, insurance and freight 到岸价（成本加运费、保险费价）。——编者注

made by the offeror, with reservation conditions such as "subject to our final confirmation".

完整的报盘应包括以下内容：

(1) 对询价表示感谢；

(2) 提供所要求的所有信息，如价格、折扣及付款条件等细节；

(3) 对交货期或装运期的承诺；

(4) 如为实盘，应注明有效期；

(5) 希望对方接受报价订购货物。

A complete offer should include the following content:

(1) express gratitude for the enquiry;

(2) provide all required information, such as prices, discounts, and payment terms details;

(3) commit to the delivery or shipment time;

(4) indicate the validity period if it is a firm offer;

(5) hope the other party accepts the quotation for ordering goods.

二、信文与范例

Letters and examples

范例1

Dear Mr. Han,

Thank you for your letter of May 5. We are glad to learn of the enquiries you have had from your customers for our raincoats. Our "D. D." range is particularly suitable for warm climates, and during the past years we have supplied this range to dealers in several tropical countries, from many of whom we have already had repeated orders. This range is popular not only because it is lightweight, but also because the material used has been specially treated to prevent excessive condensation on the inside surface.

For the quantities you mention we are pleased to quote as follows:

Payment: By irrevocable L/C at sight.

Shipment: Goods will be shipped within three or four weeks after receipt of the L/C.

This offer is subject to our final confirmation. We believe you may be interested in our other products and enclose some brochures for your reference.

We are awaiting your early orders.

Yours faithfully,

×××

范例2

Dear Sirs,

Thank you for your letter of April 18, 2015. We now have great pleasure in sending you a copy of our sample catalog and a comprehensive export price list.

As you will be able to see from our sample catalog, all the leather gloves we manufacture for export are of very high quality and are suitable for your purposes. We have reduced production costs by 5%. The prices quoted are very competitive. We feel sure that you will find that they compare very favorably with those quoted by other suppliers elsewhere in the world.

We expect payment by L/C payable within 90 days of sight and will allow you a cash discount of 10% if you are able to make payment within 30 days of invoice date. We will be able to ship any order you place with us within 30 days of your firm order.

We are looking forward to hearing from you.

Yours faithfully,

×××

第三节 还盘
Section 3 Counter-offer

一、还盘的含义和内容
The meaning and content of counter-offer

还盘，是受盘人对报盘内容不完全同意而提出修改或变更的表示，是对报盘条件进行添加、限制或其他更改的答复。还盘只有受盘人才可以做出，其他人做出无效。在接到报盘后，受盘人必须对报盘内容进行认真研究。如果受盘人认为报盘价格难以接受或对其他条件不满意，既可以拒绝接受，也可以向报盘人提出建议，要求对报盘内容进行修改。这种受盘人对报盘内容进行变更的表示被称为还盘。事实上，还盘既是受盘人对报盘的拒绝，又是受盘人以报盘人的地位提出的新报盘。

A counter-offer is a proposal of modification or amendment made by the offeree, who does not fully agree with the content of the offer. It is a response to adding, restricting, or otherwise changing the conditions of the offer. Only the offeree can make a counter-offer, and any other offer made is invalid. After receiving the offer, the offeree must carefully study the content of the offer. If the offeree finds the offer price difficult to accept or is not satisfied with other conditions, he can either refuse to accept it or make suggestions to the offeror to modify the offer content. The expression of the offeree making changes to the offered content is called a counter-offer. In fact, a counter-offer is both a rejection of the offer by the offeree and a new offer proposed by the offeree in the position of the offeror.

还盘信函应包括以下内容：

（1）对报盘人的报盘表示感谢；

（2）对由于某种原因无法接受报盘表示遗憾，同时解释原因；

（3）对希望修改的交易条件提出建议；

（4）希望对方能够接受提出的建议。

The counter-offer letter should include the following content:

(1) express gratitude to the person who made the offer;

(2) regret for not being able to accept the offer due to certain reasons, and explain the reasons;

(3) propose amendments to the desired transaction term;

(4) express the hopes for acceptance.

二、信文与范例

Letters and examples

范例1

Dear Mr. Liu,

Thank you for your letter of April 18. We note that you have indicated that our quoted prices are not sufficiently competitive and have requested a discount of 7.5% on your order, which is valued at USD 6,500.

We would like to emphasis that we have endeavored to limit our prices to the minimum in view of the very fine quality of our products, and so we regret that you still consider that they are rather too high for your market.

As a special concession, however, and as this is the first order that you have placed with us, we are willing to offer you the discount of 7.5% that you request on your order worth USD 6,500. While this is possible on this occasion, we would also like to point out that our labor costs are continually increasing, and so we regret that we cannot guarantee that we will be able to offer you these highly favorable terms in future.

The terms that we now offer are firm for 28 days only, and so we look forward to receiving your order in the near future.

We trust that you will be able to market our shoes very effectively in the United Kingdom and look forward to doing further business with you.

Sincerely,

×××

范例2

Dear Ms. Judy Jordan,

We are in receipt of both your offer of June 19, along with the catalogue and samples.

While appreciating the special design and good quality of your products, we find your price is rather too high for Chinese market. We have to point out that Japan-made men's cashmere sweater of this quality is available in our market, all of them are at prices about 15% below yours.

Such being the case, we have to ask you to consider if you can make a reduction in your price, say 15%. As we are ready to purchase many other cashmere products later this year, you may think it worthwhile to make a concession for a potential major client.

We are anticipating your early reply.

Sincerely yours,

Jim Li

第四节 接受
Section 4 Acceptance

一、接受的含义
The meaning of acceptance

如果受盘人认为能够接受报盘的全部内容和条件，那么就可向报盘人订购商品。这种买方或卖方同意对方在报盘中提出的各项交易条件，并愿意按照这些条件达成交易、订立合同的表示被称为接受，即法律上所称的“承诺”。

If the offeree believes that he can accept all the contents and conditions of the offer, he can place an order for the goods with the offeror. The agreement of the buyer or seller to the various transaction conditions proposed by the other party in the offer and their willingness to enter into a transaction or contract in accordance with these conditions is called acceptance, which is legally referred to as a "commitment".

二、接受的条件
The conditions of acceptance

作为一项有效接受，必须具备以下四个条件：

（1）接受只能由受盘人做出；

（2）接受必须是无条件的，完全同意报盘中提出的各项交易条件；

（3）接受的方式必须符合报盘的要求；

（4）接受必须在报盘规定的有效期内做出。

For an acceptance to be legally valid, the following four conditions must be met:

(1) the acceptance can only be madc by the offeree;

(2) the acceptance must be unconditional, fully agreeing to the various trading conditions proposed in the offer;

(3) the acceptance method must comply with the requirements of the offer;

(4) the acceptance must be made within the validity period specified in the offer.

三、信文与范例
Letters and examples

范例

Dear Mr. Zhao,

Thank you very much for your quotation on your men's cashmere sweater, along with the catalogue and samples.

We found both the design and quality of your products meet our requirements and the prices you quoted are satisfactory. We also note that you will allow us a discount of 5% on an order of no less than 10,000 pieces. We therefore take pleasure of placing you the order as follows, which we commend to your immediate and best attention:

Quantity: 10,000 pieces

Specification: men's cashmere sweaters

Catalogue No.: XL M10

Prices: USD 20 each

Please note that as these goods are urgently required in our market, we should be obliged if you could dispatch the goods as soon as possible. If this first order proves satisfactory, we shall be happy to place further orders with you.

Sincerely yours,

×××

第五节 重点短语与句型
Section 5 Key Phrases and Sentence Patterns

一、常用单词与短语
Common words and phrases

1. transaction negotiation 交易磋商
2. contract 合同

3. oral 口头的
4. written 书面的
5. enquiry 询盘
6. business behavior 业务行为
7. legal binding force 法律上的约束力
8. specifications 规格
9. quality 品质
10. quantity 数量
11. packaging 包装
12. shipping 装运
13. samples 样品
14. general enquiry 一般询盘
15. specific enquiry 具体询盘
16. catalogue 目录
17. price list 价目表
18. quotation sheets 报价单
19. illustrated photo prints 图片
20. commodity name 商品名称
21. unit price 单价
22. time of shipment 装船期
23. terms of payment 付款方式
24. letters 信文
25. offer 报盘
26. quotation 报价
27. tender offer 要约
28. firm offer 实盘
29. non-firm offer 虚盘
30. final confirmation 最后确认
31. payment 付款
32. L/C 信用证
33. shipment 装运
34. validity period 有效期
35. counter-offer 还盘
36. offeree 受盘人
37. modify 修改
38. change 更改
39. regret 遗憾
40. suggest 建议

41. firm　确定的
42. acceptance　接受
43. commitment　承诺
44. unconditional　无条件的
45. comply with　符合
46. catalogue No.　目录编号
47. dispatch　发运
48. satisfactory　满意的
49. further orders　进一步订单
50. hand-made gloves　手工手套
51. genuine leather　真皮
52. growing demand　日益增长的需求
53. price　价格
54. men's cashmere sweater　男士羊绒衫
55. high-quality textiles　高品质纺织品
56. import　进口
57. catalogues　目录
58. sample books　样本册
59. CIF Dalian prices　CIF 大连价格

二、常用句型

Common sentence patterns

1. We are pleased to tell you that we are interested in...
我们很高兴地告诉您，我们对……感兴趣。
2. There is a growing demand here for...
这里对……的需求日益增长。
3. We wish you would send us...
我们希望您能寄给我们……
4. We should find it most helpful if you could also send us...
如果您能同时寄给我们……，我们将非常感激。
5. We are a leading dealer in...
我们是……的主要经销商。
6. We are very much interested in...
我们对……非常感兴趣。
7. We would appreciate your sending us...
我们将非常感谢您寄给我们……
8. Please give us detailed information on...
请提供有关……的详细信息。

9. We hope this will be a good start for a long and profitable business relation.
我们希望这将是长期且有利可图的业务关系的良好开端。

10. Thank you for your letter of...
感谢您……的来信。

11. We are glad to learn of the enquiries you have had from your customers for...
我们很高兴得知您的客户对……的询盘。

12. We are pleased to quote as follows:
我们很高兴报如下价格:

13. Payment: by irrevocable L/C at sight.
付款:凭即期不可撤销信用证。

14. Shipment will be effected within... after receiving the L/C.
收到信用证后……内装运。

15. This offer is subject to our final confirmation.
本报盘以我方最后确认为准。

16. We are awaiting your early orders.
我们期待您早日下单。

17. We now have great pleasure in sending you...
我们现在很高兴地寄给您……

18. We feel sure that you will find that they compare very favorably with those quoted by other suppliers.
我们确信您会发现它们与其他供应商的报价相比非常有利。

19. We expect payment by L/C payable within... of sight
我们期望付款方式为见票后……天内付款的信用证。

20. We will allow you a cash discount of... if you are able to make payment within... of invoice date.
如果您能在发票日期后……天内付款,我们将给予您……的现金折扣。

21. We will be able to ship any order you place with us within... of your firm order.
我们将在您下达订单后……内装运任何订单。

22. We are looking forward to hearing from you.
我们期待您的回复。

23. We note that you have discounted our quoted prices not sufficiently competitive.
我们注意到您认为我们报的价格不够有竞争力。

24. We regret that you still consider that they are rather too high for your market.
我们为您仍然认为它们对您的市场来说太高感到遗憾。

25. As a special concession, however, and as this is the first order that you have placed with us, we are willing to offer you...
然而,作为特别让步,并且这是您第一次向我们下单,我们愿意向您提供……

26. While this is possible on this occasion, we would also like to point out that...

虽然这次可以做到，我们还想指出……

27. The terms that we now offer are firm for... only.

我们现在提供的条款有效期为……天。

28. We trust that you will be able to market our... very effectively in...

我们相信您将能够在……非常有效地销售我们的……

29. We look forward to doing further business with you.

我们期待与您进一步开展业务。

30. We are in receipt of both your offer and the catalogue and samples.

我们收到了您的报价以及目录和样品。

31. While appreciating the special design and good quality of your products, we find your price is rather too high for...

虽然我们赞赏您（公司）产品的特殊设计和优良品质，但我们发现您的报价对……来说过高。

32. We have to point out that... is available in our market, all of them are at prices about... below yours.

我们必须指出，……在我们的市场上有售，所有这些产品的价格都比您的低约……

33. We have to ask you to consider if you can make reduction in your price, say...

我们必须请您考虑是否可以降低价格，比如说……

34. As we are ready to purchase many other... later this year, you may think it worthwhile to make a concession for a potential big client.

因为我们准备在今年晚些时候购买许多其他……，您可能会认为为一个潜在的大客户做出让步是值得的。

35. We are anticipating your early reply.

我们期待您早日回复。

36. We found both the design and quality of your products meet our requirement.

我们发现您产品的设计和质量都符合我们的要求。

37. The prices you quoted are satisfactory.

您报的价格令人满意。

38. We also note that you will allow us a discount of... on an order of no less than...

我们还注意到，您将允许我们在不少于……的订单上享受……的折扣。

39. We therefore take pleasure of placing you the order as follows.

因此，我们很高兴向您下达如下订单。

40. If this first order proves satisfactory, we shall be happy to place further orders with you.

如果这第一笔订单令人满意，我们很乐意继续向你们下单。

课后练习

Ⅰ. 选词填空。

Fill in the blanks with the appropriate words.

(quality; samples; hand-made; copy; textiles; catalogue; pattern-book; UK; sight)

1. We are pleased to tell you that we are interested in ____________ gloves in a variety of genuine leather.
2. There is a growing demand here for gloves of high ____________.
3. We wish you would send us a ____________ of your illustrated catalogue.
4. We should find it most helpful if you could also send us ____________ of the various leather.
5. We are a leading dealer in high-quality ____________ in China.
6. We would appreciate your sending us catalogues, sample books or even ____________ if possible.
7. We now have great pleasure in sending you a ____________ and a comprehensive export price list.
8. We expect payment by L/C payable within 90 days of ____________.
9. We are in receipt of both your offer and the ____________ and samples.
10. We trust that you will be able to market our shoes very effectively in the ____________.

Ⅱ. 将下列句子翻译为英文。

Translate the following sentences into English.

1. 我们很高兴地告诉您，我们对各种真皮手工手套感兴趣。
2. 这里对高品质手套的需求日益增长。
3. 我们希望您能寄给我们您所希望购买的手套的图录副本，以及价格和付款条款的详细信息。
4. 如果您能同时寄给我们各种皮革的样品，我们将非常感激。
5. 我们是中国高品质纺织品的主要经销商。
6. 如果可能的话，我们希望您能寄给我们目录、样本册甚至样品。
7. 我们现在很高兴地寄给您样本册和全面的出口价目表。
8. 我们期望付款方式为见票后 90 天内付款的信用证。
9. 我们收到了您的报价以及目录和样品。
10. 我们相信您将能够在英国非常有效地销售我们的鞋子。

Ⅲ. 写作。

Writing.

You are the purchasing manager of a textile company in China. You are interested in cashmere products from an Australian exporter. Write an enquiry letter to them, requesting detailed information about men's cashmere sweaters. Your letter should include the following points:

1. Introduce your company and your position.

2. Express your interest in Australian cashmere products and explain why.

3. Request a catalogue, samples, and CIF Shanghai price quotations for men's cashmere sweaters.

4. Enquire about the terms of payment and any possible discount policies.

5. Express your anticipation of a fruitful cooperation and request a prompt response.

Ensure that your letter is well-structured, uses accurate language, and includes all the necessary details.

第四章 跨境合同订立
Chapter 4 Cross-border Contract Formation

众所周知，没有协议或合同来约束缔约方，商业合作将无法达成。合同是两个或多个有资格的当事方之间的协议，在该协议中，要约被提出并接受，并且每一方都受益。在跨境电商中，商业合同通常是指双方订立并可依法执行的协议，根据该协议，双方相互承诺出售或购买某种特定商品，转让或获得某种工业产权或专有技术，或提供或接受某种服务。它可以是正式的、非正式的、书面的、口头的，也可以是通俗易懂的。本章将详细介绍跨境贸易中电子商务合同的特点及电子合同签订的操作要点等，旨在帮助学生全面系统地掌握签订跨境合同的内容与方法技巧。

学习目标

1. 熟悉跨境合同订立的各种形式。
2. 熟悉跨境合同中各条款的内容与订立的方法与技巧。
3. 掌握跨境签订跨境合同的方法与技巧。
4. 掌握跨境合同签订过程中的即时沟通与信文写作方法。

思政目标

1. 学习合同订立，培养契约精神。
2. 注重合同条款，培养严谨态度。
3. 了解国际惯例，培养规则意识。

第一节 合同的订立
Section 1 Conclusion of Contracts

一、合同的签订
Signing of contract

买卖双方经过交易磋商，对交易的条件或条款取得一致意见后，即可签订书面合同。合同可由买卖双方任何一方起草，并由双方签字。

After negotiations and reaching consensus on the terms or conditions of the transaction, the buyer and seller can sign a written contract. The contract can be drafted by either party and signed by both parties.

常见的书面形式有正式的合同、确认书、协议书、备忘录、订单、委托订购单等。

Common written forms include formal contracts, confirmations, agreements, memoranda, orders, and indentures.

二、合同成立的时间

Time of contract establishment

在国际贸易中，买卖双方的合同于何时订立是一个十分重要的问题。根据《联合国国际货物销售合同公约》和《中华人民共和国民法典》的规定，合同的订立必须经过报盘与接受两个步骤，合同于接受生效时成立。

In international trade, when the contract between buyer and seller is concluded is a very important issue. According to provisions of *United Nations Convention on Contracts for the International Sale of Goods* and *Civil Code of the People's Republic of China*, the formation of a contract must go through two steps: offer and acceptance. The contract is established when acceptance takes effect.

实际业务中，有时双方当事人在洽商交易时约定，合同成立的时间以签约时合同上所写明的日期为准，或以收到对方确认合同的日期为准，在这两种情况下，双方的合同关系即在签订正式合同时成立。

In actual business, sometimes both parties agree during negotiations that the date of contract formation shall be based on the date stated in the contract at the time of signing, or the date of receipt of confirmation from the other party. In both cases, the contractual relationship between the two parties shall be established at the time of signing the formal contract.

三、合同的形式

Form of contract

在国际贸易中，书面合同的名称没有特定的限制。我国的外贸实践中，主要采用合同和确认书两种。

In international trade, there are no specific restrictions on the name of a written contract. In China's foreign trade practice, there are mainly two types: contracts and confirmation letters.

（一）合同

Contract

交易成立后，由当事人的一方将交易内容制成合同，然后由双方共同签署，这种合同的内容比较全面、详细。由卖方制作的称为“售货合同”；由买方制作的称为“购货合同”；如果是由买卖双方互派代表一同制作，当场签字的，则可称为“购销合同”，但这种情况较少见。

After the transaction is established, one of the parties involved will compile the transaction content into a contract, which will be jointly signed by both parties. The content of this type of contract is relatively comprehensive and detailed. A "Sales Contract" is made by the seller. A "Purchase Contract" is made by the buyer. If the contract is made by representatives from both the buyer and seller and signed on the spot, it can be called a "Sales and Purchase Contract", but this situation is relatively rare.

（二）确认书

Confirmation letter

合同的简化形式，通常由一方制作确认书一式两份，拟好并签名后寄给对方，对方经审核同意并签字确认，保留一份，同时将另一份寄还。由卖方制作的称为“售货确认书”，由买方制作的称为“购货确认书”，效力与合同相等。

The simplified form of a contract usually involves one party making two copies of a confirmation letter, drafting and signing them, and sending both to the other party. The other party approves and signs it for confirmation, keeping one copy and returning the other. The sales confirmation made by the seller is called "Sales Confirmation", and the purchase confirmation made by the buyer is called "Purchase Confirmation". Both documents hold the same legal validity as a formal contract.

第二节 合同的内容
Section 2 Contents of Contracts

一、合同的组成部分
Parts of the contract

书面合同一般由三个部分组成，即合同的约首、本文和约尾。这三个部分又各自包含不同的内容。

A written contract generally consists of three parts, namely the preamble, the body, and the end of the contract. These three parts each contain different contents.

（一）约首

Preamble

约首即合同的首部，主要包括合同名称、编号、缔约日期及地点、缔约当事人名称及地址等。

The preamble refers to the first part of the contract, which mainly includes the name, number, date, and location of the contract, and the names and addresses of the contracting parties.

在国际上，合同的形式可以是口头形式、书面形式和其他形式。口头合同必须提供人证，书面形式包括电报。

Internationally, contracts may be oral, written, or in other forms. Oral contracts must provide personal evidence, and written forms include telegrams.

（二）本文

Body

合同的本文，具体规定了买卖双方的权利和义务，又可分为主要条款和一般条款两部分。主要条款包括：商品的品名、品质、数量、包装、价格、装运、保险、支付。一般条款包括：

商品检验、索赔、不可抗力、仲裁、单据。

The body of the contract specifies the rights and obligations of both the buyer and the seller and can be divided into two parts: core terms and general terms. The core terms include: product name, quality, quantity, packaging, price, shipment, insurance, and payment. The general terms include: inspection of goods, claims, force majeure, arbitration, and documents.

1. 品名条款

Product name terms

品名条款的基本内容取决于成交商品的品种和特点。一般来说，列明买卖双方成交商品的名称即可。但有些商品，因其具有不同的品种、规格型号、等级或商标，在此情况下，品名条款实际上已经演变为品质条款的综合体，在合同中通常称为“货描”。

The basic content of product name terms depends on the variety and characteristics of the traded goods. Generally speaking, it is sufficient to list the names of the goods traded between the buyer and seller. However, for some products, due to their different varieties, specifications and models, grades, or trademarks, the product name terms have actually evolved into a comprehensive set of quality terms, commonly referred to as “description of goods” in contracts.

2. 品质条款

Quality terms

品质条款的基本内容主要是借助适当的方法对成交商品品质进行描述。描述品质的方法主要包括凭规格、凭等级、凭标准、凭商标或品牌、凭说明书及图样、凭原产地证名称、凭样品等，应根据成交商品的特性、买卖双方的交易习惯和具体要求合理选用。

The basic content of quality terms is mainly to describe the quality of the traded goods through appropriate methods. The methods for describing quality mainly include specifications, grades, standards, trademarks or brands, instructions and drawings, certificates of origin names, samples, etc. They should be reasonably selected based on the characteristics of the traded goods, the trading habits of both parties, and specific requirements.

3. 数量条款

Quantity terms

数量条款的基本内容主要包括成交数量、计量单位、计量方法等。必要时，为了便于履行合同，可在数量条款中增加“溢短装条款”，包括溢短装的幅度、由何方掌握溢短装的选择权以及溢短装部分的计价方法。

The basic content of quantity terms mainly includes the transaction quantity, unit of measurement, measuring method, etc. If necessary, in order to facilitate the performance of the contract, a “over or under load clause” can be added to the quantity terms, including the extent of over or under load, who has the right to choose over or under load, and the pricing method for the over or under load part.

4. 包装条款

Packaging terms

包装条款的基本内容一般包括包装方式、包装材料、包装规格、包装标志和包装费用等。由买方提供包装标志和包装材料时，在包装条款中应规定提供的最迟日期以及未能及时提供而影响货物出运时所应承担的责任。

The basic content of packaging terms generally includes packaging methods, packaging materials, packaging specifications, packaging marks, and packaging costs. When the buyer provides packaging marks and materials, the packaging terms should specify the latest date to be provided and the responsibility to be borne when the goods are not shipped due to failure to provide them in a timely manner.

5. 价格条款

Price terms

价格条款的基本内容一般包括商品单价和总值两部分。商品单价包括计价货币、单位价格金额、计价单位和贸易术语四部分。

The basic content of price terms generally includes two parts: unit price and total amount. The unit price of goods includes four parts: pricing currency, unit price amount, pricing unit, and trade terms.

商品单价未含佣价（明佣）时，应在价格条款中规定佣金率、佣金的计算方法和佣金的支付方法。

When the unit price of the product does not include commission (explicit commission), the commission rate, calculation method of commission, and payment method of commission should be specified in the price terms.

商品单价含有折扣（明扣）时，应在价格条款中规定折扣率、折扣的计算方法和支付方法。

When the unit price of the product includes discounts (explicit deductions), the discount rate, calculation method of discounts, and payment method should be specified in the price terms.

6. 装运条款

Shipment terms

装运条款的基本内容一般包括运输方式、装运期或交货期、装运（港）与目的地（港），是否允许分批装运与转运、装运通知等。

The basic content of shipment terms generally includes the mode of transportation, shipping or delivery time, shipping (port) and destination (port), whether partial shipment and transshipment, shipment notification, etc. are allowed.

其中，在允许分批装运的情况下，必要时可根据需要在装运条款中规定批次，每次需要运货物的时间和数量。必要时可根据需要在装运条款中规定转运地点、转运的方法和转运费用的负担。关于装运通知，通常应包括发出的时间、内容、签发方式以及未发出或未及时发出而导致损失时所应承担的责任。

Among them, if partial shipment is allowed, it is necessary to specify the batch, time and quantity of each shipment in the shipping terms as needed. If necessary, the transportation location, method, and cost of transportation can be specified in the shipping terms as needed. Regarding shipping notices, they usually include the time, content, methods of issuance, and the responsibility for losses caused by failure to send or not sending in a timely manner.

当货物使用租船运输时，在装运条款中应规定装卸时间、装卸率和滞期速遣条款。

When goods are transported by chartered ships, loading and unloading time, loading and unloading rate, and demurrage and dispatch clauses should be specified in the shipping terms.

7. 保险条款

Insurance terms

当使用 FOB/FCA 或 CFR/CPT 术语出口时，只在保险条款中规定由买方负责投保即可。当使用 CIF/CIP 术语出口时，保险条款的基本内容一般包括规定由卖方负责投保、选择哪家保险公司、实用的保险条款、投保哪些险别、保险金额如何确定、险费负担、提供哪些保险单据等。

When using FOB/FCA or CFR/CPT terms for export, it is only necessary to specify in the insurance terms that the buyer is responsible for insurance. When using CIF/CIP terms for export, the basic content of the insurance terms generally includes the seller is responsible for arranging insurance, specifying which insurance company to choose, practical insurance terms, which types of insurance to purchase, how to determine the insurance amount, insurance premium burden, and what insurance documents to provide.

8. 支付条款

Payment terms

支付条款的基本内容一般包括支付工具、支付方式、支付时间与地点等。其中，支付工具应列明是使用汇票、本票还是使用支票。

The basic content of payment terms generally includes payment instruments, payment methods, payment time and location, etc. Among them, the payment instruments should specify whether to use Bill of Exchange/Draft, Promissory Note or Check.

使用汇付方式时，应在支付条款中列明汇付的方法是信汇、电汇还是票汇；使用托收支付方式时，应在支付条款中列明托收的方式是跟单托收还是光票托收，托收的条件是付款交单还是承兑交单；使用信用证支付方式时，自在支付条款中列明开证时间、开证行、信用证种类、信用证有效期及到期地点等。

When using Remittance Payment, the payment terms should specify whether the remittance method is by Mail Transfer (M/T), Telegraphic Transfer (T/T), or Demand Draft (D/D). When using Collection Payment, the payment terms should specify whether the collection method is Documentary Collection or Clean Collection, and whether the collection condition is Documents Against Payment (D/P) or Documents Against Acceptance (D/A). When using Letter of Credit (L/C), please specify in the payment terms the opening time, issuing bank, type of letter of credit, validity period, and expiration location of the letter of credit.

关于支付时间，应在支付条款中结合支付方式列明是预付、凭单付现，还是即期付款、分期付款或延期付款。

Regarding the payment time, the payment terms should be combined with the payment method to specify whether it is prepayment, cash against documents, immediate payment, installment payment, or deferred payment.

支付地点与支付方式密切关联，按照一般惯例和习惯做法，汇付的支付地点是买方注册地；托收的支付地点是买方营业地；信用证的支付地点是卖方营业地。

The payment location is closely related to the payment method. According to general conventions and practices, the payment location for Remittance is the buyer's domicile; the payment location for Collection is the buyer's place of business; the payment location of the Letter of Credit is the seller's place of business.

如果合同中没有明确规定支付方式和支付地点，根据《联合国国际货物销售合同会约》的有关规定，如买方没有义务在任何其他特定地点支付价款，他就必须在“卖方营业地”支付价款。卖方若有一个以上营业地，则在“与合同及合同的履行关系最密切的营业地”支付价款；如果没有营业地，则应在其“惯常居住地”支付价款。

If the contract does not specify the payment method and location, according to the relevant provisions of the *United Nations Convention on Contracts for the International Sale of Goods*, if the buyer is not obligated to pay the price at any other specific location, payment shall be made at the "seller's place of business". If the seller has more than one place of business, payment shall be made at the "place of business with the closest relationship to the contract and its performance". If there is no place of business, payment shall be made at the seller's "habitual residence".

9. 商品检验条款

Product inspection terms

商品检验条款的基本内容一般包括检验权、检验时间与地点、检验机构、检验技术标准与检验证书等。

The basic content of inspection terms generally includes inspection rights, inspection time and place, inspection agency, inspection technical standards and inspection certificates, etc.

10. 索赔条款

Claims terms

索赔条款的基本内容一般包括索赔的证据、索赔期限和索赔金额等。实际业务中，交易双方根据需要可以增加“违约金条款”，其内容主要包括交易双方协商确定的违约金数额，并订明履约过程中若出现当事人违约情况，则违约方应向对方支付按月违约金数额；还可以就支付违约金时有无宽限期和因违约产生的损失赔偿额的具体计算方法做出规定。

The basic content of claims terms generally includes evidence of the claim, claim period, and claim amount. In actual business, both parties to a transaction can add "penalty terms" as needed, which mainly include the amount of penalty determined through negotiation between the two parties, and specify that if a party breaches the contract during the performance process, the defaulting party should pay the other party a monthly penalty amount. It is also possible to make provisions on whether there is a grace period for paying liquidated damages and the specific calculation method for the amount of compensation for losses incurred due to the breach.

11. 不可抗力条款

Force majeure terms

不可抗力条款的基本内容一般包括不可抗力事件的性质和范围、不可抗力事件的通知和证明、不可抗力事件的处理原则和办法等。

The basic content of force majeure terms generally includes the nature and scope of force majeure events, notification and proof of force majeure events, principles and methods for handling force majeure events, etc.

12. 仲裁条款

Arbitration terms

仲裁条款的基本内容一般包括仲裁地点、仲裁机构、仲裁程序规则、仲裁裁决的效力和仲裁费用的负担等。

The basic content of arbitration terms generally includes the place of arbitration, arbitration institution, arbitration procedure rules, the effectiveness of arbitration awards, and the burden of arbitration fees.

13. 单据条款

Document terms

单据条款的基本内容一般包括单据的种类、单据的份数、对单据出具人的要求、单据关键内容的缮制要求以及单据转移的要求等。

The basic content of document terms generally includes the type of document, the number of copies of the document, requirements for the issuer of the document, requirements for the key content of the document, and requirements for document transfer.

(三) 约尾

End

约尾即合同的尾部，通常写明合同适用的文字及效力，合同正本的份数、附件及效力，以及双方当事人或其授权人的签字。

The end refers to the last part of the contract, which usually specifies the applicable language and effectiveness of the contract, the number of copies, attachments and effectiveness of the original contract, and the signatures of both parties and their authorized persons.

书面合同的内容必须符合政策，做到内容完备、条款明确、文字严密，并与交易磋商的内容相一致。书面合同一经签订，即成为约束双方当事人的法律文件。

The content of a written contract must comply with policies, achieve complete content, clear terms, rigorous wording, and be consistent with the content of the transaction negotiation. Once a written contract is signed, it becomes a legal document binding on both parties.

二、信文与范例
Letters and examples

范例1

(Order Letter)

Dear Mr. Randall,

Subject: Order for 10, 000 Pairs of Sheep Leather Gloves

Please dispatch to us 10, 000 pairs of sheep leather gloves as per the terms stated in your offer of March 29.

Would you please take special care of the quality and the packaging of this order? The leather should be of the same quality as that used in the sample. We hope that you can pack each pair in an airtight polythene bag, place a dozen pairs of gloves in a box and load 20 boxes to a strong seaworthy wooden case. We will order more if the first order with you proves to be satisfactory.

We are enclosing our Purchase Confirmation No. 2015-399 in duplicate for your signature. Please sign and return one copy for our file. Upon receipt of your confirmation, an L/C will be issued.

Sincerely, Li Ming
Import Director

范例2

(Sales Confirmation)

The buyers: Weston Co., LTD.
Address: 50 Southland Street Singapore

The sellers: DALIAN YAEMIN TRADING CO., LTD.
Address: No. 3 Chifeng Road, Dalian Development Zone, Dalian, China

Contract No.: CH/10/908
DATE: August 20, 2014

This Confirmation is made by and agreed between the BUYER and SELLER, in accordance with the terms and conditions stipulated below.

COMMODITY AND SPECIFICATIONS:
Demineralized Whey Powder
Unit Price: USD 900. 00/MT CIF Singapore

Quantity: 1,000 MT
Total amount: USD 900,000.00
COUNTRY OF ORIGIN: China
PACKING: 25kg in 4-ply paper sacks with inner polyethylene liner and big bags.
TIME OF SHIPMENT: Not later than September 30, 2014
PORT OF SHIPMENT: Dalian, China
PORT OF DESTINATION: Singapore
INSURANCE: To be covered by the seller for 110% of invoice value against ALL RISKS and WAR RISKS.
PAYMENT: To be effected by irrevocable letter of credit available by draft (s) at 90 days after B/L date sight for 100% of invoice drawn by the Sellers.
INSPECTION: The Buyers shall have the qualities, specifications, quantities of the goods carefully inspected by the local Inspection Authority, which shall issue Inspection Certificate before shipment.
This contract is in two original copies, effective since being signed/ sealed by both parties.

The Buyer: 　　　　　　　　　　The Seller:

范例3

(Purchase Contract)
Contract No.: CU080145
Date: April 5th, 2014

The Seller: Carlton International
Address: 102 Lind Road, San Francisco, California 90034, USA

The Buyer: Heyee Corporation
Address: 34 Yongquan Street, Jinnan District, Tianjin 300350, PRC

The Seller and the Buyer agree to conclude this Contract subject to the terms and conditions stated below:
1. Name and Specifications of Commodity: Cotton Prints DY 78
2. Quantity: 1% more or less allowed, 3,000 meters
3. Unit Price: USD 3.3 per meter
4. Total Amount: USD 9900
5. Terms of Delivery: FOB
6. Country of Origin and Manufacturers: The United States

7. Packing: 100 meters per waterproof polyethylene bag, each bay placed in a cardboard box
8. Shipping Marks: On the surface of each package, the package number, measurement, gross weight, net weight
9. Time of Shipment: October 2014
10. Port of Loading: San Francisco U. S. A.
11. Port of Destination: Tianjin, P. R. C.
12. Insurance:

According to the payment of the contract, insurance shall be covered by the Buyer for 110% of the invoice value against ALL RISKS

13. Terms of Payment:

(1) Letter of Credit: The Buyer shall, 7 days prior to the time of shipment or after this Contract comes into effect, open an irrevocable Letter of Credit in favor of the Seller. The Letter of Credit shall expire 15 days after the completion of loading of the shipment as stipulated.

(2) Document against payment: After shipment, the seller shall draw a sight bill of exchange on the Buyer and deliver the document through Seller's bank and N/A Bank to the Buyer against payment, i. e. D/P. The Buyer shall effect the payment immediately upon the first presentation of the bill(s) of exchange.

(3) T/T: The Buyer shall pay to the Seller total amount by T/T within 3 days against receiving the full set document or the goods after shipment.

14. Documents Required:

The Seller shall present the following documents required to the bank for negotiation/ collection:

(1) Full set of clean on board Ocean/ Combined Transportation/ Land Bills of Lading and blank endorsed marked freight prepaid/ to collect.

(2) Signed commercial invoice in 5 copies indicating Contract No., L/C No. (Terms of L/C) and shipping marks.

(3) Packing list/ weight memo in 2 copies issued by Seller.

(4) Insurance policy/ certificate in 5 copies (Terms of FOB)

(5) Shipping advice.

The Seller shall, within 24 hours after shipment effected, send by courier each copy of the above mentioned documents No. (1) to (5).

15. Shipping Advice:

The Seller shall, immediately upon the completion of the loading of the goods, advise the Buyer of the Contract No., names of commodity, loading quantity, invoice values, gross weight, name of vessel and shipment date by letter within 24 hours.

16. Inspection:

After arrival of the goods at the port of destination, the Buyer shall apply to China Commodity

Inspection Bureau (hereinafter referred to as CCIB) for a further inspection as to the specifications and quantity/ weight of the goods. If damage to the goods is found, or the specifications and/or quantity are not in conformity with the stipulations in this Contract, except when the responsibilities lies with Insurance Company or Shipping Company, the Buyer shall, within 30 days or reject the goods according to the port of destination, claim against the Seller, or reject the goods according to the inspection certificate issued by CCIB on the basis of the Rules and Regulations of Witness.

17. Claim:

Should the quality, specifications, quantity, weight and/ or packing be found not in conformity with the stipulation of this Contract, the Buyer shall give a notice of claims to the Seller and shall have the right to lodge claim against the Seller within 30 days from the date of the completion of unloading of the goods at the port of destination. The Buyer shall make a claim against the seller (including replacement of the goods) on the basis of the Rules and Regulations of Witness and all the expenses incurred therefore shall be borne by the Seller. The claims mentioned above shall be regarded as being accepted if the Seller fails to reply within ten days after the Seller received the Buyer's claim.

18. Late delivery and Penalty:

Should the Seller fail to make delivery on time as stipulated in the Contract, with the exception of Force Majeure terms specified in Clause 19 of this Contract, it shall be settled by the Witness on the basis of the Rules and Regulations of Witness.

19. Force Majeure:

The Seller shall not be responsible for the delay of shipment or non-delivery of the goods due to Force Majeure, which might occur during the process of manufacturing or in the course of loading or transit. The Seller shall advise the Buyer immediately of the occurrence mentioned above and within 3 days thereafter the Seller shall send a notice by courier to the Buyer for their acceptance of a certificate of the accident issued by the local chamber of commerce under whose jurisdiction the accident occurs as evidence thereof. Under such circumstances the Seller, however, is still under the obligation to take all necessary measures to hasten delivery of the goods. In case the accident lasts for more than 15 days, the Buyer shall have the right to cancel the Contract, The Buyer's failure on getting the export license should not be regarded as force majeure.

20. Arbitration:

Any dispute arising from or in connection with the Contract shall be settled through friendly negotiation. In case no settlement is reached, the dispute shall be submitted to China International Economic and Trade Arbitration Commission (CIETAC), South China Commission or Shanghai Sub-Commission for arbitration in accordance with its rules in effect at the time of applying for arbitration. The arbitral award is final and binding upon both parties.

This contract shall be construed in accordance with and governed by the law of P. R. C.

21. Notices:

All notice shall be written in English or Chinese and served to both parties by fax/ email/ courier. If any changes of the addresses occur, one party shall inform the other party of the change of address within 3 days after the change.

22. The terms FOB/CFR/CIF in the Contract are based on INCOTERMS® 2010 of the International Chamber of Commerce.

23. Additional clause:

N/A

24. This Contract is executed in two counterparts each in Chinese and English, each of which shall be deemed equally authentic. This Contract is in 3 copies, effective upon signing/ sealing by two parties.

Representative of the buyer	Representative of the seller
(Authorized signature):	(Authorized signature):

第三节 Section 3 重点短语与句型 Key Phrases and Sentence Patterns

一、常用单词与短语 Common words and phrases

1. contract 合同，订立合同
2. contractor 订约人，承包人
3. contractual 合同的，契约的
4. to make a contract 签订合同
5. to place/enter into a contract 订合同
6. to sign a contract 签合同
7. to draw up a contract 拟订合同
8. to draft a contract 起草合同
9. to get a contract 得到合同
10. to land a contract 得到（拥有）合同
11. to countersign a contract 会签合同
12. to repeat a contract 重复合同
13. an executory contract 尚待执行的合同
14. a nice fat contract 一个很有利的合同
15. originals of the contract 合同正本

16. copies of the contract 合同副本
17. a written contract 书面合同
18. to make some concession 做某些让步
19. agreement on general terms and conditions on business 一般经营交易条件协议
20. loan agreement 贷款协议
21. agreement on loan facilities up to a given amount 商定借款协议
22. agreement fixing price 共同定价协议
23. agreement in writing 书面协议
24. agreement of reimbursement 偿付协议
25. agreement on import licensing procedure 进口许可证手续协议
26. agreement on reinsurance 分保协议
27. agreement to resell 转售协议
28. bilateral agreement 双边协议
29. bilateral trade agreement 双边贸易协议
30. commercial agreement 商业协议
31. compensation trade agreement 补偿贸易协议
32. distributorship agreement 销售协议
33. exclusive distributorship agreement 独家销售协议
34. guarantee agreement 担保协议
35. international trade agreement 国际贸易协议
36. joint venture agreement 合营协议
37. licensing agreement 许可证协议
38. management agreement 经营管理协议
39. multilateral trade agreement 多边贸易协议
40. operating agreement 经营协议
41. partnership agreement 合伙协议
42. supply agreement 供货协议
43. trade agreement 贸易协议
44. ad referendum contract 暂定合同
45. agency contract 代理合同
46. barter contract 易货合同
47. binding contract 有约束力的合同
48. blank form contract 空白合同
49. commercial contract 商业合同
50. compensation trade contract 补偿贸易合同
51. cross license contract 互换许可证合同
52. exclusive license contract 独家许可证合同
53. export contract 出口合同

54. firm sale contract 确定的销售合同
55. formal contract 正式合同
56. forward contract 期货合同
57. illegal contract 非法合同
58. import contract 进口合同
59. indirect contract 间接合同
60. installment contract 分期合同
61. international trade contract 国际贸易合同
62. know-how license contract 专业技术许可合同
63. long term contract 长期合同
64. non-transferable license contract 不可转让合同
65. patent license contract 专利合同
66. enter into a/the contract 签订合同
67. open-end contract 暂定合同，开口合同
68. price contract 购货合同

二、常用句型
Common sentence patterns

1. Your order will not create a binding contract between both parties.

你方的订单不会成为对双方具有约束力的合同。

2. The buyer is responsible for the following costs and charges in the sale and transport of goods.

买方承担货物运输和销售中的成本和费用。

3. The buyer shall open an Irrevocable Sight Letter of Credit which is acceptable bank to the seller. This credit is to reach the seller 30 days before the month of shipment, valid for negotiation in China until the 15th day after the month of shipment.

买方应由卖方可接受的银行将不可撤销的即期信用证，于装运月份前 30 天开到卖方并至装运月份后第 15 天在中国议付有效。

4. The seller will make every effort to commence transport of the goods so that they will arrive by the delivery date.

卖方应尽一切努力启运货物以便及时交货。

5. If there is any delay, the seller will immediately notify the buyer of the delay and the reason for the delay.

如果推迟交货，卖方应立即通知买方推迟交货并说明延误的原因。

6. The buyer will have the option to renegotiate with the seller for a new delivery date.

买方有权就新的交货日期与卖方磋商。

7. All disputes arising out of the performance of, or relating to this contract, shall be settled amicably through negotiation. In case no settlement can be reached through negotiation, the case shall then be submitted to the China International Economic and Trade Arbitration Commission for

arbitration in accordance with its arbitration rules. The arbitral award is final and binding upon both parties.

凡因执行本合同所发生的或与本合同有关的一切争议，双方应通过友好协商解决。如果协商不能解决，应提交中国国际经济贸易仲裁委员会根据该会仲裁规则进行仲裁。仲裁的裁决是终局的，对双方都有约束力。

8. The parties understand and agree that law of China will be applied to interpret the contract.

双方理解并同意此合同适用于中国法律。

9. Each party is responsible for obtaining on its own account any other insurance coverage for the goods that he may desire.

买卖双方为了各自的利益为货物所投保的险种由其自行负担费用。

10. Title will be transferred to the buyer while goods are delivered to New York port, provided that the buyer has paid.

如果买方已向卖方付款，在货物到达纽约港时所有权转至买方。

11. If shipment is delayed because the buyer fails to furnish such proof timely, the seller will not be deemed to have breached the contract.

如果延迟装运是由于买方无法及时提供此类证据，在这种情况下卖方不违约。

12. The buyer covenants that the goods will be shipped to and delivered in America and that the buyer will not ship or deliver the goods to any other country.

买方同意货物被运到美国并同意货物不会被运往其他国家。

13. The buyer is entitled to inspect, or to have its agent inspect, the goods at the seller's place of business.

买方有权在卖方的营业地检验或让其代理人检验货物。

14. Within 90 days after delivery, the seller agrees to replace the goods found defective free of charges.

在交货后 90 天内，卖方应免费更换任何有瑕疵的货物。

15. The buyer will pay the price by sight draft.

买方将用即期汇票付款。

16. The buyer will be responsible for obtaining import license issued by the appropriate agency of USA government, and the seller will be responsible for obtaining export license issued by the appropriate agency of China government.

买方获得由美国政府颁发的进口许可证，卖方获得由中国政府颁发的出口许可证。

17. If either party notifies the other party that it will not or is unable to perform this agreement, the party receiving notice is entitled to cancel the agreement.

如果任何一方通知另一方不想或不能履行协议，接到通知的一方有权撤销合同。

18. The date of the cancellation will be the date on which the party receives the notice of nonperformance.

撤销的日期是收到不履行协议通知的日期。

19. It is agreed that the parties have considered what would be a reasonable estimate of the

damage each would suffer if the other were to breach this agreement.

由于一方违约而给另一方造成损失，就另一方所遭受的损失的合理估计，各方已达成一致。

20. If the seller cannot deliver the goods, the seller shall pay the buyer the sum of USD 1 million as liquidated damages.

如果卖方不能交货，卖方应向买方支付一百万美元的赔偿金。

21. All modifications of this agreement must be in writing and signed by the parties.

对本协议的任何修改都应以书面形式做出，并由双方签署。

22. The seller agrees that no reliance has been placed on any representation other than the provisions contained in the agreement.

卖方同意除本协议中的条款外，任何表述都不具可靠性。

23. To give notice pursuant to this agreement, a party must send written notice to the other party at the address stated in this agreement.

根据本协议规定，发出通知一方在协议中指定的地点发出书面通知。

24. A party shall notify the other party in writing of any change in address within 90 days after such change.

当地址发生变化时，一方必须在变动后 90 天内通知另一方。

25. To accept this offer, the buyer must sign and return it without any modifications to the seller, who must receive it no later than January 9, 2019.

如接受这一要约，买方必须在 2019 年 1 月 9 日前在不改变要约的前提下签字并返给对方。

26. This contract shall be binding on both parties as of the date on which it is signed by the seller.

本合同自卖方签约之日起对双方具有约束力。

27. Please note that your acceptance to the offer is subject to the conditions printed on the reverse of the letter.

请注意你方接受这一订单的条件在此函的背面。

28. The seller will endeavor to complete all packaging within time for the delivery date.

卖方将尽力在交货期内包装好所有的货物。

29. The delivery will be made within 90 days of our receipt of your order, unless we otherwise inform you.

除我方另行通知外，在收到你方订单 90 天内我方交货。

30. The offer will be canceled if we do not receive an order from you by September 9, 2019.

如果我方在 2019 年 9 月 9 日前未收到你方的订单，此要约撤销。

31. No alternation, deletion, or addition to these conditions will have any effect unless the seller accepts the change in writing.

除卖方以书面形式接受更改外，更改、删除和添加任何此要约中的条款均为无效。

32. If the delay in delivery results from the seller's efforts to comply with particular specifications

supplied by the buyer, the buyer will not have a right to cancel the contract.

如果延迟交货是由于卖方努力提供符合买方要求的特别规格的货物，买方无权撤销合同。

33. Under the circumstances, the seller will notify the buyer of the delay and the parties will renegotiate another delivery date.

在这种情况下卖方将通知买方延迟交货，双方重新磋商一个交货日期。

34. The seller's inability to meet the delivery date designated because the buyer has furnished particular specifications will not be a breach of contract.

由于买方提供了特定的规格，卖方不能按时交货，这并不构成违约。

35. If the buyer believes that any goods delivered are defective, the buyer will return the goods to the seller.

如果买方认为交付的货物有瑕疵，买方将把货物返还给卖方。

36. If the goods are returned to the seller, the seller will replace the goods as original order provided that the buyer requests a replacement and replacement goods can still be provided.

如果买方要求换货并且有货可换，在货物被返还之后卖方应为买方交换原定货物。

37. The seller will not consider any claim for damages or loss unless the buyer presents a separate written notice and claim to the carrier concerned.

如果买方没给相关承运人书面通知或提出索赔要求，卖方将不再考虑对货物损坏或损失的赔偿。

38. If the seller cannot complete an order because raw materials are unavailable, the seller has the right to cancel the contract.

如果卖方由于无法获得原材料而无法完成订单，卖方有权撤销合同。

39. This contract is made by and between the buyer and the seller, whereby the buyer agrees to buy and the seller agrees to sell the under-mentioned commodity according to the terms and conditions stipulated below.

兹经买卖双方同意由卖方售出、买方购进下列货物，并按下列条款签订本合同。

40. The buyer shall not alter the goods or their packaging in any way, and all advertising must specify that the seller owns the intellectual property rights.

买方不得以任何方式更改货物或其包装，所有广告必须指明卖方拥有知识产权。

41. Pursuant to the contract, whether the goods are delivered to the buyer or not, the seller will retain the title to the goods until the buyer has paid the price in full.

依据本协议，无论货物是否移交买方，卖方保留货物所有权直到买方付清全部货款。

42. Neither party may assign the agreement without the written consent of the other party.

任何一方不可不经另一方书面同意转让本合同。

43. Pursuant to the agreement, the manufacturer will retain the title to the goods until the goods are sold to the consumer.

依据本协议，货物的所有权一直归制造商所有，直到卖给客户。

44. The title of goods will pass to consumers directly from manufacturer directly.

货物所有权由制造商直接移交给客户。

45. The manufacturer has/reserve the right to change any of the prices for the goods, in which event the man will immediately inform the distributors of the changes with a new price list.

制造商有权更改货物价格，更改后立即向分销商提供一个新的价目单。

46. The manufacturers own all property rights in the marks, names and designs connected with the goods.

制造商拥有与货物有关的所有商标、名称和设计的知识产权。

47. The parties acknowledge that they intend to establish a mutually beneficial relationship, to this end, they will strive to resolve the disputes through amicable negotiation.

双方承认他们将建立一个互利互惠的关系，为此他们将努力通过友好磋商的方式解决。

课后练习

Ⅰ. 单选题。

Single choice questions.

1. We would be glad to receive your ____________ export prices on the basis of CIF Shanghai.

A. low possible　　B. possible low
C. lowest possible　　D. lower possible

2. We are ____________ exporters of all kinds of Chinese goods.

A. better-establish　　B. well-established
C. good-establishing　　D. well-establish

3. ____________ for more than 30 years, we are confident we can give our customers complete satisfaction.

A. Being in business　　B. Having been in business
C. In business　　D. We are in business

4. We should consider the said firm quite reliable for ____________ engagement as you mentioned.

A. such an　　B. such as　　C. such a　　D. such like

5. We must have the goods not later than October 20 ____________ our stock is running short.

A. when　　B. that　　C. which　　D. as

6. The export sewing machines ____________ in stout water-proof material, and in pairs in light-weight crates.

A. are wrapped... being packed　　B. are wrapping... packing
C. are wrapped... packed　　D. being wrapped... are packed

7. Of all the solutions to the disputes, the one proposed by Mr. Jackson is ____________.

A. the most perfect　　B. most perfect
C. the most nearly perfect　　D. the perfect

8. Information about the current foreign markets ____________ very important to our company.

A. is　　B. was　　C. are　　D. were

9. ____________ in the labor market, he has enrolled in a computer course.

A. Be competitive　　B. Being more competitive

C. Being competitive　　D. To be more competitive

10. Our Accounts Receivable Department has written to you three times; ____________, we have had no response to our letters.

A. consequently　　B. moreover

C. thus　　D. however

Ⅱ. 将下列句子翻译为英文。

Translate the following sentences into English.

1. 依法订立的合同，对当事人具有法律约束力。当事人应当按照约定履行自己的义务，不得擅自变更或者解除合同。依法订立的合同，受法律保护。

2. 当事人订立的合同，有书面形式、口头形式和其他形式。法律、行政法规规定采用书面形式的，应当采用书面形式。当事人约定采用书面形式的，应当采用书面形式。

3. 合同的内容由当事人约定，一般包括以下条款：

（1）当事人的名称或者姓名和住所；

（2）标的；

（3）数量；

（4）质量；

（5）价款或者报酬；

（6）履行期限、地点和方式；

（7）违约责任；

（8）解决争议的方法。

当事人可以参照各类合同的示范文本订立合同。

4. 当事人对合同的效力可以约定附期限。附生效期限的合同，自期限届至时生效。附终止期限的合同，自期限届满时失效。

5. 无效的合同或者被撤销的合同自始没有法律约束力。合同部分无效，不影响其他部分效力的，其他部分仍然有效。

6. 涉外合同的当事人可以选择处理合同争议所适用的法律，但法律另有规定的除外。涉外合同的当事人没有选择的，适用与合同有最密切联系的国家的法律。在中华人民共和国境内履行的中外合资经营企业合同、中外合作经营企业合同、中外合作勘探开发自然资源合同，适用中华人民共和国法律。

Ⅲ. 将合同内容补充完整。

Fill in the contact forms in English with the following particulars.

卖方：北京轻工产品进出口公司

买方：纽约贸易总公司

商品名称：美的空调

规格：W30 型

数量：1000 台

单价：CIF 纽约每台 90 美元

包装：纸板箱装

装运期：2019 年 3 月 31 日前自中国港口至纽约，允许分批装运和转船。

付款条件：凭不可撤销即期信用证付款，于装运期前一个月开到卖方，并于上述装运期后 15 天内在中国议付有效。

保险：由卖方根据中国人民保险公司 1981 年 1 月 1 日中国保险条款按发票金额的 110% 投保一切险和战争险。

签约日期和地点：2018 年 10 月 11 日于北京

合同号码：AC4789

CONTRACT

NO.:

The Seller:

The Buyer:

The undersigned Seller and Buyer have agreed to close the following transaction according to the terms and conditions stipulated below:

Commodity:

Specifications:

Quantity:

Unit Price:

Total Value:

Packing:

Shipping Mark:

Insurance:

Time of Shipment:

Port of Shipment:

Port of Destination:

Terms of Payment:

Done and signed in ____________ on this ____________ day of ____________, 2018 ____________.

第五章 Chapter 5 跨境商务单据 Cross-border Business Documents

在全球化的经济浪潮中，跨境商务活动已成为国际贸易的核心驱动力。然而，跨境交易的复杂性不仅体现在商品和服务的跨国流动，更在于其背后严谨的单据管理和流程规范。跨境商务单据作为国际贸易中不可或缺的重要组成部分，不仅是交易双方沟通的桥梁，更是确保交易顺利进行的关键保障。

本章将深入探讨跨境商务单据的种类、功能及其重要性。从信用证的申请与审核，到商业发票、装箱单、海运提单等各类单据的填写与使用，再到运输、保险、报关等环节的单据管理，系统地梳理跨境商务单据的全流程操作。

学习目标

1. 了解信用证的含义和流程。
2. 了解各类商务单据的基本要素、书写规范和应用技巧。
3. 掌握关于信用证的各类信函的写作。
4. 能够熟练进行催证函和修改函的写作。

思政目标

1. 学习商务单据填写，培养专业素养与严谨的态度。
2. 了解法律法规，增强合规意识。
3. 注重团队配合，培养团队协作精神。

第一节 Section 1 信用证 Letter of Credit

一、信用证的申请

Application for L/C

(一) 申请开立信用证

Application for the opening of a L/C

进口人应在合同规定的时间向中国银行或其他经营外汇业务的银行办理申请开立信用证，手续如下。

The importer shall apply for the opening of a L/C from Bank of China or other banks engaged in foreign exchange business at the time specified in the contract. The procedures are as follows.

1. 递交有关合同的副本及附件

Submit copies and attachments of relevant contracts

进口人向银行申请开证时，要向银行递交进口合同的副本以及所需附件，如进口许可证。

When the importer applies for a L/C from the bank, he must submit a copy of the import contract and the required attachments, such as the import license, to the bank.

2. 填写开证申请书

Fill out the L/C application form

进口人根据银行规定的开证申请书格式，一般填写一式三份，一份留业务部门，一份留财务部门，一份交银行。填写开证申请书，必须按合同条款的具体规定，写明对信用证的各项要求，内容要明确、完整，无表意不清的记载。

The importer usually fills out three copies of the L/C application form according to the bank's regulations, one for the business department, one for the finance department, and one for the bank. When filling out the L/C application form, it is necessary to specify the requirements for the L/C in accordance with the specific provisions of the contract terms, and the content should be clear, complete, and without any unclear records.

开证申请书是银行开立信用证的依据，也是进口人凭以审查收到的货运单据并据以向开证行付款赎单的依据。开证申请书包括两部分内容。进口人在向银行申请开证时，要向银行递交进口合同副本以及所需附件，如进口许可证，并填写开证申请书。信用证开证申请书正面的内容主要包括以下项目：

（1）申请日期；

（2）申请人名称（全称）及详细地址、联系电话等；

（3）申请开证的总金额；

（4）与申请书相关的买卖合同号码；

（5）受益人的名称（全称）及详细地址、电话号码等；

（6）要求以何种方式传递信用证（电开、信开、简电开出后紧跟着航邮寄送电报证实书）；

（7）信用证的性质（如可撤销或不可撤销、是否加具保兑、是否可转让等）；

（8）申请开证中对所需要的单据条款，包括所需单据的种类、份数，出具单据的机构以及其他特殊要求；

（9）对汇票的要求，包括汇票的付款期限、付款人、金额等；

（10）本合同项下的货物名称、规格、数量、单价、价格条件、唛头①、包装条件及所必需的描述；

（11）对于装货期、交单期及有效期限的要求；

（12）对于装运地点、交单地点及到期地点的要求；

（13）对于货物是否允许分批、是否允许转运的要求；

（14）对于国外议付行费用的要求及解释；

---

① 唛头，指进出口货物包装上的标记，通常由型号、图形或收货单位简称、目的港、件数或批号等组成。——编者注

（15）其他特殊要求;

（16）信用证内容必须注明依据 UCP 600① 开出，且各项条款与规定要符合该惯例的规定和解释。

The L/C application is the basis for banks to issue L/C, and it is also the basis for importers to review the received shipping documents and make payments to the issuing bank for redemption. The L/C application consists of two parts. When the importer applies for a L/C from the bank, he must submit a copy of the import contract and required attachments, such as an import license, to the bank and fill out the L/C application form. The content on the front of the L/C application mainly includes the following items:

(1) application date;

(2) applicant's name (full name) and detailed address, contact phone number, etc;

(3) the total amount of the L/C application;

(4) the sales contract number related to the application;

(5) the name (full name) and detailed address, telephone number, etc. of the beneficiary;

(6) what is the required method for transmitting the L/C (telegraphic opening, letter opening, short telegraphic opening followed by sending a telegraphic confirmation by airmail);

(7) the nature of the L/C (such as revocable or irrevocable, whether it is confirmed, transferable, etc.);

(8) the terms of the required documents in the application for opening a L/C, including the type and number of required documents, the issuing institution, and other special requirements;

(9) requirements for bills of exchange, including payment terms, payer, amount, etc.;

(10) the name, specifications, quantity, unit price, price conditions, marking, packaging conditions, and necessary descriptions of the goods under this contract;

(11) requirements for loading period, presentation period, and validity period;

(12) requirements for shipping location, presentation location, and expiration location;

(13) requirements for whether goods are allowed to be divided into batches and transferred;

(14) requirements and explanations for foreign negotiated bank fees;

(15) other special requirements;

(16) the content of the L/C must indicate that it is issued in accordance with UCP 600, and all terms and regulations must comply with the provisions and interpretations of this convention.

信用证背面是申请人对开证行的声明，用以明确双方责任，主要有以下几项内容：

（1）声明申请人同意按照有关国际惯例办理该信用证项下一切事宜，并承担由此产生的一切责任。

（2）声明委托银行开立信用证，并保证银行按时支付货款、手续费、利息及一切费用。

（3）声明收到单据后，申请人在规定工作日内复审单据，并在规定期限内通知银行接受与否。

---

① UCP600，指《跟单信用证统一惯例》（2007 年修订版）——编者注

（4）声明该信用证及其项下业务往来函电及单据如因邮、电或其他方式传递过程中发生遗失、延误、错漏等，银行概不负责。

（5）声明若信用证需要修改，应由申请人及时通知银行，并及时核对信用证副本或修改书副本是否与原申请书相符。

（6）声明如申请书字迹不清或词意含混而引起的后果由申请人负责。

The back of the L/C is a statement from the applicant to the issuing bank, which clarifies the responsibilities of both parties and mainly includes the following contents:

(1) Declare that the applicant agrees to handle all matters under the L/C in accordance with relevant international practices and assumes all responsibilities arising therefrom.

(2) Declare that entrust the bank to open a L/C and ensure that the bank pays the goods, handling fees, interest, and all expenses on time.

(3) Declare that upon receipt of the documents, the applicant shall review them within the prescribed working days and notify the bank of acceptance within the prescribed period.

(4) Declare that the bank shall not be responsible for any loss, delay, error or omission of the L/C and its related business letter and documents during the transmission process by mail, telegram or other means.

(5) Declare that if the L/C needs to be amended, the applicant should promptly notify the bank and verify whether the copy of the L/C or amendment is consistent with the original application.

(6) Declare that the applicant shall be responsible for any consequences arising from unclear handwriting or ambiguous meanings in the application form.

3. 缴付保证金

Pay the deposit

按照国际贸易的习惯做法，除非开证行对开证申请人有授信额度，否则，进口人向银行申请开立信用证时，应向银行缴付一定比例的保证金，其金额一般为信用证金额的百分之几到百分之几十，一般根据进口人的资信情况而定。在我国的进口业务中，开证行根据不同企业和交易的情况，要求开证申请人缴付一定比例的人民币保证金，然后开证。

According to the customary practice of international trade, unless the issuing bank has a credit limit for the applicant, the importer should pay a certain percentage of the deposit to the bank when applying for the opening of a L/C. The amount is generally several percent to several tens of percent of the L/C amount, depending on the importer's creditworthiness. In China's import business, the issuing bank requires the applicant to pay a certain percentage of RMB deposit according to the situation of different enterprises and transactions, and then issue the L/C.

4. 支付开证手续费

Pay the opening fee for the L/C

进口人在申请开证时，必须按规定支付一定金额的开证手续费。

The importer must pay a certain amount of L/C handling fee according to regulations when applying for the issuance of the L/C.

（二）开证申请书主要栏位填制说明

Instructions for filling in the main fields of the L/C application

关于不可撤销信用证开证申请书的格式和内容，各银行印制的都差不多，这里主要介绍中国银行的格式，并简单介绍申请人填制的内容、方法及注意事项。

（1）申请开证日期：在申请书右上角。

（2）传递方式：有四种，即信开（航空邮寄）、电开（电报）、快递、简电后随寄电报证实书。需要哪一种方式，在前面方框中打“×”。例如，选用信开（航空邮寄），就在“issue by airmail”前的方框中打“×”。

（3）到期日期和到期地点：信用证的到期地点可以是开证行所在地，也可以是受益人所在地。如果是开证行所在地，出口审单员一定要把握好交单时间和邮程，防止信用证失效。

（4）信用证性质：如果要在已印制好的不可撤销信用证上增加保兑或可转让等内容，也可加上。信用证号码由开证行填写。信用证有效期及到期地点由申请人填写。

（5）申请人：必须填写全称及详细地址，还要注明联系电话、传真等号码，便于有关当事人之间的联系。

（6）受益人：必须填写全称及详细地址，也要注明联系电话、传真等号码，便于联系。

（7）通知行：由开证行填写。

（8）信用证金额：必须用数字和文字两种形式表示，并且要标明币种。信用证金额是开证行付款责任的最高限额，必须根据合同的规定标示清楚，如果有一定比例的上下浮动幅度，也应标示清楚。

（9）分批与转运：应根据合同的规定明确表示“允许”或“不允许”，在选择的项目前方框中打“×”。

（10）装运条款：应根据合同的规定填写装运地（港）及目的地（港）、最晚装运日期，如有转运地（港）也应写清楚。

（11）价格术语：有 FOB、CFR、CIF 及“其他条件”四个备选项目，根据合同成交的贸易术语进行选择，如是其他条件，则在该项目后面写明。

（12）付款方式：信用证有效兑付方式有四种选择——即期支付、承兑支付、议付、延期支付，应根据合同的规定，在所选方式前的方框中打“×”。

（13）汇票要求：应根据合同的规定，填写信用证项下应支付发票金额的百分之几。如合同规定所有货款都用信用证支付，则应填写信用证项下汇票金额是发票金额的 100%；如合同规定该笔货款由信用证和托收两种方式支付，各支付 50%，则应填写信用证项下汇票金额是全部发票金额的 50%；以此类推。另外，还应填写汇票的支付期限，如即期、远期。如是远期汇票，必须填写具体的天数，如 30 天、60 天、90 天等。最后，填写付款人，根据 UCP 600 的规定，信用证项下汇票的付款人必须是开证行或指定付款行。

（14）单据条款：印制好的单据要求共 12 条，其中第 1 条到第 12 条是针对具体的单据，第 13 条是“其他单据”，即以上 12 种单据以外的单据要求，可填在第 13 条中。

（15）合同项下的货物包括：货物的名称、规格、数量、包装、单价条款、唛头等所有内容必须与合同规定一样，尤其是单价条款、数量条款不得有误。包装条款如有特殊要求，如包装规格、包装物的要求等，应具体、明确、标示清楚。

（16）附加条款：印制好的有6条，其中第1条至第6条是具体的条款要求，如需要可在前面括号里打“×”，内容不完整的，可根据合同的规定和买方的需要填写清楚。第7条是“其他条款”，即以上6条以外还有附加条款的，可填在该条款中，有几条可顺序添加几条。

（17）申请书下面是有关申请人的开户银行（填银行名称）、账户号码、执行人、联系电话、申请人（法人代表）签字等内容。

The format and content of the application for opening an irrevocable L/C are similar to those printed by various banks. Here, we mainly introduce the format of Bank of China and briefly introduce the content, methods, and precautions that the applicant should fill in.

(1) Date of application for L/C: located in the upper right corner of the application form.

(2) Delivery methods: There are four types, namely letter opening (air mail), telegraphic opening (telegram), express delivery, and telegram confirmation letter sent with a simple telegram. Which method is needed? Please mark "×" in the box in front of it. For example, if you choose letter opening (air mail), mark "×" in the box before "issue by airmail".

(3) Expiration date and location. The place of expiration of a L/C can be the location of the issuing bank or the location of the beneficiary. If it is the location of the issuing bank, the export document examiner must grasp the presentation time and postal procedures to prevent the L/C from becoming invalid.

(4) Nature of L/C: If you want to add confirmation or transferable content in the already printed irrevocable L/C, you can also add it. The L/C number is filled in by the issuing bank. The validity period and expiration location of the L/C shall be filled in by the applicant.

(5) Applicant: Full name and detailed address must be provided, along with contact phone number, fax number, etc., to facilitate communication between relevant parties.

(6) Beneficiary: Full name and detailed address must be filled in, and contact phone number, fax number, etc. must also be indicated for easy contact.

(7) Notification line: To be filled out by the issuing bank.

(8) The amount of the L/C: It must be expressed in both numerical and textual forms, and the currency must be indicated. The amount of the L/C is the maximum limit of payment responsibility of the issuing bank, which must be clearly indicated in accordance with the provisions of the contract. If there is a certain percentage of fluctuation, it should also be clearly indicated.

(9) Batch and transportation: The contract should clearly indicate whether "allowed" or "not allowed" , and mark "×" in the box in front of the selected item.

(10) Shipping terms: The shipping location (port) and destination (port), as well as the latest shipping date, should be filled in according to the contract. If there is a transshipment location (port), it should also be clearly stated.

(11) Price terms: There are four alternative items: FOB, CFR, CIF, and "other conditions". The selection is based on the trade terms used in the contract. If there are other conditions, they should be specified after the item.

(12) Payment method: There are four valid payment methods for the L/C— sight payment,

acceptance payment, negotiation and deferred payment. According to the provisions of the contract, an "×" should be marked in the box before the selected method.

(13) Bill of exchange requirement: According to the contract, the percentage of the invoice amount payable under the L/C should be filled in. If the contract stipulates that all payments shall be made by L/C, the bill of exchange amount under the L/C should be filled in as 100% of the invoice amount. If the contract stipulates that the payment for the goods shall be made through two methods — L/C and collection, with each method paying 50%, then the amount of the bill of exchange under the L/C shall be filled in as 50% of the total invoice amount; and so on. In addition, the payment term of the bill of exchange should also be filled in, such as sight or forward. If it is a forward draft, the specific number of days must be filled in, such as 30 days, 60 days, 90 days, etc. Finally, fill in the payer. According to UCP 600 regulations, the payer of the bill of exchange under the L/C must be the issuing bank or the designated paying bank.

(14) Document terms: There are a total of 12 requirements for printed documents, among which the first to twelfth requirements are for specific documents, and the thirteenth requirement is for "other documents", which means that document requirements other than the above 12 types of documents can be filled in the thirteenth requirement.

(15) The goods under the contract: They include the name, specifications, quantity, packaging, unit price terms, markings, and all other contents must be the same as those specified in the contract, especially the unit price terms and quantity terms must not be incorrect. If there are special requirements for packaging terms, such as packaging specifications, packaging material requirements, etc., they should be specific, clear, and clearly labeled.

(16) Additional terms: There are 6 printed terms, among which terms 1 to 6 are specific requirements. If necessary, you can mark "×" in the parentheses in front. If the content is incomplete, it can be filled in clearly according to the provisions of the contract and the needs of the buyer. Term 7 is "Other terms", which means that if there are additional terms beyond the above 6 terms, they can be filled in this term. Several terms can be added in sequence.

(17) Below the application form are information about the applicant's bank (insert bank name), account number, executor, contact phone number, and signature of the applicant (legal representative).

二、信用证的开立
Opening for L/C

(一) 银行开立信用证
Opening for L/C by banks

在进口人申请开证时，银行为减轻自身的风险，通常进行“三查一保”。“三查”是指审查开证申请书和开证申请人声明，审查开证申请人的资信情况，查验有关进口开证必须提供的有效文件；“一保”是指开证申请人必须向开证行缴纳开证保证金。

When the importer applys for a L/C, banks usually conduct "three checks and one guarantee" to reduce their own risks. The "three checks" refer to the examination of the L/C application and the declaration of the L/C applicant, the examination of the creditworthiness of the L/C applicant, and the verification of the valid documents required for import L/C issuance. The "one guarantee" refers to the requirement for the applicant to pay a deposit to the issuing bank for the issuance of the L/C.

1. 审查开证申请书和开证人声明

Review the L/C application and the statement of the issuer

开证申请书既是开证行开立信用证的根据，又是开证行与开证申请人之间法律性的书面契约。开证人声明是开证申请人申请开立信用证应承担的义务和责任的书面承诺。开证行收到申请人填制好的开证申请书以后，必须对以上两项内容进行审查。

The L/C application is not only the basis for the issuing bank to issue a L/C, but also a legal written contract between the issuing bank and the applicant. The statement of the issuer is a written commitment by the applicant for opening a L/C to fulfill their obligations and responsibilities. After receiving the application form filled out by the applicant, the issuing bank must review the above two items.

2. 审查开证申请人的资信情况

Review the creditworthiness of the applicant for the L/C

开证申请人的资信情况直接关系到开证银行的利益，因此，开证行要严格审核申请人的资信情况，一般要掌握以下原则：

（1）如果申请人是首次申请开证，开证银行应严格审核申请人的注册资本情况、经营状况、财务状况及经济效益，以及申请人是否有进出口经营权。

（2）如果申请人不是首次申请开证或与开证行有业务往来关系，主要审查以往的业务往来中有无不良记录以及目前的经营状况、财务状况和经济实力等。

The creditworthiness of the applicant is directly related to the interests of the issuing bank. Therefore, the issuing bank should strictly review the applicant's creditworthiness and generally adhere to the following principles:

(1) If the applicant is applying for a L/C for the first time, the issuing bank should strictly review the applicant's registered capital, operating status, financial status, and economic benefits, as well as whether the applicant has import and export operating rights.

(2) If the applicant is not applying for the issuance of a L/C for the first time or has business dealings with the issuing bank, the main focus is on examining whether there are any adverse records in previous business dealings, as well as the current operating conditions, financial status, and economic strength.

3. 审查开证时应提供的有效文件

Review the valid documents to be provided during issuance of the L/C

开证行在接受开证申请书时，应查验申请人同时提供的有效文件，如进口许可证、贸易进口付汇核销单、有关部门的登记文件等。

When accepting an application for opening a L/C, the issuing bank should review the valid documents provided by the applicant, such as import license, trade import payment verification form, registration documents from relevant departments, etc.

4. 收取开证保证金

Collect the deposit for opening the L/C

信用证一经开出，开证行就要承担第一性付款的责任，所以，开证行为了保证自身资金的安全和信誉，对不同的开证申请人采取不同的办法，收取不同比例的保证金或抵押品，或第三者出具的担保等，主要是为了防止申请人违约、破产或因为市场行情的变动导致申请人无力付款赎单的风险。

Once a L/C is issued, the issuing bank is responsible for the first payment. Therefore, the issuing bank ensures the safety and reputation of its own funds by adopting different methods for different applicants, such as collecting different proportions of margin or collateral, or third-party guarantees, mainly to prevent the risk of default, bankruptcy, or inability to pay for the redemption due to changes in market conditions.

（二）催开信用证

Writing for urging the opening of L/C

在买卖双方签订合同之后，买方迟迟没有开出信用证的情况下，为了确保合同顺利执行，卖方应该去函要求买方按照合同的要求开立信用证。催开信用证的函电内容一般包括：

（1）提及合同及其项下的货物；

（2）敦促买方开立信用证；

（3）提醒买方开证时注意信用证条款与合同条款一致。

After the contract is signed between the buyer and seller, if the buyer has not yet opened the L/C, in order to ensure the smooth execution of the contract, the seller should send a letter requesting the buyer to open the L/C according to the requirements of the contract. The formal demand letter for L/C usually include:

（1）mention the contract and the goods under it;

（2）urge the buyer to open a L/C;

（3）remind the buyer to ensure that the L/C terms are consistent with the contract terms when opening the L/C.

范例

Dear Sirs,

With reference to the goods under our Sales Confirmation No. 5207, we wish to draw your attention to the fact that the delivery date is approaching, but we have not yet received the covering L/C.

Please do your utmost to expedite same, so that we may execute the order smoothly. In order to avoid subsequent amendments, please see to it that the L/C stipulations are in exact accordance with the terms of the Confirmation.

We hope to hear favorably from you soon.

Sincerely yours,

×××

三、信用证的审核与修改

Examination and amendment of L/C

（一）信用证的审核

Examination of L/C

虽然信用证的内容在合同中已有规定，但往往因买方的疏忽或立场不同，卖方可能会接到并非完全符合合同规定的信用证。为了确保交易的安全，除了平时多注意进口国的政治经济形势以及加强对买方的征信调研外，卖方收到信用证后，必须详细审核信用证所列的条件。例如：

（1）开证银行的信用是否良好？

（2）是否为信用证正本？信用证副本或预备通知均为无效信用证。

（3）信用证中所列条件是否与买卖合同相符？

（4）受益人与申请人的名称、地址是否正确？

（5）信用证的有效期是否合理？信用证有效日期必须晚于装船日，应当合理可行。

（6）信用证金额是否正确？信用证上的金额应与商业发票一致。

（7）远期信用证上有无买方负担利息的文字？

（8）信用证是否有难以履行的条款？

（9）各条款间有无相互抵触？

（10）有无列载适用 UCP 600 的条款？

（11）信用证是否规定必须另外指示或通知才生效？

（12）信用证有效期是否以进口地时间为准或未注明以何地为准？

Although the contents of the L/C are already specified in the contract, sellers may receive a L/C that does not fully comply with the contract due to the buyer's negligence or different positions. In order to ensure the safety of transactions, in addition to paying more attention to the political and economic situation of the importing country and strengthening credit research on buyers, sellers must carefully review the conditions listed in the L/C after receiving it. For example:

(1) Is the credit of the issuing bank good?

(2) Is it the original L/C? The copy or preliminary notice of the L/C is invalid.

(3) Are the conditions listed in the L/C consistent with the sales contract?

(4) Are the names and addresses of the beneficiary and applicant correct?

(5) Is the validity period of the L/C reasonable? The validity date of the L/C must be later than

the loading date and should be reasonable and feasible.

(6) Is the amount of the L/C correct? The amount on the L/C should be consistent with the commercial invoice.

(7) Is there any text indicating that the buyer bears the interest on the forward L/C?

(8) Is there any term in the L/C that is difficult to fulfill?

(9) Are there any conflicts between the terms?

(10) Are there any terms applicable to UCP 600 listed?

(11) Does the L/C require additional instructions or notifications to take effect?

(12) Is the validity period of the L/C based on the time of import or unspecified?

(二) 信用证的修改程序

Procedures for amending L/C

在信用证有效期内，任何一方的任何修改，都必须经买卖双方协商一致同意后，由申请人通过开证行办理修改。开证行可依据申请人提交的信用证修改申请书受理该笔业务。

During the validity period of the L/C, any amendment made by either party must be agreed upon by both the buyer and seller through consultation, and the applicant shall handle the amendment through the issuing bank. The issuing bank may accept the business based on the L/C amendment application submitted by the applicant.

1. 申请人提交信用证修改申请书

The applicant submits a L/C amendment application

信用证修改申请书必须由原信用证的申请人填写，并提交到原开证行办理修改业务。信用证修改申请书的主要内容有：

(1) 信用证修改申请书提交的日期；

(2) 所需修改的原信用证编号；

(3) 修改的内容，一般先列出原信用证的有关条款，再写出相应的修改条款。

The application for amendment of the L/C must be filled out by the applicant of the original L/C and submitted to the original issuing bank for amendment. The main contents of the L/C amendment application include:

(1) the date of submission of the L/C amendment application;

(2) the original L/C number that needs to be amended;

(3) the amended content that usually first lists the relevant terms of the original L/C, and then writes the corresponding amended terms.

2. 开证行审查并受理

Review and acceptance by the issuing bank

原开证行接到原信用证申请人的信用证修改申请书后，必须按照申请书所列信用证编号，调出原信用证副本对照审核。审核的主要内容有：

(1) 信用证修改申请书中的编号是否正确？

(2) 所要求修改的条款内容是否符合国际惯例和本国法律？

（3）所要求修改的条款对开证行有无不利之处？

（4）所要求修改的条款之间有无相互矛盾之处，与原信用证其他条款有无相互矛盾之处？如有，应提醒申请人同时作相应的修改，使修改后的信用证各条款相互吻合、前后协调；

（5）如提出增加信用证总金额，则要增收保证金。

After receiving the L/C amendment application from the original L/C applicant, the original issuing bank must retrieve a copy of the original L/C for comparative review according to the L/C number listed in the application. The main contents of the review include:

（1）Is the number in the L/C amendment application correct?

（2）Whether the requested amended terms comply with international conventions and domestic laws?

（3）Is there any adverse effect on the issuing bank of the requested amended terms?

（4）Are there any contradictions between the requested amended terms and with other terms of the original L/C? If so, the applicant should be reminded to make corresponding amendments to ensure that the amended terms of the L/C are consistent and coordinated.

（5）If it is proposed to increase the total amount of the L/C, a deposit must be added.

开证行审核无误后，根据修改申请书的要求，按原信用证的传递路线向各有关当事人发出信用证修改通知书。开证行应收取修改手续费。如修改手续费由受益人支付，应在修改通知书中列明，该单到付款时一并扣除。

After the issuing bank reviews that there are no errors, according to the requirements of the amendment application, it shall issue a L/C amendment notice to all relevant parties along the original transmission route of the L/C. The issuing bank shall charge a amendment handling fee. If the amendment fee is to be paid by the beneficiary, it should be specified in the amendment notice and deducted together with the payment upon receipt of the order.

3. 改证函

Amendment of L/C

卖方在收到信用证后，如果审核信用证时发现与合同条款不符或无法办到的条款，必须及时要求对方进行修改。函电的内容包括：

（1）提及对方的信用证；

（2）指出信用证的错误或存在的问题；

（3）提出修改的具体要求；

（4）希望对方早日修改信用证。

After receiving the L/C, the seller must promptly request the other party to make amendments if any terms are found to be inconsistent with or impossible to fulfill during the review of the L/C. The content of the letter includes:

（1）mention the other party's L/C;

（2）identify errors or issues in the L/C;

（3）propose specific requirements for amendments;

(4) express the hope that the other party can amend the L/C as soon as possible.

范例

Dear Mr. Johnson,

Thank you for sending us your L/C No. 651 issued by the Bank of New York. However, on checking its terms, we regret to find that there are some mistakes in your L/C, please amend the above L/C as follows:

(1) Term 15: Date of Expiry has been changed from 101115 to 101215;

(2) Term 24: Date of First Shipment has been changed from 100901 to 101001;

(3) Term 32: Goods should be insured for 120% of the invoice value, note for 130%.

We will proceed with the shipment as soon as we confirm the above amendments.

Your prompt reply is highly appreciated.

Sincerely,

Zhang Yi

第二节 商务单证
Section 2 Business Documents

一、商业发票
Commercial invoice

商业发票是卖方向买方开立的，对整个交易和所交货物有关内容的总体说明，是一张发货价目清单。买方凭发票核对货物及了解货物的品质、规格、价值等情况。

A commercial invoice is issued by the seller to the buyer, providing an overall description of the entire transaction and the goods delivered. It is a list of shipping prices. The buyer verifies the goods and understands the quality, specifications, value, and other information of the goods based on the invoice.

商业发票是国际商务单据的核心单据，其主要作用有以下几点：

(1) 是货运单据的核心，也是装运货物总的说明；

(2) 是进出口商收付货款和记账与核算的依据；

(3) 是在没有汇票时，出口商可凭发票向进口商收款；

(4) 是进出口双方报关及纳税的基本依据；

(5) 是缮制报关单、产地证、报检单、投保单等其他单据的依据。

Commercial invoice is the core document of international business documents, and its main functions are as follows:

(1) It serves as the central component of shipping documents and provide a overall description of the goods being shipped;

(2) It forms the basis for importer and exporter to receive or pay for goods, as well as for bookkeeping and accounting;

(3) When there is no draft (bill of exchange), the exporter can collect payment from the importer with the invoice;

(4) It is the primary basis for customs declaration and taxation by both parties;

(5) It is the basis for preparing other documents such as customs declaration forms, certificates of origin, inspection forms, insurance policies, etc.

二、装箱单
Packing list

(一) 装箱单的含义
The meaning of packing list

装箱单、重量单和尺码单等包装单据是商业发票的一种补充单据，是将商品的不同包装规格条件、不同花色和不同重量逐一分别详细列表说明的一种单据。它是买方收货时核对货物的品种、花色、尺寸、规格和海关验收的主要依据。

Packing list, weight list, size list and other packaging documents are supplementary documents to commercial invoices, which are detailed lists and explanations of different packaging specifications, colors and weights of goods one by one. It is the main basis for the buyer to check the variety, color, size, specifications, and customs acceptance of the goods when receiving them.

装箱单的内容一般包括合同号、发票号、出单日期、运输标志、品名、包装规格、包装件数、毛净重等。填写装箱单时，必须与货物实际包装相符，并与发票、提单等单据相一致。

The contents of packing list generally include the contract number, invoice number, invoice date, transportation mark, product name, packaging specifications, number of packages, gross and net weight, etc. When filling out the packing list, it must match the actual packaging of the goods and be consistent with documents such as invoices and bills of lading.

(二) 装箱单的作用
The functions of packing list

装箱单的作用如下：

(1) 是出口商缮制发票及其他单据时计量、计价的基本资料；

(2) 是出口商清点数量或重量以及销售货物的依据；

(3) 是海关查验货物的凭证；

(4) 是公证或商检机构查验货物的参考资料。

The functions of packing list are as follows:

(1) It is the basic information for measuring and pricing when exporters prepare invoices and other documents;

(2) It is the basis for exporters to count the quantity or weight and sell goods;

(3) It is a certificate for customs inspection of goods;

(4) It is a reference material for notary or inspection agencies to inspect goods.

三、汇票
Bill of exchange

出口收汇中使用的汇票，是指用于托收和信用证收汇方式中，出口商向进口商或银行签发的，要求后者即期或在一个固定的日期或在可以确定的将来时间，对某人或某指定人或持票人支付一定金额的无条件的书面支付命令。

The bill of exchange used in export collection refers to an unconditional written payment order issued by the exporter to the importer or bank in the collection and L/C collection methods, requiring the latter to pay a certain amount of money to someone or a designated person or holder at sight or on a fixed date or at a determinable future time.

作为可以支取信用证金额的凭证，汇票在本质上是一种票据，而不是单据。但作为信用证交易单证的组成部分，汇票所记载内容也必须符合信用证条款和 UCP 600 的相关规定。通常，由于出票人为出口商，收汇单证中的汇票属于商业汇票。

As a voucher for withdrawing the amount of a L/C, a bill of exchange is essentially an instrument, not a document. But as an integral part of the L/C transaction document, the contents of the bill of exchange must also comply with the terms of the L/C and the relevant provisions of UCP 600. Usually, due to the fact that the drawer is an exporter, the bill of exchange in the receipt document belongs to a commercial bill of exchange.

托收和信用证方式下，通常使用跟单汇票，较少用光票。延期付款信用证无须提交汇票。

Under the collection and L/C methods, documentary bills of exchange are usually used, and bare bills are less commonly used. A deferred payment L/C does not require submission of a bill of exchange.

第三节　运输与保险单证
Section 3　Shipment Documents and Insurance Documents

一、出口托运委托书
Booking note

托运是指出口企业自己或委托外运公司（或有权代理对外货运业务的单位）向承运单位或其代理人办理货物的对外运输业务。

Consignment refers to the process where an exporting enterprise, either independently or by entrusting a international transportation company (or an entity authorized to handle international freight services), arranges the international shipment of goods with the carrier or its agent.

海运方式有两种：传统散货运输和现代集装箱运输。这两种运输方式分别使用不同格式的出口托运委托书。

There are two types of sea transportation: traditional bulk cargo transportation and modern container transportation. These two modes of transportation use different formats of booking notes.

出口托运委托书（也称托运单、托单），是托运人向承运人或其代理签发的以作租船订舱的专用凭证。它的主要作用如下：

（1）出口托运委托书是租船订舱的依据。如果出口货物数量大，需要整船运输，出口企业可办理租船运输；如果出口数量不大，则可租订班轮舱位或租订非班轮的部分舱位。

（2）出口托运委托书是运输合同的组成部分。其中包含托运人与承运人双方就某批货物运输而产生的各自的权利和义务。

（3）出口托运委托书是签发提单等运输单据的依据。运输单据中的许多栏目中的数据和信息必须严格按照出口托运委托书上的信息填写。

（4）出口托运委托书是承运人收取运杂费的凭证。它是收费凭证之一，缺少出口托运委托书，托运人有权拒付。

The booking note, is a special document issued by the shipper to the carrier or its agent for the purpose of chartering a ship and booking cargo space. Its main functions are as follows:

(1) The booking note is the basis for chartering and booking cargo. If the quantity of exported goods is large and requires full-ship transportation, the exporting enterprise can handle charter transportation. If the quantity of exported goods is not large, it can rent liner space or rent some non-liner space.

(2) The booking note is an integral part of the transportation contract. It includes the respective rights and obligations of the shipper and the carrier arising from the transportation of a certain batch of goods.

(3) The booking note is the basis for issuing transportation documents, such as bills of lading. The data and information in many columns of the transportation document must be strictly filled in according to the information on the booking note.

(4) The booking note is a document for the carrier to collect transportation and miscellaneous fees. It is one of the payment vouchers; without a booking note, the shipper has the right to refuse payment.

二、海运提单
Bill of lading

海运提单是用以证明海上货物运输合同和货物已由承运人接收或装船，以及承运人保证据以交付货物的单证。根据提单中载明的向记名人交付货物，或者按照指示人的指示交付货物，或者向提单持有人交付货物的条款，构成承运人据以交付货物的保证。

A bill of lading is a document used to prove the contract of carriage of goods by sea and that the goods have been received or loaded by the carrier, as well as the carrier's guarantee of delivery of the goods. According to the terms stated in the bill of lading for delivering goods to a named person or delivering goods according to the instructions of the instructing person, or delivering goods to the holder of the bill of lading, it constitutes a guarantee for the carrier to deliver the goods.

在国际货物运输中，提单是最具特色、最完整的运输单据。在国际贸易中，提单是一种有价证券，同时代表物权和债权。在各国有关运输法律中，提单都被认定是一份非常重要的法律文件，提单上权利的实现必须以交还提单为要件。

In international cargo transportation, the bill of lading is the most distinctive and complete transport document. In international trade, a bill of lading is a valuable security that represents both property rights and creditor's rights. In the relevant transportation laws of various countries, the bill of lading is recognized as a very important legal document, and the realization of the rights on the bill of lading must be based on the return of the bill of lading.

提单的作用主要表现在：

(1) 是海上货物运输合同的证明；

(2) 是货物已由承运人接收或装船的收货证据；

(3) 是承运人必须凭以交付货物的物权凭证。

The main functions of a bill of lading are as follows:

(1) It is proof of the contract for the carriage of goods by sea;

(2) It is evidence of receipt of goods by the carrier or loaded onto the ship;

(3) It is a document of title that the carrier must use as the basis for delivering the goods.

三、装运通知

Shipping advice

装运通知，是出口商向进口商发出货物已于某月某日或将于某月某日装运某船的通知。装运通知的内容通常包括货名、装运数量、船名、装船日期、契约或信用证号码等。这项通知，大多以电报方式为之，但也有用航邮方式的。装运通知的作用在于方便买方投立保险、准备提货手续或转售；出口商作此项通知时，有时会附上或另行寄上货运单据副本，以便进口商明了装货内容。若碰到货运单据正本迟到的情况，仍可及时办理担保提货。

A shipping advice refers to a notification sent by the exporter to the importer, specifying that the goods have been or will be shipped on a designated vessel on a specified date within a given month. The contents of the shipping advice usually include the name of the goods, the quantity to be shipped, the name of the vessel, the date of loading, the contract or L/C number, etc. This notification is mostly sent by telegram, but it can also be sent by airmail. The purpose of a shipping advice is to facilitate the buyer in placing insurance, preparing for delivery procedures, or reselling. Exporters may sometimes attach or send copies of shipping documents when making this notification, so that importers can understand the contents of the shipment. Even if the original shipping documents are delayed, the guarantee for delivery can still be processed in a timely manner.

四、投保单

Insurance application

投保人在运输工具起运前，备妥货物并确定装运日后应及时办理投保，即投保人向保险人表示订立保险合同的意愿，提出投保申请。投保人必须将有关要求告诉保险公司，向保险人提出要约或询价，填写投保申请单，并随附发票或提单等。保险公司对此审核无误后，以此为依据出具保险单或其他保险单据，收取保险费。

The insured shall promptly effect insurance after preparing the goods and confirming the shipment date but before the departure of the transport vehicle. This means the insured must express the intention to enter into an insurance contract with the insurer and submit the insurance application. The insured must inform the insurance company of the relevant requirements, submit an offer or enquiry to the insurer, fill out the insurance application form, and attach an invoice or bill of lading, etc. After verifying the accuracy of this, the insurance company shall issue an insurance policy or other insurance documents based on this and charge insurance premiums.

投保单一般是保险人根据不同险种事先设计内容格式，由投保人在投保时填写，投保人应根据贸易、运输、货物的实际情况（如采用信用证方式，还需按来证要求），明确写出需投保的险别，提出相关的保险要求，并告之货物及装运情况，投保单所写明的事实内容，是保险人据此作为风险衡量、保费计费、合同订立（出保单）的依据。

The insurance application is generally designed by the insurer in advance according to different types of insurance, and filled out by the insured at the time of insurance. The insured should clearly state the types of insurance to be insured based on the actual situation of trade, transportation, and goods (if using a L/C, relevant insurance requirements should also be met), and inform the goods and shipping situation. The factual content stated in the insurance application is the basis for the insurer to measure risks, charge premiums, and enter into contracts (issue insurance policies) based on this.

各企业的投保申请格式不完全一致，但无论哪种格式，都包括以下这些主要内容：

（1）投保人名称；

（2）发票号码和标记；

（3）包装及数量（件数）；

（4）货物名称；

（5）保险金额；

（6）运输工具；

（7）开航日期；

（8）赔付地及币制；

（9）运输路程；

（10）承保险别；

（11）投保单位签章和投保日期。

The insurance application formats of various enterprises are not completely consistent, but regardless of the format, they all include the following main contents:

(1) name of the insured;
(2) invoice number and shipping marking;
(3) packaging and quantity (number of units);
(4) name of goods;
(5) insured amount;
(6) transportation vehicles;
(7) date of departure;
(8) claims settlement location and currency;
(9) transportation distance;
(10) type of insurance coverage;
(11) authorized signature and date of application by the insured entity.

第四节 Section 4 认证、检验检疫与报关单证 Certification, Inspection Quarantine and Customs Declaration Documents

一、报检单 Application for inspection

报检单是报检人根据有关法律、行政法规或合同约定申请检验检疫机构对其某种货物实施检验检疫、鉴定的书面凭证，它表明了报检人正式向检验检疫机构提出检验检疫、鉴定的申请。报检单体现的是一种行政法律关系上的权利义务关系，主要表现在以下方面。

An application for inspection is a written document issued by the applicant to the inspection and quarantine institution for inspection, quarantine, and appraisal of a certain type of goods in accordance with relevant laws, administrative regulations, or contractual agreements. It indicates that the applicant has formally submitted an application for inspection, quarantine, and appraisal to the inspection and quarantine institution. The application for inspection reflects an administrative legal relationship of rights and obligations, mainly manifested in the following aspects.

首先，作为报检人，其义务就是对法检商品必须履行报检义务，并如实填写报检单相关事项；其次是报检人要对报检单内容的真实性负责，若不如实填写，应承担相应的法律责任。同时，报检人拥有在规定的时限内获得检验检疫证书或者通关凭证的权利。

Firstly, as an applicant, one' s obligation is to fulfill the inspection obligation for legally inspected goods and truthfully fill in the relevant matters on application for inspection. Secondly, the applicant shall be responsible for the authenticity of the contents of application for inspection. If the applicant fail to fill in the form truthfully, he shall bear corresponding legal responsibilities. At the same time, the applicant has the right to obtain the inspection and quarantine certificate or customs clearance certificate within the prescribed time limit.

对检验检疫机构来说，其权利就是要求报检人按规定的时间、地点向检验检疫机构报检，并如实填报。检验检疫机构的义务就是按时依法实施检验、检疫，并在规定的时限内出具检验检疫证书。

For inspection and quarantine institutions, their right is to require the applicant to report to the inspection and quarantine institution at the prescribed time and place, and truthfully fill in the information. The obligation of inspection and quarantine institutions is to carry out inspection and quarantine on time and in accordance with the law, and issue inspection and quarantine certificates within the prescribed time limit.

二、原产地证明书
Certificate of origin

一般原产地证是出口商应进口商的要求提供的、由公证机构、政府或出口商出具的证明货物原产地和制造地的一种证明文件。它通常用于不使用海关发票或领事发票的国家（地区），以确定对货物征税的税率。若信用证或合同未作具体规定，它一般由出入境检验检疫局出具。

A general certificate of origin is a document provided by an exporter at the request of an importer, issued by a notary public, government, or exporter, to prove the origin and place of manufacture of goods. It is commonly used in countries (regions) that do not use customs or consular invoices to determine the tax rate for goods. If the L/C or contract does not specify, the certificate of origin is generally issued by the Exit-Entry Inspection and Quarantine Bureau.

另外，根据进口商的不同要求，进口国海关除了认可由出入境检验检疫局或中国国际贸易促进委员会签发的中华人民共和国原产地证外，有时也认可由出口商、生产厂家等单位出具证明货物原产地的文件。

In addition, according to the different requirements of importers, the customs of the importing country not only recognize the certificate of origin of the People's Republic of China issued by the Exit-Entry Inspection and Quarantine Bureau or the China Council for the Promotion of International Trade, but also sometimes recognize documents issued by exporters, manufacturers, and other units to prove the origin of the goods.

原产地证明书分为一般原产地证、普惠制原产地证、区域性经济集团互惠原产地证专用原产地证等。如果我国与进口国签订了普惠制关税互惠协定就应提供普惠制原产地证，签订其他协议的提供相应的原产地证，否则提供一般原产地证。

The certificate of origin is divided into general certificate of origin, Generalized System of Preferences (GSP) certificate of origin, and regional economic group reciprocal certificate of origin special certificate of origin. If China has signed a GSP tariff reciprocity agreement with the importing country, it should provide a GSP certificate of origin. If other agreements are signed, corresponding certificates of origin should be provided. Otherwise, a general certificate of origin should be provided.

三、报关单
Customs declaration document

进出口货物报关单是指进出口货物收发货人或其代理人，按照海关规定的格式对进出口货物的实际情况做出书面声明，以此要求海关对其货物按适用的海关制度办理通关手续的法律文书。它在对外经济贸易活动中具有十分重要的法律地位。它既是海关监管、征税、统计以及开展稽查和调查的重要依据，又是加工贸易进出口货物核销，以及出口退税和外汇管理的重要凭证，也是海关处理走私、违规案件，及税务、外汇管理部门查处骗税和套汇犯罪活动的重要证书。

The customs declaration document for import and export goods refers to a legal document in which the consignee or their agent makes a written declaration of the actual situation of the import and export goods in accordance with the format prescribed by the customs, in order to require the customs to handle the customs clearance procedures for their goods in accordance with the applicable customs system. It holds a very important legal position in foreign economic and trade activities. It is not only an important basis for customs supervision, taxation, statistics, and inspection and investigation, but also an important certificate for the verification of imported and exported goods in processing trade, export tax rebates, and foreign exchange management. It is also an important certificate for customs to handle smuggling and violation cases, and for tax and foreign exchange management departments to investigate and deal with tax fraud and foreign exchange fraud activities.

第五节　重点短语与句型
Section 5　Key Phrases and Sentence Patterns

一、常用单词与短语
Common words and phrases

1. revocable L/C　可撤销信用证
2. irrevocable L/C　不可撤销信用证
3. confirmed L/C　保兑信用证
4. unconfirmed L/C　不保兑信用证
5. transferable L/C　可转让信用证
6. untransferable L/C　不可转让信用证
7. divisible L/C　可分割信用证
8. indivisible L/C　不可分割信用证
9. revolving L/C　循环信用证
10. L/C with T/T reimbursement clause　带电汇条款信用证
11. without recourse L/C　无追索权信用证

12. with recourse L/C　有追索权信用证
13. documentary L/C　跟单信用证
14. clean L/C　光票信用证
15. deferred payment L/C　延付信用证
16. anticipatory L/C　预支信用证
17. back-to-back L/C　对背信用证
18. reciprocal L/C　对开信用证
19. traveler's L/C（circular L/C）　旅行信用证
20. UCP 600　《跟单信用证统一惯例》（第600号出版物）
21. commercial invoice　商业发票
22. packing list　装箱单
23. bill of exchange　汇票
24. bill of lading　海运提单
25. shipping advice　装运通知
26. insurance application　投保单
27. certificate of origin　原产地证明书
28. customs declaration document　报关单
29. sight payment　即期支付
30. deferred payment　延期支付
31. acceptance payment　承兑支付
32. negotiation payment　议付支付
33. partial shipment　分批装运
34. transshipment　转运
35. inspection certificate　检验证书
36. quarantine certificate　检疫证书
37. booking note　出口托运委托书
38. freight forwarder　货运代理
39. international transportation company　外运公司
40. customs broker　报关行
41. freight prepaid　运费预付
42. freight collect　运费到付
43. FOB（free on board）　船上交货
44. C&F（cost and freight）　成本加运费
45. CIF（cost, insurance and freight）　成本、保险加运费
46. FAS（free alongside ship）　船边交货
47. EXW（ex works）　工厂交货
48. DDP（delivered duty paid）　完税后交货
49. GSP（Generalized System of Preferences）　普惠制

二、常用句型
Common sentence patterns

1. We would like you to open an irrevocable L/C for the approximate invoice amount with a British bank.

我们希望你方请一家英国银行开立与发票金额大致相当的不可撤销信用证。

2. We are informed that the L/C in our favor amounting to USD 600,000 has been opened.

我们得到通知以我方为受益人、金额为60万美元的信用证已开出。

3. We hereby open Irrevocable Letter of Credit No. 434 in favor of CITIC Trading Co. Ltd.

兹开立第434号不可撤销信用证，受益人为中国国际信托投资总公司贸易公司。

4. We will request our bankers to open L/C in your favor upon receipt of your confirmation of this order.

一收到你方关于此项订货的确认，我方便要求银行开出以你方为受益人的信用证。

5. Please do your utmost to expedite the establishment of the L/C.

请速开出信用证。

6. Please see to it that you will establish the covering L/C as soon as possible so as to enable us to effect shipment within the stipulated time limit.

请务必尽早开立相关信用证，以便使我们能够在规定的时限内安排装运。

7. The date of shipment is approaching, but we have not received your relative L/C up to date. Please let us have your reply promptly.

装船日期日益临近，但我们至今仍未收到相关信用证，请立即给我们回复。

8. As the goods against your Order No. 118 have been ready for a long time, it is advisable for you to open the covering L/C immediately so as to enable us to effect shipment within the stipulated time limit.

你方第118号订单项下的货物备妥待运已有相当时日，我们提请你方立即开立相关信用证，以便我方能在规定的时间内交货。

9. We are sorry that we could not ship the goods on a May vessel only because of the delay of your L/C. Please open the said L/C at once.

我们感到遗憾，由于贵方延误开证，我们的货不能装5月份的船。请速开立上述信用证。

10. We write to inform you that we have today established through Tokyo Bank an irrevocable documentary L/C in your favor for the amount of USD 52,000 covering 1,000 sets of TVs.

现通知你方，今天我们已通过东京银行开出以你方为受益人的1000台电视机的不可撤销信用证，总金额52000美元。

11. We have established a commercial L/C in your favor for the contracted amount through a Japanese bank.

我们已通过一家日本银行开立了以你方为受益人的相当于合同金额的商业信用证。

12. Your L/C has been received this date, but we would request you to amend it as follows.

贵方信用证今日收到，但请按下述意见修改。

课后练习

Ⅰ. 选词填空。

Fill in the blanks with the appropriate words.

(letter of credit; commercial invoice; packing list; bill of lading; insurance application; customs declaration document; certificate of origin; booking note; sight payment; deferred payment)

1. A ____________ is a document issued by the exporter to the importer, providing an overall description of the goods and the transaction.

2. A ____________ is used to prove the contract of carriage of goods by sea and that the goods have been received or loaded by the carrier.

3. The ____________ is a document issued by the shipper to the carrier or its agent for the purpose of chartering a ship and booking cargo space.

4. ____________ is a payment method where the importer pays immediately upon presentation of the documents.

5. The ____________ is a document issued by the exporter to the importer, listing the goods shipped, the quantity, and the prices.

6. A ____________ is a document issued by the insurance company to cover the risks associated with the transportation of goods.

7. The ____________ is a document issued by the customs authority to verify the origin of the goods for tariff purposes.

8. The ____________ is a document issued by the exporter to the importer, detailing the packaging specifications, weight, and quantity of the goods.

9. The ____________ is a document used by the exporter to declare the goods to the customs authorities for export clearance.

10. ____________ refers to a payment method where the importer pays at a later date, usually after a specified period.

Ⅱ. 将下列句子翻译为英文。

Translate the following sentences into English.

1. 信用证一经开出，开证行就承担了首要的付款责任。
2. 商业发票是国际商务单据的核心文件，也是报关和纳税的基本依据。
3. 装箱单是商业发票的补充文件，用于详细说明货物的包装规格和重量。
4. 海运提单是证明货物已由承运人接收或装船的法律文件。
5. 装运通知是出口商向进口商发出的货物装运信息的通知。
6. 投保单是投保人向保险公司提交的申请文件，用于购买货物运输保险。
7. 原产地证明书是证明货物生产地和制造地的文件，通常用于海关清关。
8. 报关单是进出口商向海关提交的文件，用于办理货物的进出口手续。
9. 即期支付是指进口商在收到单据后立即付款。

10. 延期支付是指进口商在未来的某个日期付款，通常用于信用证交易。

Ⅲ. 写作。

Writing.

Assume you are a salesperson for an export company. You have just received a Letter of Credit (L/C) from an overseas client. However, upon reviewing the L/C, you find that some of its terms do not match the terms of the contract and need to be amended. Please write a letter requesting the amendment of the L/C, which should include the following points:

1. Mention the L/C number and the issuing bank.
2. Point out the specific terms in the L/C that need to be amended.
3. Propose specific suggestions for the amendments.
4. Express your hope that the client will amend the L/C as soon as possible and thank them for their cooperation.

Please ensure that the letter is formatted properly and that the content is clear, polite, and professional.

第六章 Chapter 6 跨境电商概述 Overview of Cross-border E-commerce

在当今数字化时代，跨境电商已成为推动国际贸易发展的重要力量。它不仅打破了传统贸易的时空限制，还为企业和消费者提供了更加便捷、高效的交易方式。近年来，随着国家政策的支持和互联网技术的不断进步，跨境电商呈现出蓬勃发展的态势，成为外贸领域最具活力和潜力的新增长点。本章将系统介绍跨境电商的内涵、分类及其主要业务流程，帮助学生全面了解这一新兴领域的核心知识，为深入学习和实践跨境电商奠定坚实的基础。

学习目标

1. 理解跨境电商的内涵。
2. 熟悉跨境电商的分类方法。
3. 掌握跨境电商的主要业务流程。

思政目标

1. 了解跨境电商，激发创新思维。
2. 关注行业动态，培养社会责任。
3. 学习行业规范，确保合法经营。

第一节 Section 1 跨境电商内涵 The Connotation of Cross-border E-commerce

2021年，国务院办公厅印发了《国务院办公厅关于加快发展外贸新业态新模式的意见》，提出了六种新业态。六种新业态里面，跨境电商是当前发展速度最快、潜力最大、带动作用最强的一种外贸新业态。跨境电商是一种分属不同关境的交易主体通过电子商务平台达成交易，进行支付结算，并通过跨境物流及异地仓储送达商品完成交易的国际商业活动。跨境电商的概念有狭义和广义之分。

In 2021, the General Office of the State Council issued the *Opinions of the General Office of the State Council on Accelerating the Development of New Forms and Modes in Foreign Trade*, proposing six new forms of trade. Among these, cross-border e-commerce is currently the fastest developing, most promising, and most driving new foreign trade format. Cross-border e-commerce is an international commercial activity in which trading entities belonging to different customs territories reach transactions through e-commerce platforms, conduct payment settlements, and complete transactions through cross-border logistics and remote warehousing delivery of goods. The connotation of cross-border e-commerce can be divided into a narrow sense and a broad sense.

狭义的跨境电商可以理解为跨境零售，是指分属不同关境的交易主体通过网络完成交易，进行支付结算，并利用邮政快递、商业快递和专线物流等跨境物流方式，将商品送达消费者手中的商业活动。

Narrowly defined cross-border e-commerce can be understood as cross-border retail, which refers to the commercial activity in which trading entities belonging to different customs territories complete transactions through the Internet, make payments and settlements, and use cross-border logistics methods such as postal express delivery, commercial express delivery, and dedicated line logistics to deliver goods to consumers.

广义的跨境电商可以理解为"传统外贸+互联网"，是指分属不同关境的交易主体，利用网络将传统外贸中的展示、洽谈以及成交等环节电子化，并借助跨境物流方式运送商完成交易的一种商业活动。

In a broad sense, cross-border e-commerce can be understood as "traditional foreign trade + Internet", which refers to a kind of business activity in which trading entities belonging to different customs territories use the Internet to electronically display, negotiate and conclude transactions in traditional foreign trade, and complete transactions with the help of cross-border logistics carriers.

第二节 跨境电商分类
Section 2 Classification of Cross-border E-commerce

一、按商品流向分类
Classify by product flow direction

按商品流向，跨境电商可分为出口跨境电商和进口跨境电商。

According to product flow direction, cross-border e-commerce can be divided into export cross-border e-commerce and import cross-border e-commerce.

出口跨境电商，又称出境电商，是指商家通过电子商务平台达成交易、收取货款，并通过跨境物流运送本国生产或加工的商品输往国外市场的一种国际商业活动。

Export cross-border e-commerce, also known as outbound e-commerce, refers to an international commercial activity in which merchants complete transactions, collect payment through e-commerce platforms, and transport domestically produced or processed goods to foreign markets through cross-border logistics.

进口跨境电商，又称入境电商，是指商家通过电子商务平台达成交易、支付货款，并通过跨境物流运送国外商品输入本国市场的一种国际商业活动。

Import cross-border e-commerce, also known as inbound e-commerce, refers to an international commercial activity in which merchants complete transactions, pay for goods through e-commerce platforms, and transport foreign goods into the domestic market through cross-border logistics.

二、按商业模式分类

Classified by business mode

按商业模式，跨境电商主要有 B2B、B2C、C2C 三种模式。

According to business modes, cross-border e-commerce mainly has three modes: B2B, B2C, and C2C.

B2B（business to business），又称在线批发，是一种分属不同关境的企业与企业之间通过互联网进行产品、服务、信息交换的商业模式。目前在中国跨境电商市场交易中，B2B 跨境电商市场交易规模占总交易规模的 80%以上，代表企业主要有敦煌网、中国制造网、阿里巴巴国际站和环球资源网。

B2B (business to business), also known as online wholesale, is a business mode in which enterprises belonging to different customs territories exchange products, services and information through the Internet. At present, in the cross-border e-commerce market transactions in China, B2B cross-border e-commerce market transactions account for more than 80% of the total transaction scale, and representative enterprises mainly include DHgate, Made-in-China. com, Alibaba. com, and Global Resources. com.

B2C（business to customer），是指分属不同关境的跨境电商企业直接面向个人消费者开展在线销售产品和服务，通过跨境电商平台达成交易、进行支付结算，并通过跨境物流送达商品完成交易的一种国际商业活动。B2C 跨境电商和 C2C 跨境电商统称为在线零售。

B2C (business to customer), refers to an international business activity in which cross-border e-commerce enterprises belonging to different customs territories directly sell products and services to individual consumers online, complete transactions, make payment settlements through cross-border e-commerce platforms, and deliver goods through cross-border logistics to complete transactions. B2C cross-border e-commerce and C2C cross-border e-commerce are collectively referred to as online retail.

C2C（customer to customer），是指分属不同关境的个人卖方对个人买方进行网络零售商业活动，由个人卖家通过第三方跨境电商平台发布产品和服务信息，国外的个人消费者进行筛选，最终通过跨境电商平台达成交易、进行支付结算，并通过跨境物流送达商品完成交易的一种国际商业活动。

C2C (customer to customer), refers to an international commercial activity in which individual sellers belonging to different customs territories engage in online retail business activities with individual buyers. Individual sellers publish product and service information through third-party cross-border e-commerce platforms, and foreign individual consumers screen and ultimately complete transactions through cross-border e-commerce platforms, payment settlements, and delivery of goods through cross-border logistics.

目前我国跨境电商出口以 B2B 和 B2C 为主，进口以 B2C 为主。

At present, China's cross-border e-commerce exports are mainly B2B and B2C, while imports are mainly B2C.

除以上三种模式之外，F2C 跨境电商也日渐兴起。F2C（factory to customer），是指从工厂到消费者。F2C 模式直接把出自工厂的产品送到国外消费者手中，可以理解为工厂借助跨境电商平台进行了产品直销。F2C 使消费者在线向工厂下订单，可能成为 B2C 的升级版模式，其最大的优势就是强有力的线下产业支撑、有效的全程品控、快速的市场反应，这是 B2C 跨境电商无法抗衡的。

In addition to the above three modes, F2C cross-border e-commerce is also increasingly emerging. F2C (factory to customer), refers to the process from the factory to the consumer. The F2C mode directly delivers products from factories to foreign consumers, which can be understood as factories using cross-border e-commerce platforms for direct product sales. F2C enables consumers to place orders with factories online, which may become an upgraded version of B2C mode. Its biggest advantages are strong offline industry support, effective full process quality control, and rapid market response, which B2C cross-border e-commerce cannot compete with.

三、按运营方式分类

Classified by operational mode

按运营方式，跨境电商主要有两种类型：平台运营跨境电商和自建网站运营跨境电商。

According to the operational mode, there are mainly two types of cross-border e-commerce: platform-operated cross-border e-commerce and self-built-website-operated cross-border e-commerce.

平台运营跨境电商是指从事跨境电商的交易主体在亚马逊、eBay 等诸多第三方跨境电商平台上开设网店从事外贸业务活动。

Platform-operated cross-border e-commerce refers to the trading entities engaged in cross-border e-commerce opening online stores on various third-party cross-border e-commerce platforms such as Amazon and eBay to engage in foreign trade business activities.

自建网站运营跨境电商，是指企业自建网站如兰亭集势、环球易购等从事相关外贸业务活动，其中，兰亭集势属于综合类跨境电商企业，环球易购属于垂直类电商企业。

Self-built-website-operated e-commerce, such as LightInTheBox and Global Easy Buy, engage in related foreign trade business activities through self built websites. Among them, LightInTheBox belongs to the comprehensive cross-border e-commerce enterprise, while Global Easy Buy belongs to the vertical-market e-commerce enterprise.

从长期发展趋势看，平台运营跨境电商和自建网站运营跨境电商两种模式的融合度日益增强。

From the perspective of long-term development trends, the integration of platform-operated cross-border e-commerce and self-built-website-operated cross-border e-commerce modes is increasingly strong.

第三节 跨境电商主要流程
Section 3 Main Processes of Cross-border E-commerce

一、出口业务流程
Export business process

跨境电商出口的流程：生产商或制造商将生产的商品在跨境电商平台上上线展示，在商品被选购下单并完成支付后，跨境电商企业将商品交付给物流商进行投递，经过出口国和进口国海关通关检验后，最终送达消费者或企业手中。有的跨境电商企业直接与第三方综合服务平台合作，让第三方综合服务平台代办物流、通关、商检等一系列环节，从而完成整个跨境电商交易的过程（图 6-1）。

The process of cross-border e-commerce export: Producers or manufacturers display their products online on cross-border e-commerce platforms. After the products are selected, ordered, and paid for, the cross-border e-commerce enterprise delivers them to the logistics providers for delivery. After customs clearance and inspection by the exporting and importing countries, they are finally delivered to consumers or enterprises. Some cross-border e-commerce enterprises directly cooperate with third-party comprehensive service platforms to handle a series of processes such as logistics, customs clearance, and inspection, thereby completing the entire process of cross-border e-commerce transactions (Fig 6-1).

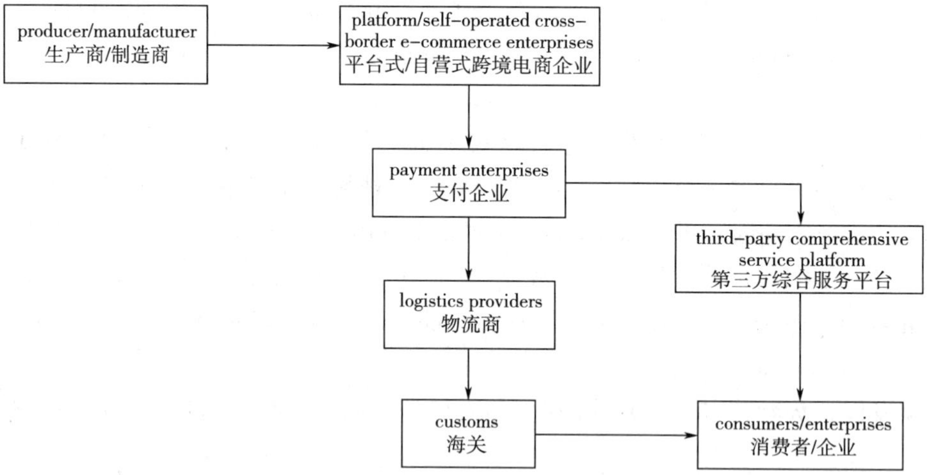

图 6-1 跨境电商出口流程

在整个跨境电商的交易过程中，可以看出跨境电商不仅是一个平台，而且需要信息技术的引领，需要快递物流的支撑。只有信息流（即卖家在网上发布所提供的产品或服务信息，消费者通过互联网搜寻需要的产品或服务信息）、物流（即产品流，消费者在网上下单，卖家委托跨境物流服务公司将产品运送到海外消费者手里）、资金流（即消费者通过第三方支付方式及时安全地付款，卖家收汇结汇）三位一体的支撑到位，跨境电商才能颠覆传统商业模式，成为中国传统贸易转型发展的战略制高点。

Throughout the entire process of cross-border e-commerce transactions, it can be seen that cross-border e-commerce is not only a platform, but also requires the guidance of information technology and the support of express logistics. Only when the information flow (that is, the seller publishes the product or service information provided online, and the consumer searches for the required product or service information through the Internet), logistics (that is, the product flow, the consumer places an order online, and the seller entrusts a cross-border logistics service company to deliver the products to overseas consumers), and capital flow (that is, the consumer makes timely and safe payments through third-party payment, and the seller collects and settles foreign exchange) are in place, can cross-border e-commerce subvert the traditional business mode and become the strategic commanding height of China's traditional trade transformation and development.

二、进口业务流程

Import business process

跨境电商进口的流程（图 6-2），除了与出口流程的方向相反外，其他内容基本相同。近年来，进口电商发展非常迅速，逐渐形成了一些典型的跨境电商进口模式，主要有海淘、海外代购平台、直发或直运平台、自营 B2C 进口、跨境导购平台等模式。

The process of cross-border e-commerce import, except that the direction of the export process is opposite, is basically the same (Figure 6-2). In recent years, import e-commerce has developed very rapidly, and some typical cross-border e-commerce import modes have gradually formed, mainly including overseas shopping, overseas purchasing platforms, direct delivery or direct shipping platforms, self-operated B2C imports, cross-border shopping guide platforms, and other modes.

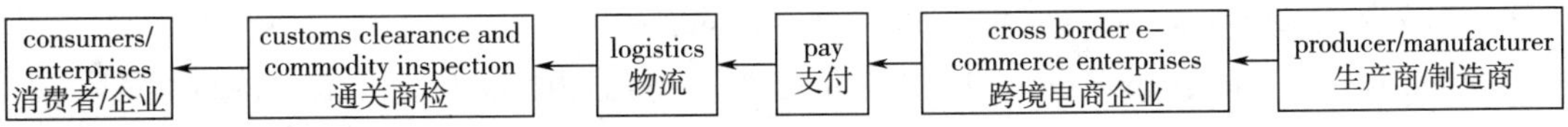

图 6-2　跨境电商进口流程

课后练习

Ⅰ. 单选题。

Single-choice questions.

1. Which of the following best describes cross-border e-commerce?

A. A business activity within the same customs territory

B. A commercial activity between different customs territories using e-commerce platforms

C. Traditional trade without the use of the Internet

D. Domestic retail business

2. What is the primary difference between narrow and broad definitions of cross-border e-commerce?

A. The narrow definition includes only B2C modes, while the broad definition includes B2B modes.

B. The narrow definition focuses on cross-border retail, while the broad definition includes traditional foreign trade enhanced by the Internet.

C. The narrow definition is limited to domestic markets, while the broad definition includes international markets.

D. There is no difference; they are interchangeable terms.

3. Which of the following is NOT a classification of cross-border e-commerce mentioned in the document?

A. By product flow direction

B. By business mode

C. By operational mode

D. By product quality

4. What does B2B stand for in the context of cross-border e-commerce?

A. Business to Business

B. Business to Customer

C. Customer to Customer

D. Factory to Customer

5. Which of the following best describes the F2C mode in cross-border e-commerce?

A. A mode where consumers place orders directly with factories

B. A mode where businesses sell products to other businesses

C. A mode where consumers sell products to other consumers

D. A mode where businesses sell products to consumers

6. What is the main advantage of the F2C mode over the B2C mode in cross-border e-commerce?

A. Lower prices for consumers

B. Stronger offline industry support and faster market response

C. Easier access to international markets

D. Higher profit margins for businesses

7. Which of the following platforms is mentioned as a representative B2B cross-border e-commerce platform?

A. Amazon

B. DHgate

C. eBay

D. Global Easy Buy

8. What is the primary difference between platform-operated and self-built-website-operated cross-border e-commerce?

A. Platform-operated cross-border e-commerce is more profitable than self-built-website-operated cross-border e-commerce.

B. Platform-operated cross-border e-commerce uses third-party platforms, while self-built-website-operated cross-border e-commerce uses company-owned websites.

C. Self-built-website-operated cross-border e-commerce is only for B2C modes.

D. There is no difference; both modes are the same.

9. Which of the following is a key component of the cross-border e-commerce export process?

A. Domestic delivery

B. Customs clearance in the exporting and importing countries

C. Local warehousing

D. In-person transactions

10. What is the main difference between export and import cross-border e-commerce processes?

A. Export involves domestic producers, while import involves foreign producers.

B. Export involves sending goods overseas, while import involves bringing goods into the domestic market.

C. Export requires payment in foreign currency, while import requires payment in domestic currency.

D. There is no difference; both processes are identical.

Ⅱ. 简答题。

Short answer questions.

1. What are the two main classifications of cross-border e-commerce by product flow direction?

2. Explain the role of information flow, logistics, and capital flow in cross-border e-commerce transactions.

3. Describe the F2C mode in cross-border e-commerce and its main advantages.

第七章 Chapter 7 跨境电商物流 Cross-border E-commerce Logistics

经济全球化的发展使得各国之间的商贸往来更加频繁，世界各国向海外出口优势产品并进口所需产品，成为促进本国经济社会发展的重要举措。随着我国经济发展进入新常态时代，跨境电商物流作为国民经济增长的新亮点，引起了国家和企业界的重视。新常态下跨境电商物流模式直接影响跨境电商的发展状况，优质的电商物流，能够促使跨境电商交易更加便利。

学习目标

1. 熟悉跨境电商物流的内涵。
2. 掌握跨境电商物流的主要模式和特征。
3. 培养跨境电商物流管理能力和意识。

思政目标

1. 了解物流环保，培养环保意识。
2. 注重团队协作，培养团队合作精神。

第一节 Section 1 跨境电商物流 Cross-border Logistics

一、跨境电商物流的内涵

The connotation of cross-border e-commerce logistics

跨境电商运作过程中涉及信息流、商流、资金流和物流。信息流、商流和资金流均可通过计算机和网络通信设备在虚拟环境下实现，但物流环节是不能在虚拟环境下实现的。国际物流系统包括仓储、运输、配送、流通加工、包装、装卸搬运和信息处理七个子系统。国际物流系统高效率、高质量、低成本的运作是跨境电商发展的保证。

The operation of cross-border e-commerce involves information flow, commercial flow, capital flow, and logistics. Information flow, commercial flow, and capital flow can all be achieved through computers and network communication devices in a virtual environment, but the logistics process cannot be realized in a virtual environment. The international logistics system includes seven subsystems: warehousing, transportation, distribution, circulation processing, packaging, loading and unloading, and information processing. The high-efficient, high-quality, and low-cost operation of the international logistics system is the guarantee for the development of cross-border e-commerce.

跨境电商物流是采用现代物流技术，利用国际化的物流网络，选择最佳的方式与路径，以最低的费用和最小的风险，对货物（商品）进行物理性移动的一项国际商业活动，从而完成国际商品交易的最终目的，旨在实现卖方交付单证、货物和收取货款，买方接收单证货款和收取货物。跨境物流交易双方分属不同国家（或地区），商品需要从供应方国家（或地区）通过跨境物流方式实现空间位置转移，在需求所在国家（或地区）内实现最后的物流与配送，分为境内物流、国际（地区间）物流与运输、目的国（或地区）物流与配送三项内容。

Cross-border e-commerce logistics is an international business activity that uses modern logistics technology, utilizes an international logistics network, selects the best way and path, and physically moves goods (commodities) with the lowest cost and minimum risk, in order to achieve the ultimate goal of international commodity transactions. It aims to realize the seller's delivery of documents, goods, and collection of payment, and the buyer's receipt of document payment and collection of goods. The two parties involved in cross-border logistics transactions belong to different countries (or regions), and the goods need to be transferred from the supplier's country or region through cross-border logistics to achieve final delivery within the demand country (or region). This is divided into three aspects: domestic logistics, international (inter regional) logistics and transportation, and destination country (or region) logistics and distribution.

二、跨境电商物流与跨境电商的关系

The relationship between cross-border e-commerce logistics and cross-border e-commerce

跨境电商必须通过线下跨境物流服务完成。跨境电商的运营涉及信息、商业、资金的流动，这些工作都可以利用计算机网络系统执行，但是，商品运输是无法在虚拟的网络完成的，必须通过跨境物流在线下对商品进行运输、储存、分拨、配送等得以实现。

Cross-border e-commerce must be completed through offline cross-border logistics services. The operation of cross-border e-commerce involves the flow of information, commerce, and capital, all of which can be executed using computer network systems. However, the transportation of goods cannot be completed in a virtual network and must be achieved through offline transportation, storage, distribution and delivery of goods through cross-border logistics.

跨境物流服务的水平决定了跨境电商的效率和效益。国际贸易的新形式表现为小量、高频次、快速发货，这就要求快速响应客户需求，利用互联网和电子商务平台，通过线跨境物流将商品尽快送达客户手中。跨境物流服务的成本、准确度和响应速度，将成为跨境电商服务的竞争项，直接影响和决定跨境电商的服务效率和经营效益。

The level of cross-border logistics services determines the efficiency and effectiveness of cross-border e-commerce. The new form of international trade is characterized by small quantity, high frequency and fast delivery, which requires rapid response to customer needs, using the Internet and e-commerce platform, and delivering goods to customers as soon as possible through online cross-border logistics. The cost, accuracy, and speed of response of cross-border logistics services will become a competitive factor for cross-border e-commerce services, directly affecting and determining the service efficiency and operational benefits of cross-border e-commerce.

三、跨境电商物流分类

Classification of cross-border e-commerce logistics

（一）主要物流模式

Main logistics modes

目前我国跨境电商物流模式主要有以下几种。

At present, there are mainly the following types of cross-border e-commerce logistics modes in China.

1. 邮政包裹模式

Postal package mode

邮政网络基本覆盖全球，比其他任何物流渠道都要广。这主要得益于万国邮政联盟和卡拉邮政组织。万国邮政联盟是联合国下设的一个关于国际邮政事务的专门机构，通过公约法规来改善国际邮政业务，发展邮政方面的国际合作。万国邮政联盟由于会员众多，且会员之间的邮政系统发展水平很不平衡，因此很难促成会员之间的深度邮政合作。2002 年，邮政系统相对发达的 6 个国家和地区（中国、美国、日本等）的邮政部门在美国召开了邮政 CEO 峰会，并成立了卡哈拉邮政组织，后来西班牙和英国也加了该组织。卡哈拉邮政组织要求所有成员的投递时限达到 98%的质量标准。如果货物没能按约定日期投递给收件人，那么负责投递的运营商要按货物价格的 100%赔付客户。这些严格的要求促使成员深化彼此合作，努力提升服务水平。据不完全统计，我国出口跨境电商 70%的包裹都是通过邮政系统投递的。其中中国邮政占据 50%左右。

The postal network basically covers the whole world, which is wider than any other logistics channel. This is mainly owing to the Universal Postal Union and the Kahala Postal Organization (KPO). The Universal Postal Union is a specialized agency under the United Nations dedicated to international postal affairs, which improves international postal services and develops international cooperation in postal services through conventions and regulations. Due to the large number of members and uneven development levels of postal systems among them, it is difficult for the Universal Postal Union to promote deep postal cooperation among its members. In 2002, the postal departments of six countries and regions with relatively developed postal systems (China, the United States, Japan, etc.) held a Postal CEO Summit in the United States and established the Kahala Postal Organization. Later, Spain and the United Kingdom also joined the organization. The Kahala Postal Organization requires all members to meet a 98% quality standard for delivery time. If the goods cannot be delivered to the recipient on a scheduled date, the operator responsible for delivery must compensate the customer 100% of the goods price. These strict requirements encourage members to deepen cooperation and strive to improve service levels. According to incomplete statistics, 70% of cross-border e-commerce packages exported from China are sold through postal services. Among them, China Post accounts for about 50%.

优势：邮政网络覆盖全球；而且，由于邮政一般为国有，有的国家甚至有税收补贴，因此非常便宜。

Advantages: The postal network covers the globe. Moreover, as postal services are generally state-owned and some countries even provide tax subsidies, they are very cheap.

劣势：一般以私人包裹方式出境，不便于海关统计，也无法享受正常的出口退税；同时，速度较慢，丢包率高。

Disadvantages: Generally, it is exported as private packages, which is not convenient for customs statistics and cannot enjoy normal export tax refunds. Meanwhile, delivery speeds are lower and the parcel loss rates tend to be higher.

2. 商业快递模式

Commercial express delivery mode

（1）国际快递模式。国际快递是指四大快递巨头，即 DHL、TNT、FedEx 和 UPS。这些国际快递商通过自建的全球网络，利用强大的 IT 系统和遍布世界各地的本地化服务，为网购中国产品的海外用户带来极好的物流体验。

优势：速度快、服务好、丢包率低，尤其是发往欧美国家非常方便。例如，使用 UPS 从中国寄包裹送到美国，最快可在 48 小时内到达，使用 TNT 从中国寄包裹到欧洲，一般 3 个工作日可到达。

劣势：价格昂贵，且资费变化较大。一般跨境电商卖家只有在客户强烈要求时效性的情况下才会使用，且会向客户收取运费。

(1) International express delivery mode. International express delivery refers to the four major express delivery giants, namely DHL, TNT, FedEx, and UPS. These international courier companies provide excellent logistics experience for overseas users who purchase Chinese products online through their self-built global network, advanced IT systems, and localized services around the world.

Advantages: Rapid delivery speed; good service; low parcel loss rates; especially convenient for shipments to European and American countries. For example, using UPS to deliver packages from China to the United States can arrive within 48 hours, while using TNT to deliver packages from China to Europe usually takes 3 working days.

Disadvantages: Higher service and significant fluctuations in tariffs. Generally, cross-border e-commerce sellers only use it when customers strongly demand timeliness, and the sellers will charge customers for shipping fees.

（2）国内快递模式。目前，我国跨境物流停留在传统物流层面，高端服务与增值服务缺失。国内快递主要是指 EMS、顺丰和“四通一达”。在跨境物流方面，“四通一达”中申通、圆通布局较早，但也是前几年才发力拓展，美国申通 2014 年 3 月才上线，圆通也是 2014 年 4 月才与 CJ 大韩通运展开合作，而中通、汇通、韵达则是近期开始启动跨境物流业务。顺丰的国际化业务则要成熟些，目前已经开通到美国、澳大利亚、韩国、日本、新加坡、马来西亚、泰国、越南等国家的快递服务，发往亚洲国家的快件一般 2~3 天可以送达。在国内快递公司中，EMS 的国际化业务是最完善的。依托邮政渠道，EMS 可以直达全球 60 多个国家和地区，费用相对四大快递巨头要低；中国境内的出关能力很强，到达亚洲国家要 2~3 天，到欧美国家则要 5~7 天。

优势：速度较快；费用低于四大国际快递巨头；EMS 在中国境内的出关能力强。

劣势：由于并非专注跨境业务，相对缺乏经验，对市场的把控能力有待提高，覆盖的海外市场也比较有限。

(2) Domestic express delivery mode. At present, China's cross-border logistics remains at the traditional logistics level, with a lack of high-end and value-added services. Domestic express delivery mainly refers to EMS, SF Express, and "Four Tong and One Da". In cross-border logistics, Shentong and Yuantong have laid out earlier in the "Four Tong and One Da" initiative, but they only made efforts to expand a few years ago. Shentong in the United States only went online in March 2014, and Yuantong only started cooperating with CJ Korean Express in April 2014. Zhongtong, Huitong, and Yunda have recently started to launch cross-border logistics business. SF Express's international business needs to be more mature. Currently, it has opened express delivery services to countries such as the United States, Australia, Korea, Japan, Singapore, Malaysia, Thailand, and Vietnam. Express shipments to Asian countries can generally be delivered within 2~3 days. Among domestic express delivery companies, EMS has the most comprehensive international business. Relying on postal channels, EMS can directly reach over 60 countries and regions worldwide, with relatively lower costs compared to the four major express delivery giants; the customs clearance capability within China is very strong, taking 2~3 days to reach Asian countries and 5~7 days to reach European and American countries.

Advantages: Faster delivery speed; costs lower than the four major international express delivery giants; EMS has the advantage of strong customs clearance capability within China.

Disadvantages: Due to not focusing on cross-border business and relatively lacking experience, the ability to control the market needs to be improved, and the coverage of overseas markets is also relatively limited.

3. 专线物流模式

Dedicated line logistics mode

跨境专线物流一般是通过航空包舱方式将货物运输到国外，再通过合作公司进行目的地配送。市面上最普遍的专线物流产品是美国专线、欧洲专线、俄罗斯专线等，也有少数物流公司推出了中东专线、南美专线、南非专线等。

Cross-border dedicated line logistics generally transport goods to foreign countries through air cargo, and then deliver them to the destination through cooperative companies. The most common dedicated logistics products on the market are the US, European, Russian dedicated line, etc. There are also a few logistics companies that have launched dedicated lines for the Middle East, South America, South Africa, etc.

优势：集中大批量货物发往目的地，通过规模效应降低成本，因此，价格比商业快递低，时效优于邮政小包，丢包率也比较低。

Advantages: Large quantities of goods are concentrated to the destination, and costs are reduced through economies of scale. As a result, the price is lower than that of commercial express delivery, the delivery speed is faster than that of postal parcels, and the parcel loss rate is also relatively lower.

劣势：相比邮政小包来说，运费成本还是高了不少，而且在国内的揽收范围相对有限，覆盖地区有待扩大。

Disadvantages: Compared to postal parcels, the shipping cost is still much higher, and the collection range in China is relatively limited, with coverage areas needing to be expanded.

4. 海外仓模式

Overseas warehouse mode

海外仓服务是指为卖家在销售目的地进行货物仓储、分拣、包装和派送的一站式控制与管理服务。确切来说，海外仓储应该包括头程运输、仓储管理和本地配送三个部分。

头程运输：中国商家通过海运、空运、陆运或者联运将商品运送至海外仓库。

仓储管理：中国商家通过物流信息系统，远程操作海外仓储货物，实时管理库存。

本地配送：海外仓储中心根据订单信息，通过当地邮政或快递将商品配送给客户。

Overseas warehouse service refers to a one-stop control and management service for sellers to store, sort, package, and deliver goods at the sales destination. Specifically, overseas warehousing should include three parts: first-mile transportation, warehouse management, and local delivery.

First-mile transportation: Chinese merchants transport goods to overseas warehouses through sea, air, land, or intermodal transportation.

Warehouse management: Chinese merchants remotely operate overseas warehouse goods through logistics information systems to manage inventory in real-time.

Local delivery: Overseas warehouse centers deliver goods to customers through local postal or courier services based on the order information.

优势：从海外直接发货给客户，相当于境内快递，较之从中国发往国外成本更低；节省了运输报关、清关等各方面复杂的操作流程所需耗费的时间，更快更有效地从海外发货；海外仓储中心配了专业的管理人员；订单和发货同步，实现自动化批量处理订单；每月的销量及剩余库存系统自动显示，并且每笔订单的物流成本一目了然；远程遥控方便快捷；客户退货直接退到海外仓储中心即可，免去了国内国外来回双清的成本、时效、弃货等各方面损失。

因为海外仓更能获得国外买家的认可，从另外一方面，如果卖家注意口碑营销，自己的商品在当地不仅能够获得买家的认可，也有利于卖家积累更多的资源去拓展市场，扩大产品销售领域与销售范围。

Advantages: Shipping directly from overseas to customers is equivalent to domestic express delivery, with lower costs compared to shipping from China to overseas. It can save time on complex operational processes such as transportation customs declaration and clearance, enabling faster and more efficient overseas shipments. Overseas warehouse centers are staffed with professional management personnel. Orders and shipments are synchronized to achieve automated batch processing of orders. The monthly sales volume and remaining inventory system are automatically displayed, and the logistics cost of each order is known daily. Remote control is convenient and fast. Customers can return their goods directly to overseas warehouse centers, eliminating the cost, timeliness, abandonment and other losses of domestic and international double clearance.

Because overseas warehouses are more likely to gain recognition from foreign buyers, on the other hand, if sellers pay attention to word-of-mouth marketing, their products can not only gain recognition from buyers locally, but also help sellers accumulate more resources to expand the market, and expand product sales areas and sales scope.

劣势：不是任何产品都适合使用海外仓，最适合的是库存周转快的热销单品，否则容易压货。同时，对卖家在供应链管理、库存管控、动销管理等方面提出了更高的要求。

对于跨境电商的卖家来说，在选择物流模式时应注意以下几个方面。首先，应该根据所售产品的特点（尺寸、安全性、通关便利性等）来选择合适的物流模式，比如大件产品（例如家具）就不适合走邮政包裹渠道，而更适合海外仓模式。其次，在淡、旺季要灵活使用不同物流模式，可以在淡季时使用中国邮政小包降低物流成本，在旺季或者大型促销活动时期采用新加坡邮政甚至比利时邮政来保证时效。最后，售前要向买家明确列出不同物流模式的特点，为买家提供多样化的物流选择，让买家根据实际需求选择物流模式。

Disadvantages: Not all products are suitable for overseas warehouses. The most suitable ones are hot-selling items with fast inventory turnover; otherwise, they are prone to overstocking. At the same time, higher requirements have been put forward for sellers in supply chain management, inventory control, and dynamic sales management.

For cross-border e-commerce sellers, they should pay attention to the following aspects when choosing a logistics mode. Firstly, they should choose a suitable logistics mode based on the characteristics of the products being sold (such as size, safety, customs clearance convenience, etc.). For example, for large products (such as furniture), they are not suitable to use postal parcel channels, but more suitable for the overseas warehouse mode. Secondly, different logistics modes should be used flexibly during peak and off-peak seasons. China Post small packages can be used during the off-season to reduce logistics costs, while Singapore Post, or even Belgium Post can be used during peak seasons or large-scale promotional events to ensure timeliness. Finally, sellers should clearly list the characteristics of different logistics modes to buyers during pre-sales, providing them with diverse logistics options and allowing them to choose logistics modes based on their actual needs.

（二）其他物流模式

Other logistics modes

1. 边境仓

Border warehouse

边境仓是指在跨境电商目的国的邻国边境内租赁或建设仓库，通过物流将商品预先运达仓库，通过互联网接受客户订单后，从该仓库进行发货。根据所处地域不同，边境仓可分为绝对边境仓和相对边境仓。海外仓的运营需要成本，商品存在积压风险，送达后的商品很难再退回国内，这些因素推动着边境仓模式的出现。一些国家的税收政策十分严格、政局不稳、货币贬值、存在严重的通货膨胀，也会刺激边境仓的出现。例如，巴西的税收政策十分严格，建海外仓的成本很高，那么可以在其相接壤国家的边境设立边境仓。

Border warehouses refer to leasing or building a warehouse within the border of neighboring countries in the destination country of cross-border e-commerce, delivering goods to the warehouse in advance through logistics, receiving customer orders through the Internet, and then shipping from the warehouse. According to different geographical locations, border warehouses can be divided into absolute border warehouses and relative border warehouses. The operation of overseas warehouses requires costs; there is a risk of product backlog; and it is difficult to return the delivered goods to the domestic market. These factors are driving the emergence of the border warehouse mode. Strict tax policies, unstable political situation, currency depreciation, and severe inflation in some countries can also stimulate the emergence of border warehouses. For example, Brazil has very strict tax policies and the cost of building overseas warehouses is high, so border warehouses can be established at the borders of neighboring countries.

绝对边境仓是指当跨境电商的交易双方所在国家相邻，将仓库设在卖方所在国家中，与买方所在国家相邻近的城市。如我国对俄罗斯的跨境电商交易，在哈尔滨或中俄边境的中方城市设立仓库。

An absolute border warehouse refers to a warehouse located in the seller's country adjacent to the buyer's country when both parties in cross-border e-commerce transactions are based in neighboring countries. For example, in China-Russia cross-border e-commerce transactions, warehouses are set up in Harbin or other Chinese cities along the China-Russia border.

相对边境仓是指当跨境电商的交易双方不相邻，将仓库设在买方所在国的相邻国家的边境城市。如我国对巴西的跨境电商交易，在与之相邻的阿根廷、巴拉圭、秘鲁等接壤国家的邻近边境城市设立仓库。相对边境仓对买方所在国而言属于边境仓，对卖方所在国而言属于海外仓。

A relative border warehouse refers to a warehouse located in a border city of a country adjacent to the buyer's country when the two parties involved in cross-border e-commerce transactions are not adjacent. For example, in China-Brazil cross-border e-commerce transactions, China has established warehouses in border cities of Brazil's neighboring countries such as Argentina, Paraguay, and Peru. Relative border warehouses belong to border warehouses for the buyer's country and overseas warehouses for the seller's country.

海外仓模式可以在买家本地仓库发货，极大地缩短了配送时间，提高了配送效率，能有效降低物流成本，解决退换货和通关商检等问题。但是，海外仓的运营成本较高，主要适用于货价较高、物流成本承担能力较强且市场销量较大的企业及电商平台。而且，海外仓在实际运用中有一定的要求和局限性，如需要考虑当地的物流发展水平与物流基础设施完善程度、当地税收政策及政局稳定性等，因此，针对一些物流设施配套不成熟或政局不稳定的国家，设立边境仓是较好的补充模式。

The overseas warehouse mode can ship goods from the buyer's local warehouse, greatly reducing delivery time, improving delivery efficiency, effectively reducing logistics costs, and solving problems such as returns and exchanges, customs clearance, and inspection. However, the operating costs of overseas warehouses are relatively higher, mainly suitable for enterprises and e-commerce platforms with high prices, strong logistics cost bearing capacity, and large market sales. Moreover, overseas warehouses have certain requirements and limitations in practical application, such as the need to consider the local level of logistics development and the completeness of logistics infrastructure, local tax policies, and political stability. Therefore, for countries with immature logistics facilities or unstable political situations, setting up border warehouses is a better supplementary mode.

边境仓的运营成本稍低于海外仓，但配送时间比海外仓慢 1~2 天。因此，边境仓与海外仓的结合可大大便利中国与类似俄罗斯、巴西等国家的双方跨境电商贸易。随着海外仓模式趋于成熟，边境仓存在的意义逐渐变为海外仓进行补货。

The operating costs of border warehouses are slightly lower than those of overseas warehouses, but the delivery time is 1~2 days slower than that of overseas warehouses. Therefore, the combination of border warehouses and overseas warehouses can greatly facilitate cross-border e-commerce trade between China and countries such as Russia and Brazil. As the overseas warehouse mode matures, the significance of the existence of border warehouses gradually shifts to overseas warehouses for replenishment.

2. 自由贸易试验区、保税区、保税港区物流

Logistics in pilot free trade zones, bonded zones, and bonded port areas

（1）自由贸易试验区。自由贸易试验区，是指在贸易和投资等方面比世界贸易组织有关规定更加优惠的贸易安排，在主权国家或地区的关境以外，划出特定的区域准许外国商品豁免关税自由进出，实质上是采取自由港政策的关税隔离区。狭义仅指提供区内加工出口所需原料等货物的进口豁免关税的地区，类似出口加工区；广义还包括自由港和转口贸易区。

2013 年 9 月至 2018 年 4 月，国务院先后批复成立上海、广东、天津、福建、辽宁、浙江、河南、湖北、重庆、四川、山西和海南 12 个自由贸易试验区。

2017 年 10 月 18 日，习近平总书记在党的十九大报告中指出，“赋予自由贸易试验区更大改革自主权，探索建设自由贸易港。”2018 年 11 月 23 日，国务院印发《国务院关于支持自由贸易试验区深化改革创新若干措施的通知》。2019 年 8 月 2 日，国务院印发《国务院关于印发 6 个新设自由贸易试验区总体方案的通知》，在山东、江苏、广西、河北、云南和黑龙江成立自由贸易试验区。

2020 年 9 月 21 日，国务院批复同意新设北京、湖南、安徽 3 个自由贸易试验区。2023 年设立新疆自由贸易试验区，目前共计 22 个。

(1) Pilot free trade zones. The pilot free trade zone refers to a trade arrangement that is more favorable than the relevant provisions of the World Trade Organization in terms of trade and investment. It is a designated area outside the customs territory of sovereign countries or regions that allows foreign goods to enter and exit freely without tariffs. Essentially, it is a tariff isolation zone that

adopts a free port policy. Narrowly defined, it only refers to areas that provide import exemption from tariffs for raw materials and other goods required for processing and export within the region, similar to export processing zones. Broadly speaking, it also includes free ports and transit trade zones.

From September 2013 to April 2018, the State Council approved the establishment of 12 pilot free trade zones in Shanghai, Guangdong, Tianjin, Fujian, Liaoning, Zhejiang, Henan, Hubei, Chongqing, Sichuan, Shanxi, and Hainan.

On October 18, 2017, General Secretary Xi Jinping pointed out in the report of the 19th National Congress of the Communist Party of China that "grant greater reform autonomy to pilot free trade zones and explore the construction of free trade ports". On November 23, 2018, the State Council issued the *Notice of the State Council on Several Measures to Support the Deepening of Reform and Innovation in Pilot Free Trade Zones*. On August 2, 2019, the State Council issued the *Notice of the State Council on issuing the Overall Plan for the Six New Pilot Free Trade Zones*, establishing six new pilot free trade zones in Shandong, Jiangsu, Guangxi, Hebei, Yunnan, and Heilongjiang.

On September 21, 2020, the State Council approved the establishment of three new pilot free trade zones in Beijing, Hunan, and Anhui. In 2023, the Xinjiang Pilot Free Trade Zone was established, bringing the current total to 22.

（2）保税区。保税区是在港口作业区和与之相连的特定区域内，具有国际中转、国际采购、国际配送、国际转口贸易、商品展示、出口加工、口岸物流等功能的特殊经济区。它是经国务院批准设立的、海关实施特殊监管的经济区域，是我国目前开放度和自由度最大的经济区域。

保税区模式是目前最常用的跨境进口电商物流配送模式。保税区的商品暂时不需要向海关缴纳进口关税、增值税、消费税等税收，只有当客户下订单之后，卖家将信息对接清关信息系统，发货出保税区进行配送时才缴纳进口税，大大降低了企业成本。

保税区最显著的特征是通过仓储前置，用“空间位移”换“时间效率”，从而通过更经济的方式降低干线运输成本。这是一种提前备货、高效通关，最后选择更经济物流企业完成“最后一公里”运输的物流运作模式。

通过自由贸易试验区或保税区仓储，可以有效利用自由贸易试验区与保税区的各类政策综合优势与优惠措施，尤其是自由贸易试验区和保税区在物流、通关、商检、收付汇、退税方面的便利，简化跨境电商的业务操作，实现促进跨境电商贸易量的目的。

这种新型的“保税备货模式”，消费者只需要承担商品价格和国内物流费用，其他风险都由卖家承担，消费者购物风险得到极大程度的降低，有利于企业大订单集货，降低商品价格，提高客户满意度，避免了传统模式下的很多不利因素。

截至 2024 年 12 月底，我国共有 169 个综合保税区，它们在我国跨境电商物流集货等方面发挥着重要作用。

(2) Bonded zones. A bonded zone is a special economic zone located within a port operation area and a specific area connected to it. It integrates multiple functions, including international transit, international procurement, international distribution, international transit trade, commodity display, export processing, and ports logistics. It is an economic region approved by the State Council

and subject to special customs supervision. It is currently the most open and free economic region in China.

The bonded zone mode is currently the most commonly used cross-border import e-commerce logistics and distribution mode. Goods in the bonded zone do not currently need to pay import tariffs, value-added tax, consumption tax and other taxes to the customs. Only after the customer places an order, the seller will connect the information to the customs clearance information system and pay the import tax when shipping out of the bonded zone for distribution, greatly reducing the cost of the enterprise.

The most prominent feature of bonded zones is the use of pre-warehousing, exchanging "spatial displacement" for "time efficiency", thereby reducing the cost of mainline transportation in a more economical way. This is a logistics operation mode that involves early stocking, efficient customs clearance, and ultimately selecting more economical logistics companies to complete the "last mile" transportation.

By using pilot free trade zones or bonded zones for warehousing, various policy advantages and preferential measures of pilot free trade zones and bonded zones can be effectively utilized, especially the convenience of logistics, customs clearance, commodity inspection, foreign exchange collection and payment, and tax refund in free trade pilot zones and bonded zones. This helps simplify cross-border e-commerce operations and boost trade volume.

This new type of "bonded stocking mode" requires consumers to bear only the price of goods and domestic logistics costs, while other risks are borne by the seller. The shopping risk of consumers is greatly reduced, which is conducive to enterprises collecting large orders, reducing product prices, improving customer satisfaction, and avoiding many unfavorable factors under traditional modes.

By the end of December 2024, there were a total of 169 comprehensive bonded zones in China, which play an important role in cross-border e-commerce logistics consolidation and other aspects in China.

（3）保税港区。随着经济全球化进程加快，保税区的不足日益显现，保税港区应运而生，成为中国进一步深化改革、扩大开放、带动区域发展的试验基地。保税港区是世界自由港在中国的一种特殊表现形式，是“中国化”的自由贸易港。与传统保税区相比，保税港区不仅是真正的“境内关外”，还享受税收、监管等各项更为优惠的政策，在跨境电商物流集货方面具有先行先试的改革示范效应。例如，2017 年 7 月 26 日在深圳前海湾保税港区建立的“全球中心仓”，通过“一区多功能、一仓多形态”的监管创新，使原来需要存储于多个地区、多个仓库的多种物流及贸易形态的货物可以在保税港区内的一个中心仓内一站式完成。

截至 2024 年，我国已批复的保税港区有上海洋山保税港区、天津东疆保税港区、辽宁大连大窑湾保税港区、海南洋浦保税港区、浙江宁波梅山保税港区、广西钦州保税港区、福建厦门海沧保税港区、山东青岛前湾保税港区、广东深圳前海湾保税港区、广东广州南沙保税港区、福建福州保税港区、重庆两路寸滩保税港区、江苏张家港保税港区、山东烟台保税港区，共 14 个。重庆两路寸滩保税港区是唯一一个位于中国内陆地区，也是第一个采取“水港+

空港”的保税港区。江苏张家港保税港区是第一个位于县域口岸的保税港区。山东烟台保税港区是全国第一家以出口加工区和邻近港口整合转型升级形成的保税港区。

(3) Bonded port areas. With the acceleration of economic globalization, the shortcomings of bonded zones are becoming increasingly apparent, and bonded port areas have emerged as experimental bases for China to further deepen reform, expand opening-up, and drive regional development. The bonded port area is a special manifestation of the world's free ports in China, and is a "Sinicized" free trade port. Compared with traditional bonded zones, bonded port areas are not only truly "inside and outside the border", but also enjoy more favorable policies such as taxation and supervision. They have a pioneering reform demonstration effect in cross-border e-commerce logistics and cargo collection. For example, on July 26, 2017, the "Global Central Warehouse" was established in the Qianhai Bay Bonded Port Area of Shenzhen. Through the innovative supervision of "multi-functional zones and multi form warehouses", various logistics and trade forms of goods that originally needed to be stored in multiple regions and warehouses can be completed in one central warehouse within the bonded port area.

As of 2024, there are 14 approved bonded port areas in China, including Shanghai Yangshan Bonded Port Area, Tianjin Dongjiang Bonded Port Area, Liaoning Dalian Dayaowan Bonded Port Area, Hainan Yangpu Bonded Port Area, Zhejiang Ningbo Meishan Bonded Port Area, Guangxi Qinzhou Bonded Port Area, Fujian Xiamen Haicang Bonded Port Area, Shandong Qingdao Qianwan Bonded Port Area, Guangdong Shenzhen Qianhai Bay Bonded Port Area, Guangdong Guangzhou Nansha Bonded Port Area, Fujian Fuzhou Bonded Port Area, Chongqing Lianglu Cuntan Bonded Port Area, Jiangsu Zhangjiagang Bonded Port Area, and Shandong Yantai Bonded Port Area. Chongqing Lianglu Cuntan Bonded Port Area is the only one located in inland China and the first bonded port area to adopt a "water port + airport" approach. Jiangsu Zhangjiagang Bonded Port Area is the first bonded port area located at a county-level port. Shandong Yantai Bonded Port Area is the first bonded port area in China formed through the integration, transformation, and upgrading of export processing zones and adjacent ports.

3. 集货物流

Consolidation logistics

集货物流是指先将商品运输到本地或当地的仓储中心，达到一定数量或形成一定规模后，通过与国际物流公司合作，将商品运到境外买家手中；或者将各地发来的商品先进行聚集，然后再批量配送；或者一些所售商品类似的跨境电商企业建立战略联盟，成立共同的跨境物流运营中心，利用规模优势或优势互补理念，达到降低跨境物流费用的目的。

Consolidation logistics refers to the transportation of goods to local or local storage centers. Once a certain quantity or scale is reached, companies collaborate with international logistics providers to deliver the goods to overseas buyers. Alternatively, it may involve gathering the goods from various places first and then delivering them in bulk. Another approach is for some cross-border e-commerce companies that sell similar products to form strategic alliances. By setting up a shared cross-border logistics operation center, they can take the advantages of scale or complementary concepts to achieve the goal of reducing cross-border logistics costs.

（三）跨境电商物流模式创新

Innovation of cross-border e-commerce logistics mode

由于跨境电商物流涉及不同关境的国内段与国外段物流，加上不同的物流模式都有优缺点。因此，跨境电子商务很难以单一物流模式实现跨境物流。伴随跨境电子商务的发展，多种物流模式共用的跨境物流模式创新解决方案应用面更广。

Since cross-border e-commerce logistics involve domestic and foreign logistics in different customs territories, and given that different logistics modes have their own advantages and disadvantages, it is difficult for cross-border e-commerce to achieve cross-border logistics through a single mode. With the development of cross-border e-commerce, innovative solutions for cross-border logistics modes that share multiple logistics modes have a wider range of applications.

跨境电商物流模式创新是指基于现有的每种物流渠道各有利弊，从解决客户需求出发，从为客户提供更优质的物流服务入手，利用现有物流条件，寻求降低物流成本、兼顾时效性与安全性的最佳物流方案。

Innovation of cross-border e-commerce logistics modes refers to the process of finding the best logistics solution that reduces logistics costs while balancing efficiency and safety. This process is based on the advantages and disadvantages of each existing logistics channel, starting with solving customer needs, providing better logistics service manpower for customers, and utilizing existing logistics conditions.

多种物流模式共用，多采用以上几种物流模式中的两种或两种以上，如“国际物流专线+海外仓”“集货物流+保税区物流”等。针对不同国家、不同商品等，采用适合的多种物流模式配合实现跨境物流，能够有效凸显各种物流模式的聚合效应。

Multiple logistics modes are shared, often using two or more of the above logistics modes, such as “international logistics dedicated lines + overseas warehouses” “consolidation logistics + bonded zone logistics” , etc. Adopting multiple suitable logistics modes to achieve cross-border logistics for different countries and products can effectively highlight the aggregation effect of various logistics modes.

四、跨境电商物流的特征

Characteristics of cross-border e-commerce logistics

（一）物流反应速度快速化

Rapidity of logistics response speed

物流服务提供商对上游、下游的物流、配送需求的反应速度越来越快，前置时间越来越短，配送间隔越来越短，物流配送速度越来越快，商品周转次数越来越多。

The response speed of logistics service providers to upstream and downstream logistics and distribution needs is getting faster; the lead time is getting shorter; the delivery interval is getting shorter; the logistics delivery speed is getting faster; and the number of product turnover times is increasing.

（二）物流功能集成化

Integration of logistics functions

现代物流着重于将物流与供应链的其他环节进行集成，包括物流渠道与商流渠道的集成、物流渠道之间的集成、物流功能的集成、物流环节与制造环节的集成等。

Modern logistics focuses on integrating logistics with other links in the supply chain, including the integration of logistics channels and commercial channels, the integration among logistics channels, the integration of logistics functions, and the integration of logistics links and manufacturing links.

（三）物流作业规范化

Standardization of logistics operations

现代物流强调功能、作业流程、作业、动作的标准化与程式化，使复杂的作业变成简单的易于推广与考核的动作。物流自动化方便物流信息的实时采集与追踪，提高整个物流系统的管理和监控水平。

Modern logistics emphasizes the standardization and proceduralizing of functions, operational processes, operations, and actions, turning complex tasks into simple actions that are easy to promote and evaluate. Logistics automation facilitates real-time collection and tracking of logistics information, thereby improving the management and monitoring level of the entire logistics system.

（四）物流信息电子化

Electronization of logistics information

由于计算机信息技术的应用，现代物流过程的可见性明显增加，物流过程中库存积压、延期交货、送货不及时、库存与运输不可控等风险大大降低，从而可以加强供应商、物流商、批发商、零售商在组织物流过程中的协调和配合以及对物流过程的控制。

Due to the application of computer information technology, the visibility of modern logistics processes has significantly increased, and the risks of inventory backlog, delayed delivery, untimely delivery, and uncontrollable inventory and transportation in the logistics process have been greatly reduced. This can strengthen the coordination and cooperation of suppliers, logistics providers, wholesalers, and retailers in organizing the logistics process, as well as their control over the logistics process.

五、跨境电商物流的难点

Difficulties in cross-border e-commerce logistics

（一）物流链条长、作业复杂

Long logistics chain and complex operations

由于增加了海外仓储配送等过程，跨境电商的整个链条比普通物流的链条广、环节多，且涉及电商、海关、国检、商检、税务、外汇等众多主体，各项信息需互联互通，其物流运作自然更为复杂、难度更大。例如，运往俄罗斯、巴西等新兴市场的物流时间往往多达数十天甚至一个月之久。

Due to the addition of overseas warehousing and distribution processes, the entire chain of cross-border e-commerce is wider and more complex than that of ordinary logistics, involving numerous entities such as e-commerce, customs, national inspection, commercial inspection, taxation, foreign exchange, etc. All information needs to be interconnected, making its logistics operation more complex and difficult. For example, logistics to emerging markets such as Russia and Brazil often take tens of days or even a month.

（二）自动化、信息化程度不高

Low level of automation and informatization

跨境电商物流涉及海量订单及海量 SKU（物理上不可分割的最小存货单位），订单商品分散，并且要快速完成订单拣选、配送以及退换货处理，因此，对物流系统自动化程度要求较高。而目前多数跨境电商企业发展时间短，自身积累不足，物流信息系统不够先进，自动化物流设备及技术先进度不够，因此订单处理滞后、效率低且错误率高、库存管理混乱甚至丢件等现象已成为困扰跨境电商发展的主要问题。

Cross-border e-commerce logistics involves a large number of orders and SKUs (Stock Keeping Units, physically the smallest indivisible inventory units), with scattered order products and the need to quickly complete order picking, distribution, and return/exchange processing. Consequently, a high level of automation is required for the logistics system. At present, most cross-border e-commerce enterprises have a short development time, insufficient self-accumulation, less advanced logistics information systems, and insufficient progress in automated logistics equipment and technology. As a result, lagging order processing, low efficiency and high error rate, chaotic inventory management, and even lost items have become the main problems hindering the development of cross-border e-commerce.

（三）仓库面积不足

Insufficient warehouse area

在跨境电商快速发展下，现有的仓库资源已难以匹配业务增速。特别是“双 11”“黑色星期五”等促销日前，陡增的订单量对现有的物流系统提出挑战，爆仓现象普遍存在。

With the rapid development of cross-border e-commerce, existing warehouse resources are struggling to keep pace with accelerated business growth rates. Especially before the promotion days such as “Double 11” and “Black Friday”, the sudden increase in order volume poses a challenge to the existing logistics system, and the phenomenon of warehouse overcrowding is widespread.

（四）流程复杂

Complex process

跨境物流涉及国内头程交货、缴费、海关清关及当地派送，如果是海外仓形式的物流渠道，还涉及海外仓内货物分拣等。

Cross-border logistics involves domestic first-mile delivery, payment, customs clearance, and local delivery. If it is a logistics channel in the form of an overseas warehouse, it also involves sorting of goods in the overseas warehouse.

此外，订单处理缓慢、物流体验差以及其他因素导致跨境电商的退换货率及消费者投诉率均比国内电商高，无形中增加了跨境电商物流管理运营的难度。

In addition, slow order processing, poor logistics experience, and other factors have led to higher return and exchange rates and consumer complaint rates in cross-border e-commerce compared to domestic e-commerce, which invisibly increases the difficulty of cross-border e-commerce logistics management and operation.

第二节 海外仓
Section 2 Overseas Warehouse

一、海外仓模式概述
Overview of overseas warehouse mode

（一）海外仓定义
Definition of Overseas Warehouse

在跨境电商中，海外仓是指由网络外贸交易平台、物流服务商单独或合作为卖家在物品销售目的地提供的货品仓储、分拣、包装、派送一站式控制与管理服务。整个流程包括头程运输、仓储管理、本地配送三个部分，即卖家将要销售的货物存储在当地的仓库，当有买家需要时，仓库立即做出响应，并及时对货物进行分拣、包装以及递送。

In cross-border e-commerce, overseas warehouse refers to a one-stop control and management service for goods storage, sorting, packaging, and delivery provided by online foreign trade trading platforms and logistics service providers individually or in cooperation for sellers at the destination of goods sales. The entire process includes three parts: first-mile transportation, warehouse management, and local delivery — the seller stores the goods to be sold in the local warehouse, and when a buyer needs them, the warehouse immediately responds and promptly sorts, packages, and delivers the goods.

（二）海外仓操作流程
Overseas warehouse operation process

1. 卖家前期准备
Seller's preliminary preparation

卖家在前期需做如下准备：

（1）在海外仓服务商提供的物流平台注册会员，开通后台账号，成为会员。

（2）在后台系统建立自己的产品信息单。

（3）备货。

（4）等候海外仓确认订单后的出货安排通知。

Sellers need to make the following preparations in the early stages:

（1）Register as a member on the logistics platform provided by the overseas warehouse service provider, open a backend account, and become a member.

(2) Create your own product information sheet in the backend system.

(3) Stock up.

(4) Wait for the shipment arrangement notification after the overseas warehouse confirms the order.

2. 海外仓使用流程

Overseas warehouse usage process

中国卖家通过海运、空运等方式将商品集中运往海外仓储中心进行存储，并通过物流服务商的库存管理系统下达操作指令。具体流程如下：

(1) 卖家将商品运至海外仓储中心，或者委托物流服务商将货发至服务商海外的仓库。这段国际货运头程可采取海运、空运等方式到达仓库。

(2) 卖家在线远程管理海外仓储。卖家使用物流商的物流信息系统远程操作海外仓储的货物数据，并且保持实时更新。

(3) 根据卖家指令进行货物操作。根据物流商海外仓储中心自动化操作设备，严格按照卖家指令对货物进行存储、分拣、包装、配送等操作。

(4) 系统信息实时更新。发货完成后系统会及时更新，以便卖家实时掌握库存状况。

Chinese sellers transport their goods to overseas warehouse centers for storage through sea and air freight, and issue operational instructions through the inventory management system of logistics service providers. The specific processes are as follows:

(1) The seller will transport the goods to an overseas warehouse center or entrust a logistics service provider to send the goods to the service provider' s overseas warehouse. This international freight first-mile can be transported to the warehouse by sea, air, or other means.

(2) The seller remotely manages overseas warehouses online. The seller uses the logistics information system of the logistics provider to remotely operate the data of goods stored overseas and maintain real-time updates.

(3) Operate the goods according to the seller' s instructions. According to the automated operation equipment of the logistics provider' s overseas warehouse center, the goods are stored, sorted, packaged, and distributed strictly according to the seller' s instructions.

(4) Update system information in real time. After the shipment is completed, the system will update in a timely manner so that the seller can grasp the inventory status in real time.

二、海外仓的功能

The functions of overseas warehouses

(一) 代收货款功能

Collection of payment function

由于跨境交易存在较大的风险，因此为解决交易风险和资金结算不便、不及时的难题，在合同规定的时限和佣金费率下，海外仓在收到货物的同时可以提供代收货款等增值业务。

Due to the significant risks associated with cross-border transactions, in order to address the challenges of transaction risks and inconvenient and untimely fund settlements, overseas warehouses can provide value-added services such as collection of payment upon receipt of goods, within the time limit and at the commission rate specified in the contract.

（二）拆包拼装功能

Disassembly and assembly function

对一般国际 B2C 跨境电商模式而言，订单数量相对较少、订单金额相对较小、频率较高且具有长距离、小批量、多批次的特点，因此为实现运输规模效应，可对零担货物①实行整箱拼装业务运输。货物到达海外仓之后，由仓库将整箱货物进行拆箱，同时根据客户订单要求，为地域环境集中的用户提供拼装业务，进行整车运输或配送。

For the general international B2C cross-border e-commerce mode, the order quantity is relatively small; the order amount is relatively small; the frequency is high; and it has the characteristics of long distance, small batch, and multiple batches. Therefore, in order to achieve the scale effect of transportation, full container assembly business transportation can be implemented for less than truckload goods. After the goods arrive at the overseas warehouse, the warehouse will unpack the entire box of goods and provide assembly services for users with concentrated regional environments according to customer order requirements for whole vehicle transportation or distribution.

（三）保税功能

Bonded function

当海外仓经海关批准成为保税仓库时，其功能和用途范围更为广泛，可简化海关通关流程和相关手续。同时，在保税仓库可以进行转口贸易，以海外仓所在地为第三国，连接卖方和买方，这种方式能够有效规避贸易制裁。保税海外仓，还提供简单加工、刷唛②等相应增值服务，能有效丰富仓库功能，提升竞争力。

When overseas warehouses are approved by customs to become bonded warehouses, their functions and uses are more extensive, which can simplify customs clearance processes and related procedures. At the same time, transit trade can be conducted in bonded warehouses, with overseas warehouses located in third countries, connecting sellers and buyers, which can effectively avoid trade sanctions. Bonded overseas warehouses also provide value-added services such as simple processing and relabelling, which can effectively enrich warehouse functions and enhance competitiveness.

（四）运输资源整合功能

Transportation resource integration function

由于国际 B2C 跨境电商订单数量相对较少、频率较高，因此，为了对国内仓库的上游供应商资源和国外仓库下游的客户资源进行更好的整合，满足物流高时效的配送要求，海外仓系统提供商将国内仓库作为共同配送的终点、将海外仓作为共同配送的起点，实现对运输资源的有效整合，实现运输规模效应，降低配送成本。

---

① 零担货物，是指一张货物运单（一批）托运的货物重量或容积不够装一车的货物（即不够整车运输条件）。——编者注

② 刷唛，专指在货物的外包装上注明收货人和货物内容的信息标志。——编者注

Due to the relatively small number and high frequency of international B2C cross-border e-commerce orders, in order to better integrate the upstream supplier resources of domestic warehouses and downstream customer resources of foreign warehouses, and meet the high delivery requirements of logistics, overseas warehouse system providers regard domestic warehouses as the endpoint of joint distribution and overseas warehouses as the starting point of joint distribution, achieving effective integration of transportation resources, realizing the scale effect of transportation, and reducing distribution costs.

一般情况下难以实现规模运输的产品，通过海外仓服务，一方面可以实现集中运输，有效减少运输成本；另一方面，在海外通过共同配送，可以更好地搭建逆向物流的运输平台，提高逆向物流货品的集货能力，降低成本费用。因为，一旦逆向物流产生阻滞，企业将面临高额的返程费用和关税征收，而海外仓的建立可以在提高逆向物流速度的同时增加客户满意度，提升客户价值。

In general, products that are difficult to transport on a large scale can utilize overseas warehouse services. On one hand, this can achieve centralized transportation, effectively reducing transportation costs. On the other hand, through joint distribution overseas, a better transportation platform for reverse logistics can be established, improving the collection capacity of reverse logistics goods and reducing costs. If reverse logistics encounters obstacles, enterprises will face high return costs and tariff collection. The establishment of overseas warehouses can increase customer satisfaction and value while improving the speed of reverse logistics.

三、海外仓选品定位与思路

Overseas warehouse selection positioning and ideas

（一）海外仓选品定位

Overseas warehouse selection positioning

海外仓选品是困扰卖家们的一个问题，究竟哪些产品必须使用海外仓？哪些产品可以选择性地使用海外仓？以全球速卖通为例，通常来说，高利润、低风险类产品以及高利润、高风险类产品适合选择使用海外仓，而低利润、低风险类产品和低利润、高风险类产品则不太适合用海外仓。

Product selection for overseas warehouses is a problem that troubles sellers. Which products must be placed in overseas warehouses? Which products can be selectively placed in overseas warehouses? Taking AliExpress as an example, high profit, low-risk products and high-profit, high-risk products are suitable for overseas warehouses, while low profit, low-risk products and low profit, high-risk products are not very suitable for overseas warehouses.

理论上，海外仓可以使覆盖的产品无限延展，不限重量和尺寸。重物流产品（如五金类产品、家具类产品、户外类产品等）特别适合用海外仓。如果企业的产品是轻物流产品，产品 SKU（库存量单位）很多，还没法对热销产品有预估，可能就不合适选择海外仓，因为海外仓要求企业对于自己产品的销售有一定的预判，然后提前囤货。当然，这些都不是绝对的选择标准，企业要根据自身的具体情况做决策。

In theory, overseas warehouses can extend the coverage of products infinitely, without limitations on weight and size. Heavy logistics products (such as hardware products, furniture products, outdoor products, etc.) are particularly suitable for overseas warehouses. If a company's products are light logistics products with many SKUs (units of inventory), it may not be suitable to choose overseas warehouses as it is not yet possible to estimate the hot selling products — overseas warehouses require companies to have a prior understanding of the sales of their products and then stock up in advance. Of course, these are not absolute selection criteria, and companies need to make decisions based on their specific circumstances.

（二）海外仓选品思路

Overseas warehouse selection ideas

海外仓选品思路应该以当地买家的市场需求为基础来构建。

（1）确定在哪个国家建立海外仓。在建仓的时候要选择可以覆盖周围市场的地方。

（2）了解当地国家买家市场需求。从当地电商平台上了解和调查。

（3）在国内寻找类似产品，开发海外仓产品。开发指标依据：单品销量，单品进仓费用，单品毛利及毛利率，月毛利，成本收益率等。

（4）运用数据工具选品。选品主要参考依据：选品专家的热销词、热搜词，搜索词分析中的飙升词。

The product selection ideas for overseas warehouses should be based on the market demand of local buyers.

(1) Determine which country to establish overseas warehouses in. When building a warehouse, choose a location that can cover the surrounding market.

(2) Understand the local buyer market demand. Learn and investigate from local e-commerce platforms.

(3) Search for similar products domestically and develop overseas warehouse products. Development indicators are based on: single product sales, single product warehouse expenses, single product gross profit and gross profit margin, monthly gross profit, cost-benefit ratio, etc.

(4) Use data tools to select products. The main reference for product selection is data analysis, including hot selling keywords and search terms of the selected product experts, as well as the skyrocketing keywords in search word analysis.

四、亚马逊 FBA

Amazon FBA

FBA（Fulfillment by Amazon），中文翻译为“亚马逊物流”，是指卖家把自己在亚马逊上销售的产品库存直接送到亚马逊当地市场的仓库中，客户下订单，由亚马逊系统自动完成后续的发货。作为世界上最大的在线零售商，在美国的菲尼克斯（凤凰城），亚马逊最大的仓库有 28 个标准足球场大小。

FBA (Fulfillment by Amazon), translated as “亚马逊物流” in Chinese. It refers to sellers directly delivering their inventory of products sold on Amazon to the warehouse in the local Amazon market, where customers place orders and the Amazon system automatically completes subsequent shipments. As the world's largest online retailer, Amazon has its largest warehouse in Phoenix, USA, which is the size of 28 standard football fields.

（一）FBA 的服务流程

FBA Service Process

FBA 是由亚马逊提供的包括仓储、拣货、打包、派送、收款、客服与退货处理的一条龙式物流服务，其服务流程主要包括以下五个方面：

（1）发送货物。卖家通过 FBA 头程运输服务商将货物发送到亚马逊海外仓库。

（2）接受并存储。亚马逊仓储接受并存储卖家货物信息。

（3）买家下单。买家搜索并购买卖家产品。

（4）分拣、打包产品。亚马逊利用先进的系统分拣、打包客户订单货物。

（5）配送及跟踪。亚马逊使用卖家选择的物流商配送产品，并为买家提供订单跟踪信息。

FBA is a one-stop logistics service provided by Amazon, including warehousing, picking, packaging, delivery, payment, customer service, and return processing. Its service process mainly includes the following five aspects:

(1) Send goods. The seller sends the goods to Amazon's overseas warehouse through an FBA first-mile shipping service provider.

(2) Accept and store. Amazon warehouse accepts and records the seller's goods information.

(3) Place order by the buyer. The buyer searches and purchases the seller's product.

(4) Sort and package products. Amazon utilizes advanced systems to sort and package customer-ordered goods.

(5) Deliver and track. Amazon uses the logistics provider selected by the seller to deliver the product and provide order tracking information to the buyer.

（二）FBA 费用构成

FBA fee composition

FBA 服务的费用主要包括订单处理费、商品分拣包装费、重量处理费、仓储管理费四个方面。

The fees for FBA services mainly include four aspects: order processing, pick & package, weight calculation, and monthly storage.

（三）FBA 的优缺点

Advantages and disadvantages of FBA

1. 优点

Advantages

FBA 的优点如下：

（1）提高排名，帮助卖家成为特色卖家和抢夺购物车，提高客户的信任度，提高销售额。

（2）丰富的物流经验。仓库遍布全世界，实现智能化管理。

（3）配送时效快（仓库大多靠近机场）。

（4）亚马逊专业客服提供 7×24 小时客户服务热线，可以提高用户体验，解决卖家的客服问题。根据亚马逊的服务条款，卖家使用 FBA，买家留下不利于 FBA 物流方面的负面评价，亚马逊拥有全权消除这个负面评价的权利。

（5）对于单价超过 300 美元的产品可免费。

The advantages of FBA include:

(1) Improve listing ranking, help sellers earn featured sellers status and secure the buy box, thereby increasing customer trust and boosting sales.

(2) With rich logistics experience. Warehouses are spread all over the world, achieving intelligent management.

(3) Its delivery speed is fast (Most warehouses are close to airports).

(4) Amazon's professional customer service provides a 7×24 hour customer service hotline, which can improve user experience and resolve seller issues. According to Amazon's terms of service, if sellers use FBA and buyers leave negative reviews that are detrimental to FBA logistics, Amazon has the full right to eliminate such negative reviews.

(5) Products with a unit price exceeding USD 300 are free of charge.

2. 缺点

Disadvantages

FBA 的缺点如下：

（1）成本较高，尤其是仓储费。

（2）客服的灵活性差（FBA 只能用英文和客户沟通，而且用邮件沟通回复不像第三方海外仓客服那样及时）。

（3）如果前期工作没做好，标签扫描出现问题会影响货物入库，甚至入不了库。

（4）退货地址只支持美国（如果卖家是做美国站点的 FBA）

（5）FBA 不会为卖家头程发货提供清关服务。

The disadvantages of FBA are as follows:

(1) The cost is relatively high, especially the storage fee.

(2) Customer service lacks flexibility (FBA can only communicate with customers in English, and replies via email are not as timely as those from third-party overseas warehouse customer service).

(3) If the preliminary work is not done well, there may be problems with label scanning, which will affect the storage of goods, or even make it impossible to store them.

(4) Return addresses are limited to the United States (for seller using FBA on Amazon US marketplace).

(5) FBA does not provide customs clearance services for sellers' first-mile shipments.

五、第三方海外仓

Third-party overseas warehouse

第三方海外仓，也就是跨境电商与第三方海外仓合作，分为租用和合作建设两种合作方式。在租用的情况下会产生操作、租用、运输物流等多重费用；在合作的情况下只产生运输物流费用。

Third-party overseas warehouses, also known as cross-border e-commerce and cooperation with third-party overseas warehouses, are divided into two types of cooperation: leasing and cooperative construction. In the case of leasing, multiple costs such as operation, rental, transportation and logistics will be incurred. In the case of cooperation, only transportation and logistics costs are incurred.

相比亚马逊的 FBA 来说，第三方海外仓交易出现问题时与客户的沟通比较及时，在清关方面也可以提供收件人和代缴关税，而且价格也优惠很多。

Compared to Amazon's FBA, third-party overseas warehouse have more timely communication with customers when problems arise. They can also provide recipients and collect customs duties on behalf of customers in terms of customs clearance, and the prices are much more favorable.

（一）第三方海外仓与 FBA 的共同点

Similarities between third-party overseas warehouses and FBA

第三方海外仓与 FBA 的共同点如下：

（1）两者都需要卖家提前备货，都具有很好的仓储管理经验，无须卖家操心仓储与配送问题。

（2）两者都可以缩短配送时间，提升客户的满意度，对店铺的销售额增长有帮助。

（3）两者都需要卖家批量发货，发货的方式一般选择空运、海运等，能有效避免物流高峰。

（4）两者都可以为买家提供退换货服务。

（5）无论是选择 FBA 仓还是第三方海外仓租用，卖家每月都需缴纳仓储费、物流费用和其他费用。

（6）产品在卖家的控制之外，但两者都提供客服服务，让卖家知悉库存情况。

The similarities between third-party overseas warehouses and FBA are as follows:

(1) Both require sellers to stock up in advance and have good warehousing management experience, so sellers do not need to worry about warehousing and distribution issues.

(2) Both can shorten delivery time, improve customer satisfaction, and contribute to the growth of store sales.

(3) Both require sellers to ship in bulk, and shipping methods such as air freight and sea freight are generally chosen to effectively avoid logistics peaks.

(4) Both can provide buyers with return and exchange services.

(5) Whether choosing FBA warehouse or third-party overseas warehouse rental, sellers need to pay monthly storage fees, logistics fees, and other expenses.

(6) The products are outside the seller's control, but both provide customer service to keep the seller informed of inventory status.

(二) 第三方海外仓与 FBA 的不同点

Differences between third-party overseas warehouses and FBA

第三方海外仓与 FBA 的不同点如下:

(1) 选品范围差异。亚马逊 FBA 仓对选品的尺寸、重量、类别有一定程度的限制,所以选品偏向于体积小、利润高、质量好的产品;如果选择第三方海外仓,选品范围比 FBA 仓广,体积大、重量大的产品也适合。换个说法,即能进入亚马逊 FBA 仓的产品必定能进入第三方海外仓,但能进入第三方海外仓的产品不一定能进入亚马逊 FBA 仓。

(2) 头程服务差异。亚马逊 FBA 仓不会为卖家提供头程清关服务;部分第三方海外仓服务商会给卖家提供头程清关服务,甚至还会有包含代缴税金、派送到仓的一条龙服务。

(3) 产品入仓要求差异。亚马逊 FBA 仓的入仓要求较为严格,需要卖家在发货前贴好外箱标签及产品标签,如果外箱标签或产品标签有破损,会要求卖家先整理,然后才能进入。亚马逊也不提供产品组装服务。第三方海外仓的入库要求没有亚马逊 FBA 仓那么高,并且在上架前会提供整理、组装产品的服务。

(4) 产品管理差异。亚马逊是默认分仓的,往往会将卖家的产品分散到不同的仓库进行混储。而第三方海外仓一般会将货物放在同一个仓库集中管理。

(5) 适用范围差异。FBA 仓只提供给在亚马逊平台上的卖家使用。而第三方海外仓则没这个要求,只要有货,无论在哪个平台售卖,都可以使用。另外,第三方海外仓还具有中转作用,如果卖家同时使用第三方海外仓与 FBA 仓,旺季时可以直接从第三方海外仓调货到 FBA 仓,节省从国内发货的时间。

但是,第三方海外仓无法为卖家提供产品推广服务,需要卖家自己通过站内、站外推广来增加曝光度,第三方海外仓不能提供售后与投诉服务,无法消除买家的差评。此外,将货物放在第三方海外仓存在潜在的安全风险。

The differences between third-party overseas warehouses and FBA are as follows:

(1) Differences in product selection range. Amazon FBA warehouses have certain restrictions on the size, weight, and category of selected products, so the selection tends to focus on products with small size, high profit, and good quality. If sellers choose a third-party overseas warehouse, the product selection range is wider than FBA warehouse, and products with large volume and weight are also suitable. In other words, products that can enter Amazon FBA warehouses will definitely enter third-party overseas warehouses, but products that can enter third-party overseas warehouses may not necessarily enter Amazon FBA warehouses.

(2) Differences in first-mile services. Amazon FBA warehouses do not provide first-mile customs clearance services for sellers. Some third-party overseas warehouse service providers will provide sellers with first-mile customs clearance services, and even offer one-stop services including tax payment and delivery to the warehouse.

(3) Differences in product warehousing requirements. The entry requirements for Amazon FBA warehouses are quite strict, requiring sellers to properly label the outer packaging and product labels

before shipping. If the outer packaging or product labels are damaged, sellers will be required to tidy them up before entering. Amazon also does not provide product assembly services. The personnel requirements for third-party overseas warehouses are not as high as those for Amazon FBA warehouses, and they will provide services for organizing and assembling products before listing.

(4) Differences in product management. Amazon defaults to warehousing and often distributes sellers' products to different warehouses for mixed storage. Third-party overseas warehouses usually store goods in the same warehouse for centralized management.

(5) Differences in scope of application. FBA warehouses are only available for sellers on the Amazon platform to use, while third-party overseas warehouses do not have this requirement. As long as there are goods available, they can be used regardless of which platform they are sold on. In addition, third-party overseas warehouses also have a transit function. If sellers use both third-party overseas warehouses and FBA warehouses, they can directly transfer goods from the third-party overseas warehouse to the FBA warehouse during peak seasons, saving time for domestic shipments.

However, third-party overseas warehouses cannot provide product promotion services for sellers, and sellers need to increase their exposure through internal and external promotion. Third-party overseas warehouses cannot provide after-sales and complaint services, and cannot eliminate buyer negative reviews. In addition, placing goods in third-party overseas warehouses poses potential security risks.

第三节 Section 3 重点短语与句型 Key Phrases and Sentence Patterns

一、常用单词与短语 Common words and phrases

1. cross-border e-commerce logistics 跨境电商物流
2. transaction preparation phase 交易准备阶段
3. cross-border trade orders 跨境贸易订单
4. cross-border business relationship 跨境商务关系
5. market research 市场调研
6. customer development 客户开发
7. credit investigation 资信调查
8. business contact 业务联系
9. communication skills 沟通技巧
10. logistics technology 物流技术
11. international logistics network 国际物流网络
12. physical movement of goods 货物物理性移动

13. international commodity transaction　国际商品交易
14. seller's delivery of documents　卖方交付单证
15. buyer's receipt of goods　买方接收货物
16. cross-border logistics services　跨境物流服务
17. efficiency and effectiveness　效率和效益
18. postal package mode　邮政包裹模式
19. commercial express delivery mode　商业快递模式
20. international express delivery　国际快递
21. domestic express delivery　国内快递
22. dedicated line logistics mode　专线物流模式
23. overseas warehouse service　海外仓服务
24. first-mile transportation　头程运输
25. warehouse management　仓储管理
26. local distribution　本地配送
27. border warehouse　边境仓
28. pilot free trade zones　自由贸易试验区
29. bonded zones　保税区
30. bonded port areas　保税港区
31. consolidation logistics　集货物流
32. innovation of cross-border e-commerce logistics mode　跨境电商物流模式创新
33. rapidity of logistics response speed　物流反应速度快速化
34. integration of logistics functions　物流功能集成化
35. standardization of logistics operations　物流作业规范化
36. electronization of logistics information　物流信息电子化
37. long logistics chain　物流链条长
38. automation and informatization　自动化、信息化
39. insufficient warehouse area　仓库面积不足
40. complex process　流程复杂
41. overseas warehouse mode　海外仓模式
42. collection of payment function　代收货款功能
43. disassembly and assembly function　拆包拼装功能
44. bonded function　保税功能
45. transportation resource integration function　运输资源整合功能
46. FBA (Fulfillment by Amazon)　亚马逊物流
47. third-party overseas warehouse　第三方海外仓

二、常用句型
Common sentence patterns

1. The operation of cross-border e-commerce involves information flow, commercial flow, capital flow, and logistics.

跨境电商运作过程中涉及信息流、商流、资金流和物流。

2. Information flow, commercial flow, and capital flow can all be achieved through computers and network communication devices in a virtual environment.

信息流、商流和资金流均可通过计算机和网络通信设备在虚拟环境下实现。

3. The international logistics system includes seven subsystems: warehousing, transportation, distribution, circulation processing, packaging, loading and unloading, and information processing.

国际物流系统包括仓储、运输、配送、流通加工、包装、装卸搬运和信息处理七个子系统。

4. The high-efficiency, high-quality, and low-cost operation of the international logistics system is the guarantee for the development of cross-border e-commerce.

国际物流系统高效率、高质量、低成本的运作是跨境电商发展的保证。

5. Cross-border e-commerce logistics is an international business activity that uses modern logistics technology.

跨境电商物流是采用现代物流技术的一项国际商业活动。

6. It selects the best way and path, and physically moves goods (commodities) with the lowest cost and minimum risk.

它选择最佳的方式与路径，以最低的费用和最小的风险，对货物（商品）进行物理性移动。

7. The two parties involved in cross-border logistics transactions belong to different countries (or regions).

跨境物流交易双方分属不同国家（或地区）。

8. The goods need to be transferred from the supplier's country or region through cross-border logistics to achieve final delivery within the demand country (or region).

商品需要从供应方国家或地区通过跨境物流方式实现空间位置转移，在需求所在国家（或地区）内实现最后的物流配送。

9. Cross-border e-commerce must be completed through offline cross-border logistics services.

跨境电商必须通过线下跨境物流服务完成。

10. The level of cross-border logistics services determines the efficiency and effectiveness of cross-border e-commerce.

跨境物流服务的水平决定了跨境电商的效率和有效性。

11. The new form of international trade is characterized by small quantities, high frequency, and fast delivery.

国际贸易的新形式表现为小量、高频次、快速发货。

12. The cost, accuracy, and response speed of cross-border logistics services will become a competitive factor for cross-border e-commerce services.

跨境物流服务的成本、准确度和响应速度将成为跨境电商服务的竞争项。

13. FBA (Fulfillment by Amazon) is a one-stop logistics service provided by Amazon, including warehousing, picking, packaging, delivery, payment, customer service, and return processing.

FBA（Fulfillment by Amazon）是亚马逊提供的包括仓储、拣货、打包、派送、收款、客服与退货处理的一条龙式物流服务。

14. The postal network basically covers the whole world, which is wider than any other logistics channel.

邮政网络基本覆盖全球，比其他任何物流渠道都要广。

15. The Universal Postal Union (UPU) is a specialized agency under the United Nations dedicated to international postal affairs.

万国邮政联盟是联合国下设的一个关于国际邮政事务的专门机构。

16. The Kahala Postal Organization requires all members to meet a 98% on-time delivery rate standard.

卡哈拉邮政组织要求所有成员的投递时限达到98%的质量标准。

17. Postal packages sent from China to the United States can typically arrive within a few days.

从中国发往美国的邮政包裹，一般几天内可以到达。

18. Lianyi focuses on cross-border e-commerce logistics supply chain services and is the only enterprise that integrates global postal channels.

联易专注于跨境电商物流供应链服务，是唯一一家集全球邮政渠道于一身的企业。

19. International express delivery refers to the four major express delivery giants, namely DHL, TNT, FedEx, and UPS.

国际快递是指四大快递巨头，即 DHL、TNT、FedEx 和 UPS。

20. These international courier companies provide excellent logistics experience for overseas users who purchase Chinese products online.

这些国际快递商为网购中国产品的海外用户带来极好的物流体验。

21. The domestic express delivery mainly refers to EMS, SF Express, and "Four Tong and One Da".

国内快递主要是指 EMS、顺丰和“四通一达”。

22. Cross-border dedicated line logistics generally transport goods to foreign countries through air cargo.

跨境专线物流一般是通过航空包舱方式将货物运输到国外。

23. The advantage of dedicated line logistics lies in its ability to consolidate large quantities of goods to a specific country or region.

专线物流的优势在于其能够集中大批量到某一特定国家或地区的货物。

24. Overseas warehouse service refers to a one-stop control and management service for sellers to store, sort, package, and deliver goods at the sales destination.

海外仓服务是指为卖家在销售目的地进行货物仓储、分拣、包装和派送的一站式控制与管理服务。

25. The overseas warehouse mode can ship goods from the buyer' s local warehouse, greatly reducing delivery time and improving delivery efficiency.

海外仓模式可以在买家本地仓库发货，大大缩短了配送时间，提高了配送效率。

26. The operation of overseas warehouses requires costs, there is a risk of product backlog, and it is difficult to return the delivered goods to the domestic market.

海外仓的运营需要成本，商品存在积压风险，送达后的商品很难再退回国内。

27. Border warehouses can be categorized as absolute border warehouses and relative border warehouses.

边境仓可分为绝对边境仓和相对边境仓。

28. The bonded zone is a special economic zone located within a port operation area and a specific area connected to it.

保税区是在港口作业区和与之相连的特定区域内的特殊经济区。

29. The bonded zone mode is currently the most commonly used cross-border import e-commerce logistics and distribution mode.

保税区模式是目前最常用的跨境进口电商物流配送模式。

30. The bonded port area is a special manifestation of the world's free ports in China, and is a "Sinicized" free trade port.

保税港区是世界自由港在中国的一种特殊表现形式，是“中国化”的自由贸易港。

31. Consolidation logistics refers to the transportation of goods to local or local storage centers, reaching a certain quantity or scale.

集货物流是指先将商品运输到本地或当地的仓储中心，达到一定数量或形成一定规模。

32. Innovation in cross-border e-commerce logistics mode refers to the process of finding the best logistics solution.

跨境电商物流模式创新是指寻找最佳物流解决方案的过程。

33. Multiple logistics modes are shared, often using two or more of the above logistics modes.

多种物流模式共用，多采用以上几种物流模式中的两种或两种以上。

34. The response speed of logistics service providers to upstream and downstream logistics and distribution needs is getting faster.

物流服务提供商对上下游的物流配送需求的响应速度越来越快。

35. Modern logistics emphasizes the standardization and proceduralizing of functions, operational processes, operations, and actions.

现代物流强调功能、作业流程、作业、动作的标准化与程序化。

36. Due to the application of computer information technology, the visibility of modern logistics processes has significantly increased.

由于计算机信息技术的应用，现代物流过程的可见性明显增加。

37. The entire chain of cross-border e-commerce is wider and more complex than that of ordinary logistics.

跨境电商的整个链条比普通物流的链条广、环节多。

38. Cross-border logistics involves domestic first-mile delivery, payment, customs clearance, and local delivery.

跨境物流涉及国内头程交货、缴费、海关清关及当地派送。

39. The overseas warehouse refers to a one-stop control and management service for goods storage, sorting, packaging, and delivery.

海外仓是指对货物仓储、分拣、包装、派送的一站式控制与管理服务。

40. The overseas warehouse mode can reduce logistics costs significantly, especially when shipping locally.

尤其是在本地发货时，海外仓模式可以显著降低物流成本。

41. Overseas warehouses can improve product exposure and boost store sales.

海外仓可以提高产品曝光率和提升店铺销量。

42. The operation of overseas warehouses is subject to uncontrollable factors such as local policies, social factors, and natural factors.

海外仓的运营受当地政策、社会因素、自然因素等不可控因素的影响。

43. Not all products are suitable for using overseas warehouses; the most suitable ones are hot-selling items with fast inventory turnover.

不是所有产品都适合使用海外仓；最适合（使用海外仓）的是库存周转快的热销单品。

44. Consolidation logistics can effectively reduce transportation costs through centralized transportation.

集货物流可以通过集中运输有效降低运输成本。

45. Innovation in cross-border e-commerce logistics mode seeks to provide better logistics services to customers.

跨境电商物流模式创新旨在为顾客提供更好的物流服务。

46. Third-party overseas warehouses can provide more timely communication with customers when problems arise.

第三方海外仓在出现问题时可以更及时地与客户沟通。

47. The combination of border warehouses and overseas warehouses can greatly facilitate cross-border e-commerce trade between China and countries such as Russia and Brazil.

边境仓与海外仓的结合可以大大便利中国与俄罗斯、巴西等国的跨境电商贸易。

48. The bonded port area has a pioneering reform demonstration effect in cross-border e-commerce logistics and cargo collection.

保税港区在跨境电商物流集货方面具有先行先试的改革示范效应。

49. Consolidation logistics can achieve centralized transportation and effectively reduce transportation costs.

集货物流可以实现集中运输，有效降低运输成本。

50. Multiple logistics modes used in conjunction can effectively highlight the aggregation effect of various logistics modes.

多种物流模式共用可以有效凸显各种物流模式的聚合效应。

51. The overseas warehouse mode can greatly reduce logistics costs and improve delivery efficiency.

海外仓模式可以大幅降低物流成本，提高配送效率。

52. The combination of border warehouses and overseas warehouses can facilitate cross-border e-commerce trade.

边境仓与海外仓的结合可以促进跨境电商贸易。

课后练习

Ⅰ. 单选题。

Single choice questions.

1. What does "FBA" stand for in the context of Amazon's services?

A. Fulfillment by Alibaba　　B. Fulfillment by Amazon

C. Free by Air　　D. Full Business Automation

2. Which of the following is NOT a subsystem of the international logistics system?

A. Warehousing　　B. Transportation

C. Information Processing　　D. Sales Force Management

3. What is the primary advantage of using postal package mode for cross-border e-commerce?

A. Speed　　B. Coverage

C. Cost　　D. Customization

4. What is one of the disadvantages of the postal package mode mentioned in the document?

A. High cost　　B. Slow speed

C. Frequent promotions　　D. Easy customs clearance

5. Which of the following is an advantage of commercial express delivery mode?

A. Low packet loss rate　　B. Coverage in few countries

C. High cost　　D. Slow speed

6. What is the significance of the combination of border warehouses and overseas warehouses for cross-border e-commerce trade?

A. It increases operational costs

B. It complicates the logistics process

C. It facilitates trade between China and countries like Russia and Brazil

D. It limits the market reach

7. What is the main purpose of a bonded zone?

A. To provide tax incentives for foreign companies

B. To offer a special economic zone for international trade

C. To restrict the movement of goods within the country

D. To eliminate the need for customs clearance

8. Which of the following is NOT a feature of the "bonded stocking mode" mentioned in the document?

A. Reduced consumer risk

B. Increased product price

C. Improved customer satisfaction

D. Simplified logistics operations

9. What is one of the challenges faced by cross-border e-commerce logistics mentioned in the document?

A. Short logistics chain

B. High automation and information level

C. Complex processes

D. Sufficient warehouse space

10. What is the meaning of "KYC" and "KYB" in the context of the document?

A. Know Your Customer and Know Your Business

B. Keep Your Customers and Keep Your Business

C. Key Customer and Key Business

D. Knowledgeable Customer and Knowledgeable Business

11. Which of the following is NOT a benefit of using overseas warehouses?

A. Faster delivery times　　B. Higher storage costs

C. Improved product exposure　　D. Enhanced customer satisfaction

12. What is one of the disadvantages of using third-party overseas warehouses compared to FBA?

A. They provide product promotion services.

B. They cannot eliminate buyer's negative reviews.

C. They offer more flexible customer service.

D. They have potential security risks.

13. What is the basic principle of Alibaba's cross-border supply chain logistics?

A. To make the right choice of service provider.

B. To minimize the use of technology.

C. To avoid international cooperation.

D. To focus solely on cost reduction.

14. What is the significance of the "Global Central Warehouse" established in the Qianhai Bay Bonded Port Area of Shenzhen?

A. It is the largest warehouse in the world.

B. It simplifies customs clearance processes.

C. It is a center for global product storage and distribution.

D. It is a tourist attraction in Shenzhen.

Ⅱ. 简答题。

Short answer questions.

1. What are the main components of the international logistics system?

2. What are the advantages and disadvantages of using the postal package mode for cross-border e-commerce logistics?

3. How does the level of cross-border logistics services affect cross-border e-commerce?

第八章 Chapter 8 跨境电商通关与报关 Customs Clearance and Declaration

随着全球化进程的加速，跨境电商已成为国际贸易的重要组成部分。然而，跨境电商的快速发展也带来了诸多挑战，其中通关与报关环节尤为关键。本章将深入探讨跨境电商通关与报关的基本流程、一达通外贸综合服务平台的通关服务及其优势，以及如何应对海关暂扣物品等问题。通过学习本章内容，学生将全面了解跨境电商通关与报关的核心要点，掌握相关操作流程和技巧，为从事跨境电商行业奠定坚实的基础。

学习目标

1. 掌握跨境电商通关与报关的基本流程。
2. 熟悉一达通外贸综合服务平台的服务内容。
3. 理解一达通外贸综合服务平台的准入条件和开通方法。
4. 掌握海关暂扣物品的处理方法。

思政目标

1. 学习通关流程，确保合规操作。
2. 了解法律法规，保障合法权益。
3. 学习通关服务，提升服务质量。

第一节 Section 1 通关与报关的基本流程 Basic Process of Customs Clearance and Declaration

跨境电商企业可以通过通关服务平台实现通关一次申报，同时海关、税务、检验检疫、外汇、市场监管等部门也可通过通关服务平台获得跨境电商产品信息，并对产品交易实现全流程监管。跨境电商零售进口商品申报前，电子商务企业或电子商务交易平台企业、支付企业、物流企业应当分别通过跨境电商通关服务平台如实向海关传输交易、支付、物流等电子信息。

Cross-border e-commerce enterprises can achieve one-time declaration of customs clearance through the customs clearance service platform. At the same time, customs, taxation, inspection and quarantine, foreign exchange, market supervision and other departments can also obtain cross-border e-commerce product information through the customs clearance service platform and achieve full process supervision of product transactions. Before declaring imported goods for cross-border e-commerce retail, e-commerce enterprises or e-commerce transaction platform enterprises, payment enterprises, and logistics enterprises shall truthfully transmit electronic information such as transactions, payments, and logistics to customs through the cross-border e-commerce clearance service platform.

一般来说，跨境电商出口报关需要经过以下六个步骤：

（1）跨境电商企业在跨境电商服务平台上备案。

（2）货物售出后，电商、物流、支付企业向“跨境电商服务平台”提交订单、支付、物流三单信息。

（3）“跨境电商服务平台”完成三单比对，自动生成货物清单，并向中国电子口岸发送清单数据。

（4）货物运往跨境电子商务监管仓库。

（5）海关通过“跨境电商服务平台”审核，确定单货相符后，货物放行出口。

（6）跨境电商企业凭报关单向国家税务总局申请退税。

Generally speaking, cross-border e-commerce export customs clearance requires the following six steps:

（1）Cross-border e-commerce enterprises register on cross-border e-commerce service platforms.

（2）After the goods are sold, e-commerce, logistics, and payment companies submit order, payment, and logistics information to the “cross-border e-commerce service platform”.

（3）The “cross-border e-commerce service platform” completes three order comparisons, automatically generates a list of goods, and sends the list data to the Chinese electronic port.

（4）The goods are transported to a cross-border e-commerce supervised warehouse.

（5）After the customs complete the review on the “cross-border e-commerce service platform” and confirm that the goods match the declared information, the goods will be cleared for export.

（6）Cross-border e-commerce enterprises can apply for tax refunds from the State Administration of Taxation with the customs declaration form.

电子商务企业或其代理人应提交《中华人民共和国海关跨境电子商务零售进出口商品申报清单》（以下简称《申报清单》），出口采取“清单核放、汇总申报”方式办理报关手续。

E-commerce enterprises or their agents shall submit the *Declaration Form for Cross-border E-commerce Retail Import/Export Goods of the General Administration of Customs of the People's Republic of China* (hereinafter referred to as the *Declaration Form*), and process export customs clearance through the “itemized clearance with consolidated declaration” mechanism.

“清单核放、汇总申报”是指跨境电商零售商品出口后，电子商务企业或其代理人应当于每月 10 日前（当月 10 日是法定节假日或者法定休息日的，顺延至其后的第一个工作日，12 月的清单汇总应当于当月最后一个工作日前完成），将上月（12 月为当月）结关的《申报清单》依据清单表头同一收发货人、同一运输方式、同一运抵国（地区）、同一出境口岸，以及清单表体同一 10 位海关商品编码、同一申报计量单位、同一币制规则进行归并，汇总形成《中华人民共和国海关进（出）口货物报关单》向海关申报。

The “itemized clearance with consolidated declaration” refers to the process where, after the export of cross-border e-commerce retail goods, e-commerce enterprises or their agents should consolidate the *Declaration Form* for the previous month (with December being the current month) before the 10th day of each month. If the 10th day of the current month falls on a statutory holiday or statutory rest day, the deadline should be postponed to the first working day thereafter. Note that the form consolidation for December must be completed before the last working day of the current month. The consolidation is based on the following criteria in the list header: the same consignee and consignor, the same transportation method, the same destination country (region), and the same exit port. Additionally, the form body should have the same 10-digit customs commodity code, the same declaration measurement unit, and the same currency. This process forms the *Customs Declaration Form for Import/Export Goods of the People's Republic of China* for declaration to Customs.

《申报清单》《中华人民共和国海关进（出）口货物报关单》应当采取通关无纸化作业方式进行申报。《申报清单》的修改或者撤销，参照海关《中华人民共和国海关进（出）口货物报关单》修改或者撤销有关规定办理。

The *Declaration Form* and *Customs Declaration Form for Import/Export Goods of the People's Republic of China* should be declared through paperless customs clearance procedures. The amendment or revocation of the *Declaration Form* shall be handled in accordance with the relevant provisions of the *Customs Declaration Form for Import/Export Goods of the People's Republic of China*.

第二节 Section 2 一达通外贸综合服务平台的通关服务 Customs Clearance Service of OneTouch Foreign Trade Comprehensive Service Platform

一、企业历史

Enterprise History

深圳市一达通企业服务有限公司成立于 2001 年，是国内第一家面向中小企业的进出口流程外包服务平台，通过互联网为中小企业和个人提供通关、物流、结汇、退税和金融等所有进出口环节服务。

Shenzhen OneTouch Business Service Co., Ltd., founded in 2001, is the first import and export process outsourcing service platform dedicated to SMEs (Small and Medium-sized Enterprises) in China. It provides all import and export services such as customs clearance, logistics, foreign exchange settlement, tax refund and finance for SMEs and individuals through the Internet.

2010 年 11 月，一达通加入阿里巴巴，是阿里巴巴旗下的外贸综合服务平台。一达通是中国专业服务于中小企业的外贸综合服务行业的开拓者和领军者，致力于推动传统外贸模式的革新。通过线上操作及建立有效的信用数据系统、整合各项外贸服务资源和银行资源，为中小企业提供专业、低成本的通关、结汇、退税及配套物流和金融服务的外贸综合平台。

OneTouch joined Alibaba in November 2010 and is a comprehensive foreign trade service platform under Alibaba. OneTouch is a pioneer and leader in China's comprehensive foreign trade service industry, specializing in serving SMEs. It is committed to promoting the innovation of traditional foreign trade modes. Through online operations and the establishment of an effective credit data system, integrating various foreign trade service resources and banking resources, it provide a professional and low-cost foreign trade comprehensive platform for SMEs, including customs clearance, foreign exchange settlement, tax refund, and supporting logistics and financial services.

二、企业发展
Enterprise development

2018 年 11 月 23 日，一达通，正式升级为跨境供应链平台。之前，一达通主要通过遍布全国的合作伙伴“一拍档”，为中小企业提供通关、结汇和退税等服务，升级为跨境供应链平台后，一达通将整合阿里巴巴国际站和菜鸟驿站等业务资源，为中小企业升级跨境支付结算、供应链金融、流通供应链和生产供应链等服务。

On November 23, 2018, OneTouch was officially upgraded to a cross-border supply chain platform. Previously, OneTouch mainly provided customs clearance, foreign exchange settlement, and tax refund services for SMEs through its nationwide partner “One Partner”. After upgrading to a cross-border supply chain platform, OneTouch will integrate business resources such as Alibaba International Station and Cainiao Station to upgrade cross-border payment settlement, supply chain finance, circulation supply chain, and production supply chain services for SMEs.

（一）三个升级加速数据信用价值落地
Three upgrades accelerate the landing of data credit value

阿里巴巴跨境供应链主要在以下几个方面实现较大升级：

（1）“一拍档”将变成“供应链拍档”。服务不再局限于报关、结汇和退税，而是将服务拓展到国际物流、信用信保、验货认证、海外仓储、贸易金融等领域。通过数字赋能，“拍档”们将具备服务能力、专家能力、物流能力、金融能力、售卖能力、整合能力。

（2）服务对象扩大，原来以国内商家为主，逐步扩大到服务海外 B 类买家，比如在物流的选择上，支持海外买家在平台下物流订单。

（3）数字化能力提升，通过在线化、数据打通、技术对接等方式，构建起数字化协同的底层履约保障系统，聚集具备服务能力、专家能力、物流能力、金融能力、售卖能力和整合能力的各类生态伙伴。

商家通过使用阿里巴巴跨境供应链的服务，可以累积和分析订单数据，能够向商家的国际站店铺前端系统提供有效的反馈，从而达到增加曝光量、询盘量和订单量的目的，实现商家和供应链平台双赢的互利目标。

有订单的店铺也将比无订单店铺多获得 3 倍的曝光量、4 倍的点击量和 4 倍的询盘量。而订单数量排名前 20% 的店铺将比无订单店铺多获得 5 倍曝光量、7 倍点击量和 8 倍的询盘量。

Alibaba's cross-border supply chain has achieved significant upgrades in the following areas:

(1) “One partner” will become “supply chain partner”. Its services are no longer limited to

customs declaration, foreign exchange settlement, and tax refund, but have expanded to include international logistics, credit insurance, inspection and certification, overseas warehouse, trade finance, and other fields. Through digital empowerment, "partners" will have service capabilities, expert capabilities, logistics capabilities, financial capabilities, sales capabilities, and integration capabilities.

(2) The service target has expanded, originally focusing on domestic merchants, gradually expanding to serve overseas B-class buyers. For example, in terms of logistics selection, it supports overseas buyers to place logistics orders on the platform.

(3) The digital capabilities has enhanced, building a digital collaborative underlying performance guarantee system through online, data integration, and technology docking, gathering various ecological partners with service capabilities, expert capabilities, logistics capabilities, financial capabilities, sales capabilities, and integration capabilities.

By using Alibaba's cross-border supply chain services, merchants can accumulate and analyse order data, enabling effective feedback into front end systems of their international store, thereby increasing exposure, enquiry volume, and order volume, and achieving a mutually beneficial goal for both merchants and supply chain platforms.

Stores with orders will also receive three times more exposure, four times more clicks, and four times more enquiries than stores without orders. The top 20% of stores with the highest order volume will receive 5 times more exposure, 7 times more clicks, and 8 times more enquiries than stores without orders.

(二) 贯通内外资金流通链路

Connect the internal and external capital circulation links

跨境供应链升级后，最受关注的模块当属跨境支付与结算业务。随着跨境贸易版图碎片化成为趋势，跨境贸易买卖方画像和支付场景也越来越丰富。如何应对不同地缘政治下的支付场景，满足商家多元的支付和账期需求，成为 B2B 企业和平台共同关注的问题。

After the upgrade of cross-border supply chain, the most concerned module is undoubtedly cross-border payment and settlement business. With the trend of fragmented cross-border trade landscape, the profiles of cross-border trade buyers and sellers and payment scenarios are becoming increasingly diverse. How to cope with payment scenarios in different geopolitical contexts and meet the diverse payment and payment terms needs of merchants has become a common concern for B2B enterprises and platforms.

为此，供应链平台打造了跨境信用保障服务产品。当买卖双方在国际平台上达成交易后，首先将会通过信用保障产品进行支付。信用保障产品可以理解为一个国际版的支付宝，是阿里巴巴旗下专业的跨境 B2B 交易体系，致力于为全球 B2B 买/卖家提供安全、高效、可视化的交易服务，整合各方资源以提供综合性跨境支付、结算、金融等服务，帮助买/卖家轻松实现“全球买/全球卖”。

To this end, the supply chain platform has developed cross-border credit guarantee service products. After the buyer and seller reach a transaction on an international platform, payment will first be made through credit guarantee products. Credit guarantee products can be understood as an international version of Alipay, which is a professional cross-border B2B transaction system under Alibaba. It is committed to providing safe, efficient and visual transaction services for global B2B buyers/sellers, integrating resources of all parties to provide comprehensive cross-border payment, settlement, finance and other services, and helping buyers/sellers easily achieve "global buying/global selling".

在跨境支付和收款上，跨境供应链的信用保障产品为卖家量身定制了专业和多元的解决方案，支持多种支付方式：T/T（含本地 T/T）、信用证、信用卡、西联、PayLater、Online Bank Payment、Online Transfer。

In terms of cross-border payments and receipts, the credit guarantee products of cross-border supply chain have tailored professional and diversified solutions for sellers, supporting multiple payment methods: T/T (including local T/T), letter of credit, credit card, Western Union, PayLater, Online Bank Payment, Online Transfer.

传统的跨境线下大额美金支付，都是通过银行来完成，平均 T/T 转账时间为 3~5 个工作日，转账成本为 30~50 美元，还存在高额的汇损。阿里巴巴跨境供应链通过搭建本地 T/T 网络，成功地将资金跨境时间缩短至 1 秒，汇款费用下降到 1 美元，同时避免了汇损的发生。在完善“货物”跨境之后，“资金”的跨境成为首要关注点，而跨境供应链将传统跨境支付链路中的资金痛点切实解决了，真正实现了降本提效的效果。现在，本地 T/T 最快 1~2 个工作日到账，信用卡实时到账（2h 内）；本地 T/T 买家支付手续费低至 1 本币，无中间行收费。

Traditional cross-border offline large dollar payments are completed through banks, with an average T/T transfer time of 3~5 working days, transfer costs of 30~50 US dollars, and high exchange losses. Alibaba's cross-border supply chain has successfully shortened the cross-border time of funds to 1 second, reduced remittance fees to 1 US dollar, and avoided exchange losses by building a local T/T network. After improving the cross-border of "goods", the cross-border of "funds" has become the primary focus, and the cross-border supply chain has effectively solved the funding pain points in the traditional cross-border payment chain, truly achieving the effect of reducing costs and improving efficiency. Now, local T/T can be credited within 1~2 working days at the fastest, and credit cards can be credited in real time (within 2 hours). Local T/T buyers pay transaction fees as low as 1 local currency, with no intermediary fees.

除此之外，大数据技术赋能下，阿里巴巴跨境供应链让原本无法预测和监控的事情尽在掌握之中。通过与 SWIFT（环球同业银行金融电讯协会）合作全球支付创新服务 SWIFT GPI（全球支付创新服务），阿里巴巴国际站实现了支付资金全链路的数字化和透明化，提高了跨境汇款的确定性。一方面，商家可以实时掌握买家支付动态、银行处理时效、扣费等信息；另一方面，则可以实时地向买家推荐最优惠的汇款路径，同时为商家提供到账时效及费用预测。

In addition, with the empowerment of big data technology, Alibaba's cross-border supply chain enables things that were previously impossible to predict and monitor to be fully under control. By collaborating with SWIFT (Society for Worldwide Interbank Financial Telecommunication) on the global payment innovation service SWIFT GPI (Global Payment Innovation Service), Alibaba International Station has achieved digitalization and transparency of the entire payment fund chain, improving the certainty of cross-border remittances. On the one hand, merchants can have real-time access to buyer payment dynamics, bank processing time, deduction and other information. On the other hand, it is possible to recommend the most favorable remittance path to buyers in real time, while providing merchants with timely payment and cost predictions.

一旦订单形成后，对于买卖家，最核心的问题就是资金的安全、资金成本效率、资金链路可视化。这个资金可以是货物的资金，也可以是服务所产生的物流服务费、金融服务费等，这些费用被称作跨境贸易服务产业费用。一达通平台实现了端到端在线上资金完全可视，数十万中小企业、上千万全球中小买家可以享受到免费的全程资金可视服务。

Once an order is formed, the core issues for buyers and sellers are the safety of funds, the efficiency of fund costs, and the visualization of the fund chain. This fund can be the funds for goods, as well as logistics service fees, financial service fees, etc. generated by services. These fees are called cross-border trade service industry fees. The OneTouch platform has achieved end-to-end online fund visibility, allowing hundreds of thousands of SMEs and millions of global small and medium-sized buyers to enjoy free full process fund visibility services.

同时，对政府来说，通过跨境供应链平台的数据和商品物流轨迹等信息，能更精准地防范和打击骗税行为，保障了外贸的真实性和有效合规。

At the same time, for the government, using data from cross-border supply chain platforms and information on product logistics trajectories can more accurately prevent and combat tax fraud, ensuring the authenticity and effective compliance of foreign trade.

经过近几年阿里巴巴国际站对支付场景的观察，在跨境贸易的大盘中有 70%的大额交易，商家会采用账期支付。有账期支付需求供应链平台推出支付与金融相结合的账期产品，并将账期服务线上化，且落实到支付环节，其链路也更加透明，助推更多的跨境贸易实现交易数字化。

After observing payment scenarios on Alibaba International Station in recent years, it has been found that 70% of large transactions in cross-border trade involve merchants using payment terms. The supply chain platform with demand for payment terms has launched payment term products that combine payment and finance, and has digitized payment term services online and implemented them in the payment process, making the chain more transparent and promoting the digitization of cross-border trade transactions.

通过大数据赋能，平台根据中小企业订单走货数据的沉淀，为客户快速提供相应额度的融资授信，解决资金难题。例如，很多美国买家实现 7 分钟完成融资授信，资金账期从 28 天延长至 90 天。

Empowered by big data, the platform quickly provides customers with corresponding financing credit lines based on the accumulation of SMEs order shipment data, solving financial difficulties. For example, many American buyers have achieved 7-minute completion of financing credit, extending the payment term from 28 days to 90 days.

PayLater 则是买家在 alibaba. com 采购时可用的一种全新支付方式，相当于国际版的花呗。当买家在线上花 10 分钟完成申请后，即可获得最高 15 万美元的信用额度。在使用 PayLater 支付时，第三方金融机构将直接垫付资金给卖家，帮助卖家安全快速收款。买家则可获得最长 6 个月的贷款期。目前 PayLater 已面向美国买家开放。

PayLater is a new payment method available to buyers when making purchases on alibaba. com, which is equivalent to the international version of Huabei. When buyers complete the application online in 10 minutes, they can receive a credit limit of up to USD 150, 000. When using PayLater payment, third-party financial institutions will directly advance funds to sellers to help them receive payments safely and quickly. Buyers can receive a loan term of up to 6 months. PayLater is currently open to buyers in the United States.

（三）加速物流“端到端”数字化

Accelerate end-to-end digitalization of logistics

在支付完成后，卖方只需要通过供应链运输平台进行查价，便可对所有费用了如指掌，从而一键选择合适的物流方案进行货物运输，并且可全程查询追踪货物运输轨迹。

After the payment is completed, the seller only needs to check the price through the supply chain transportation platform to have a clear understanding of all costs, so as to select the appropriate logistics plan for goods transportation with just one click, and can track the entire transportation trajectory of the goods.

以前，物流成本占中小企业出口成本的近 30%，而通过升级后的跨境供应链平台，物流成本能降低 10%。阿里巴巴跨境供应链重新规划了物流拍档体系，引入多方物流服务商，联合菜鸟网络打造货物运输平台，为买家/卖家提供海运拼箱、海运整柜、国际快递、国际空运、港口集运、拖车运输和海外仓、中美专线等跨境货物运输及储存中转服务，降低了国际物流成本。例如，联合菜鸟网络，让中美专线快递价格在首重和续重上比市场价格降低44%。中美海运从原来的拼箱变成“拼箱+整柜”，大大提高了时效。

Previously, logistics costs accounted for nearly 30% of the export costs for SMEs, but through the upgraded cross-border supply chain platform, logistics costs can be reduced by 10%. Alibaba's cross-border supply chain has replanned its logistics partner system, attracting multiple logistics service providers and collaborating with Cainiao Network to create a cargo transportation platform. This platform provides buyers/sellers with services such as sea freight consolidation, sea freight full container load, international express delivery, international air freight, port consolidation and trailer transportation, as well as cross-border cargo transportation and storage transfer services such as overseas warehouses and China-US dedicated lines, reducing international logistics costs. For example, by partnering with Cainiao Network, the price of express delivery between China and the United States can be reduced by 44% compared to the market price in terms of first and subsequent shipments. China-US shipping has changed from LCL to “LCL+FCL” , greatly improving efficiency.

阿里巴巴跨境供应链做物流的基本原则是做对的选择，核心是要选择对的服务商。从前的物流匹配更多以主观选择为准，而如今则是以订单为维度的匹配，买家和卖家在流通领域，更多以数据为核心作为相互选择的标准。当一个交易订单在平台上形成后，跨境供应链平台通过历史的履约情况，基于数据为客户提供 AI 线路选择和推荐算法，缩短买家、卖家的选择时间。

The basic principle of Alibaba's cross-border supply chain logistics is to make the right choice, and the core is to choose the right service provider. Previously, logistics matching was more based on subjective choices, but now it is based on order dimensions. In the field of circulation, buyers and sellers rely more on data as the core criterion for mutual selection. After a transaction order is formed on the platform, the cross-border supply chain platform provides customers with AI route selection and recommendation algorithms based on historical performance data, shortening the selection time for buyers and sellers.

（四）推动通关退税持续迭代

Promote continuous iteration of customs clearance and tax refund

在通关事务上，一达通从 2000 年开始做尝试，如今，一达通为客户提供“2+N”和“3+N”服务。“2+N”是指出口代理服务，为客户提供通关和结汇两个环节的服务，而退免税申报由客户自行在当地完成，无须信保交易手续费。发货后信保额度立即释放，客户可累积信保数据，同时享受快速退税和融资贷款；而 3+N 是指外贸综合服务，为客户提供通关、结汇、退税及配套的物流、金融服务等“一揽子”外贸服务。

In terms of customs affairs, OneTouch has been trying since 2000. Nowadays, OneTouch provides customers with “2+N” and “3+N” services. “2+N” refers to export agency services, providing customers with both customs clearance and foreign exchange setelement services. Customers can complete tax refund and exemption declarations locally without the need for credit insurance transaction fees. After shipment, the credit insurance limit is immediately released, allowing customers to accumulate credit insurance data while benefiting from fast tax refunds and financing loans. And “3+N” refers to comprehensive foreign trade services, providing customers with a “package” of foreign trade services such as customs clearance, foreign exchange setelement , tax refunds, and supporting logistics and financial services.

中小企业退税，无论自主退税，还是代理服务退税，都比较关心以下两点：①退税成本多少？②退税出现异常比例的大小或者出现异常之后（如函调）处理能力如何？

Small and medium-sized enterprises are more concerned about the following two points when it comes to tax refunds, whether processed independently or through agency services: ① How much is the cost of tax refunds? ② What is the size of the abnormal proportion of tax refunds or the handling ability after the occurrence of abnormalities (such as correspondence investigation)?

阿里巴巴跨境供应链通过和相关政府部门合作搭建了基于区块链的退税平台，使用户可以查看到不可篡改的买家/卖家的交易情况、流通情况、报关资料申报情况等。基于这些信息的积累可以有效地降低成本，为客户提供更便捷、更具有前瞻性和确定性的退税融资服务。阿里巴巴跨境供应链希望帮助更多有操作能力、有极强本地化通关事务能力的公司做数字化平台，进一步高效、低成本地为中国的中小企业提供流通、通关的服务能力。

Alibaba's cross-border supply chain has built a blockchain-based tax refund platform in collaboration with government departments. This platform allows users to view tamper-proof transactions, circulation, and customs declaration information of buyers and sellers. The accumulation of this information can effectively reduce costs and provide customers with more convenient, forward-looking, and deterministic tax refund financing services. Alibaba's cross-border supply chain hopes to help more companies with operational capabilities and strong local customs clearance capabilities become digital platforms, further providing efficient and low-cost circulation and customs clearance services for SMEs in China.

虽然阿里巴巴跨境供应链的信用保障服务已经覆盖了全球200多个国家和地区；物流体系、关检、汇税以及买家支付服务也已全面支持国内商家往海外走货，但要成为一个能持续稳定为全球中小卖家提供确定性履约保障服务的数字化协同平台，阿里巴巴跨境供应链仍需克服诸多挑战。

Although Alibaba's cross-border supply chain credit guarantee services have covered over 200 countries and regions worldwide. The logistics system, customs inspection, foreign exchange taxes, and buyer payment services have fully supported domestic merchants to ship overseas. However, in order to become a digital collaborative platform that can continuously and stably provide deterministic performance guarantee services for global small and medium-sized sellers, Alibaba's cross-border supply chain still needs to overcome many challenges.

未来，跨境供应链还将通过IoT（物联网）和区块链等新技术，打造一个涵盖供应链拍档、报关行、国际物流和贸易金融于一体的生态体系，并通过阿里巴巴的EWTP（Electronic World Trade Platform，世界电子贸易平台）倡议，把中国跨境供应链模式推广到海外，赋能全球中小企业更好地做贸易。

In the future, cross-border supply chains will also use new technologies such as IoT and blockchain to create an ecosystem that integrates supply chain partners, customs brokers, international logistics, and trade finance. Through Alibaba's EWTP (Electronic World Trade Platform) initiative, the Chinese cross-border supply chain mode will be promoted overseas, empowering global SMEs to better trade.

阿里巴巴跨境供应链平台已服务全国近20万家出口企业。除打造全球跨境供应链外，阿里巴巴中小企业国际贸易事业部的另外两大重点方向是：中国商家卖全球，全球商家卖全球。

Alibaba's cross-border supply chain platform has served nearly 200, 000 export enterprises nationwide. In addition to building a global cross-border supply chain, the other two key directions of Alibaba's International Trade Division for SMEs are: Chinese merchants selling globally, and global merchants selling globally.

三、一达通准入条件

Access conditions for OneTouch

1. 企业类型

Enterprise types

企业类型：非境外；个人或非出口综合服务尚未覆盖地区企业（如福建莆田等）。

Enterprise types: non overseas; individuals or enterprises located in regions not yet covered by comprehensive export services (e. g., Putian, Fujian, etc.).

2. 出口产品

Export products

出口的产品在一达通可以出口的产品范围内。

The exported products are within the scope of products that OneTouch can export.

3. 开票人资质

Qualifications of the issuer

对于不同的开票人，资质要求不同。

(1) 与一达通签约的企业注册地在浙江省的，开票人要求为：

生产型工厂，具有一般纳税人资格且一般纳税人认定时间≥6 个月。

委外加工型企业，需具有一般纳税人工厂资格、具备出口产品的生产线、具备后加工的环节。

(2) 与一达通签约的企业注册地在福建省的，开票人要求为：

生产型工厂，具有一般纳税人资格，一般纳税人认定时间≥1 年。

(3) 与一达通签约的企业注册地在河南省的，开票人要求为：

生产型工厂，具有一般纳税人资格，一般纳税人认定时间≥2 年。

(4) 与一达通签约的企业注册地在其他省份的，开票人要求为：

生产型工厂，具有一般纳税人资格，一般纳税人认定时间>2 年，且开票人注册地非内蒙古赤峰巴林右旗、福建莆田、天津武清区（武清区的自行车及其零配件、电动车及其零配件企业除外）；HS 编码是 61 章的产品开票人，需满足一般纳税人认定时间满 2 年。

For different issuers, qualification requirements vary.

(1) For enterprises contracted with OneTouch and registered in Zhejiang Province, the issuer's requirements are:

A production-oriented factory has the qualification of a general taxpayer, with a recognition period of at least 6 months as a general taxpayer.

Outsourced processing enterprises need to have general taxpayer factory qualifications, production lines for export products, and post-processing links.

(2) For enterprises contracted with OneTouch and registered in Fujian Province, the issuer's requirements are:

A production-oriented factory has the qualification of a general taxpayer, with a recognition period of at least 1 year as a general taxpayer.

(3) For enterprises contracted with OneTouch and registered in Henan Province, the issuer's requirements are:

A production-oriented factory has the qualification of a general taxpayer, with a recognition period of at least 2 years as a general taxpayer.

(4) If the registered address of the enterprise signed with OneTouch is in another province, the

issuer's requirements are:

A production-oriented factory has the qualification of a general taxpayer, with a recognition period of more than 2 years as a general taxpayer, and the issuer's registered address is not in Balin Right Banner, Chifeng, Inner Mongolia, Putian, Fujian, or Wuqing District, Tianjin (excluding bicycle and its parts, electric vehicle and its parts enterprises in Wuqing District); HS code is a product issuer under Chapter 61 and must meet the requirement of being recognized as a general taxpayer for at least 2 years.

四、开通一达通的方法

The method to activate OneTouch

如果用户有阿里巴巴国际站账号，则可以在申请一达通服务时直接输入国际站账号和密码登录。用户根据页面提示留下联系方式等信息，会有客户经理联系用户处理相关事宜。如果用户没有阿里巴巴国际站账号，可以先免费注册阿里巴巴国际站账号，然后再登录到一达通平台点击申请一达通服务，后续流程同上。如果提交后长时间没有反馈，用户可通过在线人工提交加急处理。

If users have Alibaba International Station accounts, they can directly enter their accounts and passwords to log in when applying for OneTouch services. According to the prompts on the page, the users will leave their contact information and other information, and a customer manager will contact the users to handle relevant matters. If users don't have Alibaba International Station accounts, they can first register for free Alibaba International Station accounts, and then log in to the OneTouch platform and click to apply for OneTouch services. The subsequent process is the same as above. If there is no feedback for a long time after submission, users can submit urgent processing through online manual submission.

五、一达通提供的服务

The services provided by OneTouch

一达通提供的服务主要有：通关（报关及报检）、结汇、退税等政务服务，以及金融、物流等商务服务。一达通将政务服务称为基础服务，将商务服务称为增值服务。

The services provided by OneTouch mainly include government services such as customs clearance (customs declaration and inspection), foreign exchange settlement, tax refund, as well as business services such as financial and logistics. OneTouch refers to government services as basic services and business services as value-added services.

(一) 通关服务

Customs clearance services

客户以一达通名义完成全国各口岸海关、商检的申报，可享受绿色通关通道。

Customers, who complete the declaration of customs and inspection at various ports across the country on behalf of OneTouch, can enjoy green clearance channels.

客户通过一达通通关时，具体流程如下：

（1）联系拍档/一达通对接人告知需求。

（2）自行在下单系统自助下单或委托拍档/一达通对接人辅助下单。

（3）核对下单及出货信息后选择“提交订单”。

（4）按系统指引签署“出口服务委托函”。

（5）一达通安排通关（或下载报关资料安排自行报关）。

（6）通关放行（自行报关部分需要客户及时上传报关底单至订单系统）。

The specific processes for customers to clear customs through OneTouch are as follows:

(1) Inform your partner/OneTouch contact person of the requirements.

(2) Place orders on your own in the ordering system or entrust your partner/OneTouch contact person to assist with the order.

(3) After verifying the order and shipping information, select “Submit Order”.

(4) Sign the “Export Service Authorization Letter” according to the system guidelines.

(5) OneTouch arranges customs clearance (or downloads customs declaration materials to arrange self-declaration).

(6) Customs clearance and release (for self-declaration, customers need to upload the customs declaration form to the order system in a timely manner).

（二）结汇服务

Foreign exchange settlement services

一达通可为客户提供方便、快捷的结汇服务，以及外汇保值服务，提前锁定未来结汇或者购汇的汇率成本，防范汇率波动风险。

OneTouch can provide customers with convenient and efficient foreign exchange settlement services and foreign exchange hedging services, locking in the exchange rate costs of future foreign exchange settlements or purchases in advance to prevent the risk of exchange rate fluctuations.

（三）退税服务

Tax refund services

一达通可为企业与个人正规、快速地办理退税，加快资金周转。

OneTouch can handle tax refunds for enterprises and individuals in a formal and fast manner, and to accelerate capital turnover.

（四）金融服务

Financial services

一达通为客户提供的金融服务包括流水贷服务、结余增值服务、锁汇保服务等。一达通流水贷是由阿里巴巴联合银行共同推出，向使用一达通出口基础服务的客户提供的无抵押、纯信用贷款服务。该服务通过银行风控审核，由银行直接对企业法人授信，真正实现“信用=财富”，助力中国外贸中小企业的发展。

The financial services provided by OneTouch to customers include revolving loan services, balance appreciation services, and lock-up guarantee services. A OneTouch revolving loan is a collateral free and clean credit facility jointly launched by Alibaba and Banks, provided to customers who use OneTouch's export basic services. This service has passed the bank's risk-control review and allows the bank to directly grant credit to corporate entities, truly realizing the principle of "credit equals wealth" and helping the development of SMEs in China's foreign trade.

锁汇保即远期外汇保值，一达通免费代客户向银行购买远期外汇合约，锁定未来某一时间段到账外汇（固定金额、币种）的结汇汇率。

The lock-up guarantee service refers to the preservation of forward foreign exchange value. OneTouch purchases forward foreign exchange contracts from banks on behalf of customers for free, locking in the settlement exchange rate of foreign exchange (fixed amount, currency) received at a certain time in the future.

（五）物流服务

Logistics services

阿里巴巴国际物流包括海运、空运（普货空运和国际快递）、陆运三大板块。通过整合船运公司和货代资源，一达通为客户提供安全及价格100%透明的整柜拼箱服务；物流专家按需为客户定制最佳物流方案，持续降低物流成本。

Alibaba International Logistics includes three major segments: sea freight, air freight (general cargo air freight and international express delivery), and land freight. By integrating the resources of shipping companies and freight forwarders, OneTouch provides customers with safe and 100% transparent full container load (FCL) services. Logistics experts customize the best logistics solutions for customers as needed, continuously reducing logistics costs.

第三节 被海关暂扣物品的处理
Section 3 Handling of Goods Temporarily Detained by Customs

国际快递货物被海关扣关或者不允许清关存在以下几种原因：

（1）货物描述填写不详细、不清楚。海关要求重新提供证明函，具体说明货物的品名及其用途。

（2）货物申报价值过低（海关有理由怀疑逃税）。

（3）国际快递货物单、证不齐全。海关要求提供必需的单、证，如进口许可证、3C认证。

（4）敏感货物，属于进、出口国家禁止或者限制进口、出口的物品。

There are several reasons why international express delivery goods are detained or not allowed to clear customs by customs:

(1) The description of goods is not detailed or clear. The customs requires a new certificate to be provided, specifying the name and purpose of the goods.

(2) The declared value of the goods is too low (Customs has reason to suspect tax evasion).

(3) The international express delivery bill of lading and certificate are incomplete. Customs requires the provision of necessary documents and certificates, such as import licenses and 3C certification.

(4) Sensitive goods refer to items that are prohibited or restricted from import or export by importing or exporting countries.

货物一旦被扣关，发件人或收件人应尽量配合海关，提供相关的文件。当然，卖家要做好相关工作，尽量避免海关扣货情况发生。

(1) 选择安全的递送方式，如航空挂号小包和 EMS，且 EMS 就算是被海关扣货，还是能够免费退回到发货地点。

(2) 了解各国政策，如澳大利亚虽然通关容易，但是电池类产品是海关不允许的，因此电池或者带电池的产品尽量不发往澳大利亚。如果一定要卖带电池的产品，可以向客户解释后不发电池只发产品。

(3) 重量越重的包裹被海关扣货的可能性越大。

(4) 不同产品被海关扣货的概率不同，如电子产品被扣的概率相对较高。

Once the goods are detained, the sender or recipient should try their best to cooperate with the customs and provide relevant documents. Of course, the seller should do a good job in related work and try to avoid customs detention as much as possible.

(1) Choose safe delivery methods such as air registered parcels and EMS. Even if EMS is seized by customs, it can still be returned to the shipping location for free.

(2) Understand the policies of various countries, such as Australia. Although its customs clearance is easy, battery products are not allowed by customs. Batteries or products with batteries should be avoided from being sent to Australia as much as possible. If sellers must sell products with batteries, they can explain to the customer and only ship the product without the battery.

(3) The heavier the package, the more likely it is to be seized by customs.

(4) The probability of different products being detained by customs varies. Eletronic products, for example, face a higher risk of detention.

第四节 重点短语与句型
Section 4 Key Phrases and Sentence Patterns

一、常用单词与短语
Common words and phrases

1. customs clearance and declaration for cross-border e-commerce 跨境电商通关与报关
2. customs clearance service platform 通关服务平台
3. one-time declaration 一次申报
4. full process supervision 全流程监管
5. itemized clearance with consolidated declaration 清单核放、汇总申报
6. paperless operation 无纸化作业
7. tax refund application 退税申请

8. foreign trade comprehensive service platform 外贸综合服务平台
9. import and export process outsourcing 进出口流程外包
10. cross-border supply chain platform 跨境供应链平台
11. digital collaboration 数字化协同
12. fund chain visualization 资金链路可视化
13. payment terms 账期支付
14. cross-border payment and settlement 跨境支付与结算
15. credit guarantee service 信用保障服务
16. "end-to-end" digitalization of logistics 物流"端到端"数字化
17. customs supervised warehouse 海关监管仓库
18. customs clearance and release 通关放行
19. tax refund financing service 退税融资服务
20. credit data system 信用数据系统
21. supply chain finance 供应链金融
22. overseas warehousing 海外仓储
23. international logistics 国际物流
24. cross-border fund transfer 资金跨境
25. exchange rate locking 汇率锁定
26. customized logistics solutions 物流方案定制
27. customs clearance agency service 通关代理服务
28. green clearance channel 绿色通关通道
29. customs commodity code 海关商品编码
30. OneTouch platform 一达通平台
31. export agency service 出口代理服务
32. foreign exchange hedging service 外汇保值服务
33. logistics cost reduction 物流成本降低
34. goods list data 货物清单数据
35. accumulation of transaction data 交易数据沉淀
36. customs review 海关审核
37. payment dynamics monitoring 支付动态监控
38. tax refund cost 退税成本
39. customs declaration form for goods 货物报关单
40. logistics trajectory tracking 物流轨迹追踪

二、常用句型

Common sentence patterns

1. Cross-border e-commerce enterprises can achieve one-time declaration of customs clearance through the customs clearance service platform.

跨境电商企业可以通过通关服务平台实现通关一次申报。

2. E-commerce enterprises or their agents shall submit the *Declaration Form for Cross-Border E-commerce Retail Import/Export Goods of the General Administration of Customs of the People's Republic of China*.

电子商务企业或其代理人应提交《中华人民共和国海关跨境电子商务零售进出口商品申报清单》。

3. The "itemized clearance with consolidated declaration" refers to the process where e-commerce enterprises or their agents should consolidate the *Declaration Form* by the 10th of each month.

"清单核放、汇总申报"是指跨境电商零售商品出口后，电子商务企业或其代理人应当于每月 10 日前将上月结关的《申报清单》进行归并。

4. The *Declaration Form* and *Customs Declaration Form for Import/Export Goods of the People's Republic of China* should be declared through paperless customs clearance procedures.

《申报清单》和《中华人民共和国海关进（出）口货物报关单》应当采取通关无纸化作业方式进行申报。

5. OneTouch joined Alibaba in November 2010 and is a comprehensive foreign trade service platform under Alibaba.

一达通于 2010 年 11 月加入阿里巴巴，是阿里巴巴旗下的外贸综合服务平台。

6. OneTouch provides customs clearance, foreign exchange settlement, tax refund, and supporting logistics and financial services.

一达通提供通关、结汇、退税及配套物流和金融服务。

7. The service target has expanded from domestic merchants to overseas B-class buyers.

服务对象从国内商家逐步扩大到服务海外 B 类买家。

8. Credit guarantee products can be understood as an international version of Alipay.

信用保障产品可以理解为一个国际版的支付宝。

9. The cross-border supply chain platform has successfully shortened the cross-border time of funds to 1 second.

跨境供应链平台成功地将资金跨境时间缩短至 1 秒。

10. Merchants can have real-time access to buyer payment dynamics and bank processing time.

商家可以实时掌握买家支付动态和银行处理时效。

11. The platform provides customers with AI route selection and recommendation algorithms based on historical performance data.

平台通过历史履约情况，为客户提供基于数据的 AI 线路选择和推荐算法。

12. OneTouch provides "2+N" and "3+N" services for customs clearance and foreign trade.

一达通提供"2+N"和"3+N"的通关和外贸综合服务。

13. The tax refund platform allows users to view tamper-proof KYC (Know Your Customer) and KYB (Know Your Business) transactions.

退税平台允许用户查看不可篡改的 KYC（了解您的用户）和 KYB（了解您的业务）交易情况。

14. Alibaba's cross-border supply chain aims to empower global SMEs to trade better.

阿里巴巴跨境供应链旨在赋能全球中小企业更好地开展贸易。

15. Once an order is formed, the core issues for buyers and sellers are the safety and efficiency of funds.

一旦订单形成，买卖双方最核心的问题是资金的安全性和效率。

16. The payment term products combine payment and finance to make the payment process more transparent.

账期产品结合支付与金融，使支付环节更加透明。

17. The platform provides customers with corresponding financing credit lines based on the accumulation of order shipment data.

平台根据订单走货数据的沉淀，为客户快速提供相应额度的融资授信。

18. After the payment is completed, sellers can select the appropriate logistics plan with just one click.

支付完成后，卖家可以一键选择合适的物流方案。

19. The customs clearance service includes declaration of customs and inspection at various ports.

通关服务包括在各口岸的海关和商检申报。

20. OneTouch arranges customs clearance or provides customs declaration materials for self-declaration.

一达通安排通关或提供报关资料供客户自行报关。

21. The platform offers foreign exchange settlement services with lower costs and faster processing.

平台提供低成本、快速处理的外汇结算服务。

22. Tax refund services help enterprises and individuals accelerate capital turnover.

退税服务帮助企业与个人加快资金周转。

23. OneTouch offers collateral-free and clean credit facilities through bank partnerships.

一达通与银行合作，提供无抵押、纯信用贷款服务。

24. The platform locks in the exchange rate for future foreign exchange settlements to prevent the risk of exchange rate fluctuations.

平台锁定未来结汇的汇率，防范汇率波动风险。

25. Logistics experts customize the best logistics solutions for customers, continuously reducing logistics costs.

物流专家为客户定制最佳物流方案，持续降低物流成本。

26. The customs require a new certificate specifying the name and purpose of the goods.

海关要求重新提供证明函，具体说明货物的品名及其用途。

27. The declared value of the goods is too low, causing suspicion of tax evasion by customs.

货物申报价值过低，海关有理由怀疑逃税。

28. The international express delivery bill of lading and certificate are incomplete.

国际快递货物单、证不齐全。

29. Sensitive goods are prohibited or restricted from import or export by the importing or exporting countries.

敏感货物属于进、出口国家禁止或限制进出口的物品。

30. The sender or recipient should cooperate with customs to provide relevant documents.

发件人或收件人应尽量配合海关，提供相关的文件。

31. Choose safe delivery methods such as air registered parcels and EMS.

选择安全的递送方式，如航空挂号小包和 EMS。

32. Understand the policies of various countries to avoid detention by customs.

了解各国政策，避免海关扣货情况发生。

33. Heavier packages are more likely to be seized by customs.

包裹越重，被海关扣货的可能性越大。

34. Electronic products have a relatively higher probability of being detained by customs.

电子产品被海关扣货的概率相对较高。

35. The platform provides free full-process fund visibility services for SMEs.

平台为中小企业提供免费的全程资金可视服务。

课后练习

Ⅰ. 判断题。

True or False questions.

1. Cross-border e-commerce enterprises can complete customs clearance through a one-time declaration on the customs clearance service platform.

2. E-commerce enterprises are required to submit the *Declaration Form for Cross-border E-commerce Retail Import/Export Goods of the General Administration of Customs of the People's Republic of China* to customs before declaring imported goods.

3. The "itemized clearance with consolidated declaration" mechanism requires e-commerce enterprises to consolidate the *Declaration Form* before the 10th day of each month.

4. OneTouch is a comprehensive foreign trade service platform under Alibaba that provides services such as customs clearance, foreign exchange settlement, and tax refund.

5. Credit guarantee services offered by cross-border supply chain platforms are designed to provide secure and efficient payment solutions for B2B transactions.

6. The cross-border supply chain platform has increased the time required for cross-border fund transfers to several days.

7. OneTouch offers "2+N" and "3+N" services, where the "N" stands for additional logistics and financial services provided by the platform.

8. The tax refund platform built by Alibaba's cross-border supply chain uses blockchain technology to ensure the integrity and security of transaction data.

9. PayLater is a payment method available to buyers on Alibaba. com, allowing them to receive a credit limit of up to $150, 000.

10. Customs clearance services provided by OneTouch include arranging customs clearance and providing customs declaration materials for self-declaration.

Ⅱ. 简答题。

Short answer questions.

1. What are the main reasons for goods being detained or not allowed to clear customs according to the document?

2. How does OneTouch's "2+N" and "3+N" service mode differ in terms of customs clearance, foreign exchange settlement, and tax refund?

3. Explain the benefits of the "itemized clearance with consolidated declaration" mechanism for cross-border e-commerce retail exports.

第九章 Chapter 9 跨境电商支付 Cross-border E-commerce Payment

跨境电商与跨境支付相互依存、彼此影响，跨境支付是跨境电商的重要环节，除了汇率、税费、政策、基础设施等制约外，还涉及不同货币之间能否通用、能否实现通汇通兑、不同货币间的汇率波动等问题。跨境电商在交易的过程中离不开跨境支付，了解跨境支付方式及其支付流程是跨境电商最基本的生存之道。

学习目标

1. 了解跨境电商支付的基础理论知识。
2. 熟悉跨境电商支付的结算方式和基本程序。
3. 掌握跨境电商支付的业务流程与操作规程。
4. 培养解决跨境电商支付实际问题的能力。

思政目标

1. 学习支付方式，培养支付安全意识。
2. 了解支付工具，提升金融素养。
3. 强调诚信支付，树立良好信誉。

第一节 Section 1 国际货款结算方式 International Payment Settlement Methods

一、普通银行电汇
Ordinary bank telegraphic transfer

（一）电汇
Telegraphic transfer

电汇是汇出行应汇款人的申请，用加押电报或者 SWIFT（环球同业银行金融电信协会）的形式指示汇入行付款给收款人的一种汇款方式。电汇的特点是速度快，但是手续费较高，因此只有在金额较大时或者比较紧急的情况下才使用电汇。

Telegraphic Transfer（T/T） is a remittance method in which the remitting bank, upon the request of the remitter, instructs the receiving bank to make payment to the payee through a tested cable or SWIFT（Society for Worldwide Interbank Financial Telecommunication）. The characteristic of T/T is fast speed, but the transaction fees are relatively high, so it is only used for large amounts or in urgent situations.

目前，全球大多数国家的银行都使用 SWIFT 系统。SWIFT 成立于 1973 年，总部设在比利时的布鲁塞尔，同时在荷兰阿姆斯特丹和美国纽约分别设立交换中心，并为参加方开设集线中心，为国际金融业务提供快捷、准确、优良的服务。SWIFT 运营着世界级的金融电文网络，银行和其他金融机构通过它与同业交换电文来完成金融交易。除此之外，SWIFT 还向金融机构提供软件和服务，其中大部分的用户都在使用 SWIFT 网络。SWIFT 系统的使用为银行的结算提供了安全、可靠、快捷、标准化、自动化的通信服务，从而大大提高了银行的结算速度。

At present, banks in most countries around the world use the SWIFT system. SWIFT was founded in 1973 and is headquartered in Brussels, Belgium. It has established switching centers in Amsterdam, the Netherlands, and New York, USA, and opened national concentrations for participating members to provide fast, accurate, and excellent services for international financial business. SWIFT operates a world-class financial messaging network, through which banks and other financial institutions exchange messages with each other to complete financial transactions. In addition, SWIFT also provides software and services to financial institutions, with the majority of users using the SWIFT network. The use of SWIFT system provides secure, reliable, fast, standardized, and automated communication services for bank settlement, greatly improving the settlement speed of banks.

在实际的跨境电商进出口中，T/T 分为预付、即期和远期。现在比较多采用的是 30% 预付和 70% 即期。T/T 付款有以下三种方式：①前款 T/T，先收款，后发货，在发货前预付货款对买方来说风险较大。②后款 T/T，先发货，后收款，对卖方来说风险较大。③先订金，再余款。外贸业务中，出口商对一般熟悉的客户会采用 T/T 付款，经常是发货前预付部分货款，余款在到货后付清，通常情况下，电汇常用的是预付 30% 货款作为定金，另外 70%的余款见提单付款。定金的比例越大，出口商的风险越小。

In actual cross-border e-commerce import and export, T/T is divided into prepaid, spot, and forward. Nowadays, what is more commonly used is 30% prepayment and 70% spot payment. There are three ways of T/T payment: ① T/T in advance, which means receiving payment first and shipping later. Prepaying the payment before shipping carries a higher risk for the buyer. ② Post payment T/T, shipping first and receiving payment later, poses a higher risk for the seller. ③ Deposit first, then pay the remaining balance. In foreign trade business, exporters usually use T/T payment for familiar customers. They often prepay a portion of the payment before shipment and pay the remaining balance after arrival. Usually, T/T is used to prepay 30% of the payment as a deposit, and the remaining 70% is paid according to the bill of lading. The larger the deposit ratio, the lower the risk for the exporter.

（二）电汇业务当事人

Parties involved in T/T business

电汇有四个当事人：汇款人、收款人、汇出行和汇入行。

汇款人是债务人，通常是跨境电商中的进口方。

收款人是债权人，通常为跨境电商中的出口方。

汇出行是受汇款人委托汇出汇款的银行，在跨境电商中通常为进口方所在地银行。

汇入行是解付行，是受汇出行委托解付汇款的银行，通常为出口方所在地银行。

There are four parties involved in T/T: remitter, payee, remitting bank, and receiving bank.

The remitter is the debtor, usually the importer in cross-border e-commerce.

The payee is the creditor, usually the exporter in cross-border e-commerce.

The remitting bank is the bank entrusted by the remitter to remit the money, usually located in the importer's country for cross-border e-commerce.

The receiving bank, also known as the paying bank, is entrusted by the remitting bank to remit the money, usually located in the exporter's country.

（三）电汇业务基本程序

Basic procedures for T/T business

电汇业务基本程序包括下列步骤：

（1）汇款人填写汇款申请书，交款给汇出行，申请书上说明使用电汇方式。

（2）汇出行接受申请，向汇款人开立电汇回执。

（3）汇出行根据电汇申请书向汇入行发出电报或 SWIFT 电文，委托汇入行解付汇款给收款人。

（4）汇入行收到汇款指示后，核对密押，缮制电汇通知书通知收款人收款。

（5）收款人收到通知后在收据联上盖章，交给汇入行。

（6）汇入行借记汇出行账户取出头寸①，解付汇款给收款人。

（7）汇入行将借记通知书寄给汇出行，通知它汇款解付完毕，资金从债务人流向债权人，完成一笔电汇汇款。

The basic procedure for T/T business includes the following steps:

(1) The remitter fills out the remittance application form and makes the payment to the remitting bank. The application form specifies the use of T/T.

(2) The remitting bank accepts the application and issues a T/T receipt to the remitter.

(3) The remitting bank sends a telegram or SWIFT message to the receiving bank based on the remittance application, entrusting the remitting bank to remit the money to the payee.

(4) After receiving the remittance instructions, the receiving bank will verify the security code and prepare a T/T notification to notify the payee to receive the payment.

(5) After receiving the notification, the payee shall stamp the receipt and hand it over to the receiving bank.

(6) The receiving bank debits the account of the remitting bank, withdraws the funds, and release the remittance to the recipient.

(7) The receiving bank sends a debit notification to the remitting bank, notifying it that the remittance has been completed. The funds have flowed from the debtor to the creditor, completing

① 头寸，即“款项”，是金融行业常用到的一个词。——编者注

a T/T.

二、PayPal 和国际支付宝
PayPal and Escrow

（一）PayPal 的支付与结算
PayPal's payment and settlement

1. PayPal 的介绍
Introduction to PayPal

PayPal 于 1998 年 12 月由彼得·蒂尔和麦克斯·拉夫琴建立。eBay 于 2002 年 10 月以 15 亿美元收购了 PayPal，2015 年 6 月 27 日 PayPal 业务和 eBay 拆分为两家独立上市的公司，从 eBay 体系剥离后，PayPal 实现了高速增长，成为支付巨头。

PayPal was established in December 1998 by Peter Thiel and Max Levchin. eBay acquired PayPal for USD 1.5 billion in October 2002, and on June 27, 2015, the PayPal business and eBay were split into two independent publicly traded companies. After being spun off from the eBay, PayPal achieved rapid growth and became a payment giant.

2. PayPal 的类型
Types of PayPal

PayPal 账户分三种类型：个人账户、高级账户和企业账户。用户可根据实际情况进行注册，个人账户可以升级为高级账户进而升级为企业账户。反之，企业账户也可以降为高级账户或者个人账户。

（1）个人账户。个人账户适用于在线购物的买家用户，主要用于付款，可以收款，但比高级账户或企业账户少一些商家必备的功能和特点，如查看历史交易记录的多种筛选功能、商家费率、网站集成、快速结账等集成工具，因此不建议卖家选择。

（2）高级账户。高级账户适用于在线购物或在线销售的个人商户，可以付款、收款，并可享受商家费率、网站付款标准、快速结账等集成工具以及集中付款功能，帮助商家拓展海外销售渠道，提升销售额，推荐进行跨境交易的个人卖家使用。

（3）企业账户。企业账户适用于以企业或团体名义经营的商家用户，特别是使用公司银行账户进行提现的商家用户。企业账户拥有高级账户的所有商家功能，可设立多个子账户，适合大型商家使用，便于每个部门设立子账户进行收款。另外，企业账户需要添加以企业名义开设的电汇银行账户进行转账，若添加个人名义开设的电汇银行账户可能会导致转账失败。

PayPal accounts are divided into three types: personal accounts, advanced accounts, and enterprise accounts. Users can register according to their actual situation. Personal accounts can be upgraded to advanced accounts and then upgraded to enterprise accounts. Conversely, enterprise accounts can also be downgraded to advanced accounts or personal accounts.

(1) Personal account. Personal accounts are suitable for online shopping buyers and users, mainly used for payment and receiving payments. However, they lack some essential functions and features for merchants compared to advanced accounts or enterprise accounts, such as multiple

filtering functions for viewing historical transaction records, merchant rates, website integration, quick checkout and other integrated tools. Therefore, it is not recommended for sellers to choose.

(2) Advanced account. Advanced accounts are suitable for individual merchants who shop or sell online. They can make payments, receive payments, and enjoy integrated tools such as merchant rates, website payment standards, quick checkout, and centralized payment functions. They help merchants expand overseas sales channels, increase sales revenue, and are recommended for individual sellers who conduct cross-border transactions.

(3) Enterprise account. Enterprise accounts are suitable for merchant users who operate in the name of a company or group, especially those who use the company's bank account for withdrawals. Enterprise accounts have all the merchant functions of advanced accounts and can set up multiple sub accounts, suitable for large merchants to use. Each department sets up sub accounts for receiving payments. In addition, enterprise accounts need to add a T/T bank account opened under the corporate name for transfer. Adding a T/T bank account opened under a personal name may result in transfer failure.

3. PayPal 的优势

Advantages of PayPal

PayPal 的优势表现在以下几个方面：

（1）全球用户广。PayPal 在全球 190 多个国家和地区有超过 2.2 亿用户，已实现在 24 种外币之间进行交易。

（2）品牌效应强。PayPal 在欧美普及率极高，是全球在线支付的代名词，强大的品牌优势能使网站轻松吸引众多海外客户。

（3）资金周转快。PayPal 独有的即时支付、即时到账的特点，能够实时收到海外客户发送的款项。最短仅需 3 天，即可将账户内款项转至国内银行账户，助力企业及时、高效地开拓海外市场。

（4）安全保障高。完善的安全保障体系、丰富的防欺诈经验、业界最低的风险损失率（仅 0.27%，是传统交易方式的 1/6），这些均可确保交易顺利进行。

（5）使用成本低。无注册费用、无年费，手续费仅为传统收款方式的 1/2。

（6）采用数据加密技术。注册或登录 PayPal 的站点时，PayPal 会验证登录者的网络浏览器是否正在运行安全套接字层 3.0（SSLv3）或更高版本。传送过程中，信息受到加密密钥长度达 168 位的 SSL 保护。

（7）具有循环结账功能。定期为客户开具账单、支付会员费或提供租用服务和分期付款计划。

PayPal's advantages are reflected in the following aspects:

(1) Global user base. PayPal serves over 220 million users in more than 190 countries and regions worldwide, supporting transactions in 24 foreign currencies.

(2) Strong brand recognition. PayPal has a high popularity rate in Europe and America, and is synonymous with global online payments. Its strong brand advantage can easily attract numerous

overseas customers to the website.

(3) Fast turnover of funds. PayPal's unique features of instant payment and instant receipt allow for real-time receipt of payments from overseas customers. In just 3 days, the funds in the account can be transferred to a domestic bank account, helping enterprises to timely and efficiently explore overseas markets.

(4) High security guarantee. A comprehensive security system, rich experience in fraud prevention, and the industry's lowest risk loss rate (only 0.27%, which is 1/6 of traditional trading methods) all ensure smooth transactions.

(5) Low cost of use. There is no registration fee, no annual fee, and the handling fee is only half of the traditional payment method.

(6) Data encryption technology. When registering or logging into PayPal's website, PayPal verifies whether the login's web browser is running Secure Socket Layer 3.0 (SSLv3) or higher. During transmission, the information is protected by SSL with an encryption key length of 168 bits.

(7) Circular checkout. Regularly bill customers, pay membership fees, or offer rental services and installment plans.

4. PayPal 的支付流程

Process of PayPal's payment

付款人通过 PayPal 支付一笔款项给商家或收款人的流程，可以分为以下几个步骤：

(1) 只要有一个电子邮件地址，付款人即可注册 PayPal 账户，通过验证成为其用户，并提供信用卡或者相关银行资料，增加账户金额，将一定数额的款项从其开户时登记的账户转移至 PayPal 账户下。

(2) 当付款人启动向第三方付款流程时，必须先进入 PayPal 账户，指定特定的汇出金额，并提供收款人的电子邮件账号给 PayPal。

(3) 接着 PayPal 向商家或者收款人发送电子邮件，通知其有等待领取或转账的款项。

(4) 如商家或者收款人也是 PayPal 用户，其决定接受后，付款人所指定的款项即移转给收款人。若商家或者收款人没有 PayPal 账户，商家或收款人按 PayPal 电子邮件内容指示联网进入网页注册，取得一个 PayPal 账户。因此，也有人称 PayPal 的这种销售模式是一种“邮件病毒式”的商业拓展方式，它使 PayPal 越来越多地占有市场。

The process of a payer paying a sum of money to a merchant or payee through PayPal can be divided into the following steps:

(1) As long as there is an email address, the payer can register a PayPal account, become its user through verification, and provide credit card or related bank information to increase the account amount, transferring a certain amount of funds from the account registered at the time of opening the account to the PayPal account.

(2) When the payer initiates the payment process to a third party, he must first enter his PayPal account, specify a specific remittance amount, and provide the recipient's email account to PayPal.

（3） Then PayPal sends an email to the merchant or payee, notifying them of pending payments for collection or transfer.

（4） If the merchant or payee is also a PayPal user, and he decides to accept, the payment specified by the payer will be transferred to the payee. If the merchant or payee does not have a PayPal account, the merchant or payee should follow the instructions in the PayPal email to register on the website and obtain a PayPal account. Therefore, some people also call PayPal's sales mode a "viral email" business expansion method, which has enabled PayPal to increasingly occupy the market.

（二） 国际支付宝

Escrow

在全球速卖通平台做生意，离不开国际支付宝的保驾护航。

Doing business on the AliExpress platform is inseparable from the escort of Escrow.

1. 国际支付宝的介绍

Introduction to Escrow

国际支付宝由阿里巴巴与支付宝联合开发，是旨在保护国际在线交易中买卖双方的交易安全所设的一种第三方支付担保服务，全称为 Escrow Service。

Escrow, jointly developed by Alibaba and Alipay, is a third-party payment guarantee service designed to safeguard transaction security for buyers and sellers in international online transactions. Its full name is Escrow Service.

国际支付宝的服务模式与国内支付宝类似：交易过程中先由买家将货款打到第三方担保平台的国际支付宝账户中，然后由第三方担保平台通知卖家发货，买家收到商品后确认，货款放于卖家，至此完成一笔网络交易。

The service mode of Escrow is similar to that of domestic Alipay: During a transaction, the buyer first sends the payment to the Escrow account on the third-party guarantee platform, and then the third-party guarantee platform notifies the seller to deliver the goods. After the buyer receives the goods, it confirms that the payment is placed in the seller, and then an online transaction is completed.

2. 国际支付宝账号申请

Account application of Escrow

如果卖家已经拥有了国内支付宝账号，无须再另外申请国际支付宝账户。只要卖家是全球速卖通的用户，就可以直接登录"My Alibaba"后台（中国供应商会员）或"我的全球速卖通"后台（普通会员）管理收款账户，绑定国内的支付宝账户即可。如果卖家还没有国内支付宝账号，可以先登录支付宝网站申请国内的支付宝账号，再绑定即可。

If the seller already has a domestic Alipay account, it is unnecessary to apply for an Escrow account. As long as the seller is a user of AliExpress, he can directly log in to the "My Alibaba" backend (for Chinese suppliers members) or "My AliExpress" backend (for regular member) to manage his receiving account and bind it to the domestic Alipay account. If the seller does not have a domestic Alipay account, he can first log in to the Alipay website to apply for one, and then complete the binding.

绑定国内支付宝账户后，卖家就可以通过支付宝账户收取人民币。国际支付宝会按照买家支付当天的汇率，将美元兑换成人民币支付到卖家的国内支付宝或银行账户中。卖家还可以通过设置美元收款账户的方式来直接收取美元。

After binding the domestic Alipay account, the seller can collect RMB through the Alipay account. Escrow will convert US dollars into RMB according to the exchange rate of the buyer on the day of payment to the seller' s domestic Alipay or bank account. Sellers can also set up a USD receiving account to directly receive US dollars.

3. 国际支付宝账户使用

Use of Escrow account

国际支付宝账户是支付宝为从事跨境交易的国内卖家建立的资金账户管理平台，主要功能包括对交易的收款、退款和提现等。国际支付宝账户是多币种账户，包含美元账户和人民币账户。目前，只有全球速卖通与阿里巴巴国际站会员才能使用。

Escrow Account is a fund account management platform established by Alipay for domestic sellers engaged in cross-border transactions. Its main functions include collection, refund and withdrawal of transactions. Escrow Account is a multi-currency account, including a USD account and an RMB account. Currently, only members of AliExpress and Alibaba International Station can use it.

支付宝系统上线后，提现功能较之前有了一些改变，用户提现不再限制在 100 元交易金额之内，而是可根据自身需要对账户中“可提现金额”做全部或者部分提现，大大降低了用户的提现成本。

After the Alipay system went online, the withdrawal function has changed a lot. The user' s withdrawal is no longer limited to 100 yuan of transaction amount, but can withdraw all or part of the “withdrawable amount” in the account according to their own needs, greatly reducing the user' s withdrawal cost.

4. 国际支付宝与国内支付宝的区别

Difference between Escrow and domestic Alipay

国际支付宝的第三方担保服务是由阿里巴巴国际站同国内支付宝联合提供支持的。全球速卖通平台只是在买家端将国内支付宝改名为国际支付宝。这是因为根据对买家调研的数据发现买家群体更加喜欢和信赖国际支付宝，认为国际支付宝可以保护买家的交易安全。

The third-party guarantee service of Escrow is jointly supported by Alibaba International Station and domestic Alipay. On the buyer side, the AliExpress platform only changed the name of Alipay to Escrow. This is because according to data from buyer research, it has been found that the buyer community prefers and trusts Escrow more, believing that Escrow can protect the transaction security of buyers.

而在卖家端，全球速卖通平台依然沿用“国际支付宝”这一名称，只是国际支付宝相应的英文名称变成“Escrow”.

On the seller side, the AliExpress platform retains the term "International Alipay", but the corresponding English of Alipay is translated as "Escrow".

第二节 信用卡支付
Section 2 Credit Cards Accepted

在欧美发达国家，信用卡的使用频率非常高，发行量也很大。常见的信用卡组织有VISA、万事达、美国运通、大来等。因此，在跨境支付中，信用卡支付成为一种较为常见的支付方式。

In developed countries across Europe and North America, credit cards are used very frequently and have a large issuance volume. Common credit card organizations include VISA, MasterCard, American Express, Diners Club, etc. Therefore, in cross-border payment, credit card payment has become a common payment method.

一、信用卡的基本知识
Basic knowledge of credit cards

信用卡由卡号、CVV 码、有效期、发卡行信息组成。卡号是由 16 位数字组成，4 开头的是 VSA 卡，5 开头的是万事达卡，62 开头的属于银联卡，35 开头的属于 JCB 卡，34、37 开头的属于美国运通卡，30、36 开头的属于大来卡。第 16 位数字根据前面数位数字规则推算而成。人们一般是根据前六、后四位数字来查看交易记录。VISA 卡为 CVV 码，万事达卡为 CVC 码，其号码在信用卡的背面。有效期是指信用卡能有效使用的期限。发卡行是签发信用卡的银行。

A credit card consists of a card number, CVV code, expiration date, and issuing bank information. The card number is composed of 16 digits. VISA cards start with 4, MasterCard cards start with 5, UnionPay cards start with 62, JCB cards start with 35, American Express cards start with 34 or 37, and Diners Club cards start with 30 or 36. The 16th digit is calculated based on the rule of the preceding digit. People usually view transaction records using the first six and last four digits. VISA cards have a CVV code, while Mastercards have a CVC code, which is located on the back of the credit card. The validity period refers to the period during which the credit card is valid. The issuing bank is the bank that issues credit cards.

威士国际组织是一个单一法人机构，是目前世界上最大的信用卡组织。它的总部设在美国旧金山市，VISA 将全球业务分为亚太地区、加拿大、中欧—东欧、欧盟、拉丁美洲—加勒比海地区以及美国，共六大区域，其区域总部和办事处分别设在伦敦、巴黎、东京、新加坡、悉尼、多伦多、法兰克福和迈阿密。它的前身是美洲银行信用卡公司，1959 年开始发行“美洲信用卡”。1974 年美洲银行信用卡公司与几家银行联手合作共同发起成立了国际信用卡服务组织。1976 年改称威士国际组织，并以“VISA”为该组织的标志。当前，威士国际组织已经成为一个拥有超过 21000 万多家会员银行、特约商户达 2200 多万家、发卡量达十亿多张

（不包括 Interlink 卡）的大型国际组织。

VISA International Service Association is a single legal entity and currently the largest credit card organization in the world. Its headquarters is located in San Francisco, USA. It divides its global business into six regions: Asia Pacific, Canada, Central and Eastern Europe, European Union, Latin America and the Caribbean, and the United States. Its regional headquarters and offices are located in London, Paris, Tokyo, Singapore, Sydney, Toronto, Frankfurt, and Miami. Its predecessor was the Bank of America Credit Card Company, which began issuing "America Credit Cards" in 1959. In 1974, Bank of America Credit Card Company collaborated with several banks to jointly establish the International Credit Card Service Organization. In 1976, it was renamed Visa International Service Association and adopted "VISA" as its logo. Nowadays, It has become a large international organization with over 210 million member banks, over 22 million authorized merchants, and over one billion issued cards (excluding Interlink cards).

万事达卡国际组织于 1966 年成立于美国，在北美和欧洲的业务量远超过其他卡组织。万事达卡国际组织的前身是美国加利福尼亚州几家银行机构成立的美国西部银行卡协会。截至 2024 年，万事达卡国际组织在全球拥有超 1.3 亿家特约商户，这些特约商户遍布全球 210 个国家和地区。万事达卡国际组织是服务于金融机构（如商业银行、储蓄银行、储蓄和放款协会、存款互助会）的非营利性全球会员协会，其宗旨是为会员提供全球最佳支付系统和金融服务。万事达卡国际组织目前已经发展成为仅次于威士国际组织的世界第二大信用卡国际组织。

MasterCard Worldwide was founded in the United States in 1966 and has a much larger business volume in North America and Europe than other card organizations. The predecessor of MasterCard Worldwide was the Western Bank Card Association, established by several banking institutions in California, USA. As of 2024, MasterCard Worldwide has over 130 million authorized merchants worldwide, spanning 210 countries and regions. MasterCard Worldwide is a non-profit global membership association serving financial institutions (such as commercial banks, savings banks, savings and lending associations, and mutual aid societies). Its mission is to provide its members with the world's best payment systems and financial services. Mastercard Worldwide has now developed into the world's second largest credit card international organization after Visa International Service Association.

大来于 1950 年成立于美国，是世界上第一个信用卡组织。现在是六大信用卡组织里体量最小的。国内只有中国工商银行和它合作发行了信用卡。

Diners Club was founded in the United States in 1950 and was the world's first credit card organization. Now it is the smallest among the six major credit card organizations in terms of size. Only Industrial and Commercial Bank of China has cooperated with it to issue credit cards domestically.

美国运通的总部在美国，成立于 1941 年，于 1958 年开始发行运通卡，目前是世界上第三大信用卡组织。美国运通公司主要通过其三大分支机构运营：美国运通旅游，美国运通财务顾问及美国运通银行。它既是卡组织又是发卡行，业务量在全球不如 VISA、万事达、银联。该卡定位于顶级群体，无额度上限（中国的百夫长黑金卡为合作发行的信用卡，所以存在额度限制），持卡人多为各国政要、亿万富豪及社会名流。

American Express is headquartered in the United States and was founded in 1941. It began issuing American Express cards in 1958 and is currently the third largest credit card organization in the world. American Express operates primarily through its three major branches: American Express Travel, American Express Financial Advisor, and American Express Bank. It is both a card organization and an issuing bank, with less business volume globally than VISA, MasterCard, and UnionPay. This card is targeted at the top group, with no credit limit (China's Centurion Black Gold Card is a cooperative credit card, hence there is a limit), and the cardholders are mostly politicians, billionaires, and social celebrities from various countries.

吉士美于 1981 年成立于日本，在日本和东南亚占有很强的地位，国内只有几家银行和 JCB 合作发卡。

JCB (Japan Credit Bureau Card) was founded in Japan in 1981 and holds a strong position in Japan and Southeast Asia. Only a few banks in China cooperate with JCB to issue cards.

中国银联成立于 2002 年 3 月，是经国务院同意、中国人民银行批准设立的中国银行卡联合组织，总部设于上海。银联是最年轻的卡组织。银联在 160 多个国家和地区发卡，是目前世界上发卡量最大的卡组织。

Founded in March 2002, China UnionPay is a joint organization of Chinese bank cards approved by the State Council and the People's Bank of China, with its headquarters in Shanghai. UnionPay is the youngest card organization. Issued cards in over 160 countries and regions, it is currently the largest card issuing organization in the world.

以前，国内发行的外币信用卡会同时支持两种卡组织，也就是我们常说的双标信用卡，通常会是银联+VISA、银联+万事达、银联+美国运通、银联 +JCB 以及银联+大来。目前国内已经逐渐停发双标信用卡，以发行单标卡为主。单标信用卡多为芯片卡，双标信用卡均为磁条卡。

Previously, foreign currency credit cards issued domestically would support two types of card organizations simultaneously, commonly known as dual standard credit cards, which are usually UnionPay + VIA, UnionPay + Mastercard, UnionPay + American Express, UnionPay + JCB, and UnionPay + Diners Club. At present, the issuance of dual standard credit cards has gradually stopped in China, and single standard cards are mainly issued. Single standard credit cards are chip cards, while dual standard credit cards are both magnetic stripe cards.

在申请信用卡的时候，如果只在国内使用信用卡，办一张银联信用卡就可以；如果想要出国海淘，就要办理其他组织的信用卡。

When applying for a credit card, if you only use it domestically, you can apply for a UnionPay credit card; if you want to go shopping overseas, you need to apply for a credit card from another organization.

二、信用卡支付网关

Credit card payment gateway

国际信用卡支付网关是指专业提供国际信用卡收款的银行支付接口，通常也称信用卡支付通道。信用卡支付网关涉及的对象有：发卡行、持卡人、卡组织、收单行、第三方支付平台。

International credit card payment gateways refer to professional bank payment interfaces that provide international credit card payments, commonly known as credit card payment channels. The objects involved in credit card payment gateways include issuing banks, cardholders, card organizations, acquiring banks, and third-party payment platforms.

按照是否需要密码验证，信用卡支付通道分为 3D 通道和非 3D 通道。

3D 通道：3D 通道是卡组织为了保证交易的安全性，为信用卡添加的密码验证。因为涉及发卡行、收单行以及卡组织三个领域，所以称作 3D 通道。有些发卡行不支持 3D 验证，申请 3D 验证服务需要首先向发卡行提出申请。3D 验证只有在在线购物的时候才能起作用。虽然 3D 验证服务是免费的，但由于其相对复杂且不符合国际支付惯例，所以一般不用。

非 3D 通道：反之，非 3D 通道不需要密码验证。非 3D 通道符合国际使用信用卡习惯，比较便捷地为外贸商家解决跨境收款难题，从而提高商务交易效率。

Credit card payment gateway are categorized into 3D channel and non-3D channel based on whether password authentication is required.

3D channel：3D channel is a password verification added by card organizations for credit cards to ensure transaction security. Because it involves three domains：issuing banks, acquiring banks, and card organizations, it is called a 3D channel. Some issuing banks do not support 3D verification, and applying for 3D verification services requires first submitting an application to the issuing bank. 3D verification only works when shopping online. Although 3D verification services are free, they are generally not necessary due to their complexity and lack of compliance with international payment conventions.

Non-3D channel：Conversely, non-3D channel does not require password verification. Non-3D channel complys with international credit card usage habits, conveniently solving cross-border payment problems for foreign trade merchants, thereby improving business transaction efficiency.

按照订单支付结果显示时间，信用卡支付通道分为实时通道和延时通道。

实时通道：买家在填写支付页面信息并单击确认交易后，买家能立即收到由第三方支付公司与银行发送的支付结果。由于此种支付通道是由风控系统自动控制的，会阻隔一部分高风险交易。

延时通道：延时通道的目的在于有效控制交易风险，8～24 小时内显示订单支付的结果（待处理、支付成功、支付失败）。该段时间内，银行、网关等多重关口有效控制风险，再配合人工审核每一笔交易订单，有效保障交易安全。

Credit card payment gateway are classified into real-time channel and delayed channel based on the timing of payment result display for orders.

Real-time channel：After filling in the payment page information and clicking confirm the transaction, the buyer can immediately receive the payment result sent by the third-party payment company and the bank. Due to the automatic control of this payment channel by the risk control system, it may block some high-risk transactions.

Delayed channel: The purpose of the delay channel is to effectively control transaction risks and display the results of order payments (pending, successful, failed) within 8~24 hours. During this period, multiple checkpoints such as banks and gateways effectively monitor risks, and cooperate with manual review of each transaction order to effectively ensure transaction security.

第三节 Section 3 跨境支付账户介绍——全球速卖通
Introduction to Cross-border Payment Accounts — AliExpress

全球速卖通是阿里巴巴旗下面向全球市场打造的在线交易平台，被广大卖家称为国际版“淘宝”。与淘宝类似，卖家将商品信息上传至平台，通过全球速卖通平台发布给海外买家。其发货流程与国内类似，卖家使用国际快递与220多个国家和地区的买家达成交易，赚取外汇。全球速卖通平台支持多样化的支付方式，卖家只需要设置双币收款账户即可接受所有买家的支付。

AliExpress is an online trading platform created by Alibaba for the global market, known as the international version of “Taobao” by a large number of sellers. Like Taobao, sellers upload items as online information and publish them to overseas buyers through the AliExpress platform. Similar to the domestic shipping process, the platform facilitates transactions with buyers from over 220 countries and regions using international express delivery, enabling sellers to earn foreign exchange. The AliExpress platform supports diverse payment methods, and sellers only need to set up dual-currency payment accounts to accept payment from all buyers.

第四节 Section 4 重点短语与句型
Key Phrases and Sentence Patterns

一、常用单词与短语
Common words and phrases

1. cross-border e-commerce payment 跨境电商支付
2. international payment settlement method 国际货款结算方式
3. T/T (Telegraphic Transfer) 电汇
4. SWIFT (Society for Worldwide Interbank Financial Telecommunication) 环球同业银行金融电信协会
5. prepayment 预付
6. spot payment 即期支付
7. forward payment 远期支付
8. remitter 汇款人

9. payee　收款人
10. remitting bank　汇出行
11. receiving bank　汇入行
12. PayPal　贝宝（PayPal 在中国的称呼）
13. personal account　个人账户
14. advanced account　高级账户
15. enterprise account　企业账户
16. third-party payment guarantee service　第三方支付担保服务
17. AliExpress　全球速卖通
18. credit cards accepted　信用卡支付
19. VISA　维萨
20. MasterCard　万事达
21. American Express　美国运通
22. Diners Club　大来
23. UnionPay　银联
24. CVV（Card Verification Value）code　信用卡验证码
25. expiration date　有效期
26. issuing bank　发卡行
27. payment gateway　支付网关
28. 3D channel　3D 通道
29. non-3D channel　非 3D 通道
30. real-time channel　实时通道
31. delay channel　延时通道
32. risk control　风险控制
33. transaction security　交易安全
34. Escrow　国际支付宝
35. multi-currency account　多币种账户
36. account application　账号申请
37. account management　账户管理
38. currency conversion　货币兑换
39. online transactions　网络交易
40. electronic payments　电子支付
41. financial transactions　金融交易
42. international financial business　国际金融业务
43. automated communication services　自动化通信服务
44. secure and reliable　安全可靠
45. standardized services　标准化服务
46. automated services　自动化服务

47. payment process　支付流程
48. email notification　电子邮件通知
49. registration process　注册流程
50. account verification　账户验证

二、常用句型
Common sentence patterns

1. T/T is a remittance method in which the remitting bank, upon the request of the remitter, instructs the remitting bank to make payment to the payee through a tested cable or SWIFT.

电汇是汇出行应汇款人的申请，用加押电报或 SWIFT 的形式指示汇入行付款给收款人的一种汇款方式。

2. SWIFT operates a world-class financial messaging network, through which banks and other financial institutions exchange messages with peers to complete financial transactions.

SWIF 运营着一个世界级的金融电文网络，银行和其他金融机构通过它与同业交换电文以完成金融交易。

3. T/T is divided into prepaid, spot, and forward.

电汇分为预付、即期和远期。

4. There are three ways of T/T payment: ① T/T in advance, ② Post payment T/T, ③ Deposit first, then pay the remaining balance.

电汇付款有以下三种方式：①前款 T/T，②后款 T/T，③先订金，再余款。

5. PayPal was established in December 1998 by PeterThiel and Max Levchin.

PayPal 于 1998 年 12 月由 Peter Thiel 和 Max Levchin 建立。

6. PayPal accounts are divided into three types: personal accounts, advanced accounts, and enterprise accounts.

PayPal 账户分为三种类型：个人账户、高级账户和企业账户。

7. Personal accounts are suitable for online shopping buyers and users, mainly used for payment and receiving payments.

个人账户适用于在线购物的买家用户，主要用于付款和收款。

8. Advanced accounts are suitable for individual merchants who shop or sell online.

高级账户适用于在线购物或在线销售的个人商户。

9. Enterprise accounts are suitable for merchant users who operate in the name of a company or group.

企业账户适用于以企业或团体名义经营的商家用户。

10. PayPal has over 220 million users in more than 190 countries and regions worldwide.

PayPal 在全球 190 多个国家和地区拥有超过 2.2 亿用户。

11. PayPal's unique features of instant payment and instant receipt allow for real-time receipt of payments from overseas customers.

PayPal 独有的即时支付、即时到账的功能，可实时接收海外客户的款项。

12. A comprehensive security system, rich experience in fraud prevention, and the industry's lowest risk loss rate ensure smooth transactions.

完善的安全保障体系、丰富的防欺诈经验、业界最低的风险损失率，确保交易顺利进行。

13. The process of a payer paying a sum of money to a merchant or payee through PayPal can be divided into the following steps.

付款人通过 PayPal 支付一笔款项给商家或收款人的流程可以分为以下步骤。

14. If the merchant or payee is already a PayPal user, then the payment will be transferred to his PayPal account.

如果商家或收款人已经是 PayPal 的用户，那么该笔款项就汇入他拥有的 PayPal 账户。

15. Escrow is a third-party payment guarantee service designed to protect the transaction security of buyers and sellers in international online transactions.

国际支付宝是一种第三方支付担保服务，旨在保护国际在线交易中买卖双方的交易安全。

16. The service mode of Escrow is similar to that of domestic Alipay.

国际支付宝的服务模式与国内支付宝类似。

17. If the seller already has a domestic Alipay account, it is unnecessary to apply for an Escrow account.

如果卖家已经拥有了国内支付宝账号，则无须再申请国际支付宝账户。

18. Escrow will convert US dollars into RMB according to the exchange rate of the buyer on the day of payment to the seller.

国际支付宝会按照买家支付当天的汇率，将美元兑换成人民币支付给卖家。

19. Escrow Account is a fund account management platform established by Alipay for domestic sellers engaged in cross-border transactions.

国际支付宝账户是支付宝为从事跨境交易的国内卖家建立的资金账户管理平台。

20. The third-party guarantee service of Escrow is jointly supported by Alibaba International Station and domestic Alipay.

国际支付宝的第三方担保服务是由阿里巴巴国际站与国内支付宝共同提供支持。

21. In developed countries in Europe and North America, credit cards are used very frequently and have a large issuance volume.

在欧美发达国家，信用卡的使用频率非常高，发行量也很大。

22. A credit card consists of a card number, CVV code, expiration date, and issuing bank information.

信用卡由卡号、CVV 码、有效期、发卡行信息组成。

23. VISA is currently the largest credit card organization in the world.

VISA 是目前世界上最大的信用卡组织。

24. MasterCard has a much larger business volume in North America and Europe than other card organizations.

MasterCard 在北美和欧洲的业务规模远超其他卡组织。

25. American Express is both a card organization and an issuing bank.

美国运通既是卡组织，又是发卡行。

26. JCB holds a strong position in Japan and Southeast Asia.

JCB 在日本和东南亚占有很强的地位。

27. UnionPay is the largest card issuing organization in the world.

银联是世界上发卡量最大的卡组织。

28. International credit card payment gateways refer to professional bank payment interfaces that provide international credit card payments.

国际信用卡支付网关是指专业提供国际信用卡收款的银行支付接口。

29. 3D channel is a password verification added by card organizations for credit cards to ensure transaction security.

3D 通道是卡组织为信用卡添加的密码验证，以确保交易安全。

30. Non-3D channel does not require password verification.

非 3D 通道不需要密码验证。

31. Real-time channel allows buyers to immediately receive the payment result sent by the third-party payment company and the bank.

实时通道使买家能够立即收到由第三方支付公司和银行发送的支付结果。

32. The purpose of the delay channel is to effectively control transaction risks.

延时通道的目的是有效控制交易风险。

33. AliExpress is an online trading platform created by Alibaba for the global market.

全球速卖通是阿里巴巴旗下面向全球市场打造的在线交易平台。

34. Sellers can manage their payment accounts through "My Alibaba" or "My AliExpress".

卖家可以通过"My Alibaba"或"My AliExpress"管理他们的收款账户。

35. Escrow Account includes USD account and RMB account.

国际支付宝账户包含美元账户和人民币账户。

36. Only members of AliExpress and Alibaba International station can use Escrow Account.

只有全球速卖通与阿里巴巴国际站的会员才能使用国际支付宝账户。

37. Users can withdraw all or part of the withdrawable amount in the account according to their own needs.

用户可以根据自身需要对账户中的可提现金额进行全部或部分提现。

38. The AliExpress platform uses the term "Escrow" on the seller side.

全球速卖通平台在卖家端使用"Escrow"一词。

39. Except for UnionPay, the other five major card organizations still cannot carry out RMB clearing business in China.

除了银联以外，其他五大卡组织依然无法在中国开展人民币清算业务。

40. Single standard credit cards are chip cards, while dual standard credit cards are magnetic stripe cards.

单标信用卡多为芯片卡，而双标信用卡均为磁条卡。

41. Domestic issuance of dual standard credit cards has gradually stopped in China, and single

standard cards are mainly issued.

中国国内已经逐渐停发双标信用卡，主要以发行单标卡为主。

42. If you only use the credit card domestically, you can apply for a UnionPay credit card.

如果只在国内使用信用卡，可以办理一张银联信用卡。

43. If you want to go shopping overseas, you need to apply for a credit card from another organization.

如果想要出国海淘，需要办理其他组织的信用卡。

44. Some people also call PayPal's sales mode a "viral email" business expansion method.

有人也称 PayPal 的销售模式为“病毒式电邮”的商业扩展方式。

45. The larger the deposit ratio, the lower the risk for the exporter.

定金的比例越大，出口商的风险越小。

46. PayPal achieved rapid growth and became a payment giant after being spun off from the eBay system.

PayPal 从 eBay 体系剥离后实现了快速增长，成为支付巨头。

47. The service scope of MasterCard has reached all over the world.

MasterCard 的服务范围已遍及全球。

48. American Express cardholders are mostly politicians, billionaires, and social celebrities from various countries.

美国运通卡的持卡人多为各国政要、亿万富豪及社会名流。

课后练习

Ⅰ. 单选题。

Single choice questions.

1. What does T/T stand for in the context of international payment methods?

A. Telegraphic Transfer　　B. Telephone Transfer

C. Traveler's Transfer　　D. Trade Transaction

2. Which of the following is a characteristic of the Telegraphic Transfer (T/T)?

A. Slow speed　　B. High fees

C. Low security　　D. Fast speed

3. In which year was SWIFT founded?

A. 1968　　B. 1973

C. 1985　　D. 1990

4. What is the full form of the term used for a payment guarantee service similar to Alipay in international transactions?

A. Escrow Service　　B. E-check Service

C. Digital Payment Service　　D. Online Wallet Service

5. PayPal was acquired by eBay in what year?

A. 2001 B. 2002

C. 2003 D. 2004

6. Which type of PayPal account is suitable for individual merchants who shop or sell online?

A. Personal account B. Advanced account

C. Enterprise account D. Non-profit account

7. How many users does PayPal have worldwide?

A. Over 100 million B. Over 150 million

C. Over 220 million D. Over 250 million

8. Which of the following is a feature of PayPal that allows for real-time receipt of payments from overseas customers?

A. Instant payment and instant receipt B. Delayed payment and receipt

C. Scheduled payment and receipt D. Batch payment and receipt

9. What is the name of the service that protects the transaction security of buyers and sellers in international online transactions on the AliExpress platform?

A. Alipay B. Escrow

C. PayPal D. Visa

10. Which of the following is a major credit card organization that is part of the international payment system?

A. VISA B. VISP

C. VIVA D. VIA

11. What is the name of the largest credit card organization in the world?

A. MasterCard B. American Express

C. VISA D. UnionPay

12. Which of the following is a requirement for using a 3D channel for credit card transactions?

A. It requires password verification.

B. It does not require any additional security measures.

C. It is only used for offline transactions.

D. It is mandatory for all international transactions.

13. What is the purpose of a delay channel in credit card transactions?

A. To speed up transaction processing

B. To effectively control transaction risks

C. To reduce the cost of transactions

D. To increase the number of transactions processed

14. Which platform is referred to as the international version of "Taobao"?

A. Alibaba B. eBay

C. Amazon D. AliExpress

15. What type of cards are dual standard credit cards?

A. Chip cards
B. Magnetic stripe cards
C. Contactless cards
D. Both A and C

Ⅱ. 简答题。

Short answer questions.

1. What are the three types of PayPal accounts, and which one is recommended for individual sellers conducting cross-border transactions?

2. How does the international Alipay (Escrow) service protect the transaction security of buyers and sellers in international online transactions?

3. What are the differences between 3D channel and non-3D channel in the context of international credit card payment gateways?

第十章 跨境电商客户沟通
Chapter 10 Cross-border E-commerce Customer Communication

客户服务的好坏直接影响到跨境电商经营的好坏，良好的客户关系能为店铺带来更多的回头客及好评，帮助店铺可持续运营。本章以全球速卖通为例，从跨境电商客户服务的基本原理讲起，对沟通模板、沟通方式、纠纷处理技巧做具体论述，旨在帮助学生更好地掌握跨境电商客户沟通的方法与技巧，并且掌握预防、处理纠纷的主要流程与方法。

学习目标

1. 了解跨境电商客户关系管理的主要内容。
2. 熟悉跨境电商客户沟通的方法与技巧。
3. 了解跨境电商经营过程中的纠纷处理流程。
4. 掌握客户沟通以及纠纷处理中的信文写作方法。

思政目标

1. 学习沟通模板，培养沟通能力。
2. 学习纠纷处理，增强服务意识。
3. 注重团队协作，培养团队合作精神。

第一节 客户沟通模板
Section 1 Customer Communication Templates

用英文与客户沟通，需要做到以下几点：一是清楚，即用词肯定、准确，内容主旨清晰；二是简洁，即用简短的语句清晰表达观点，尽量避免使用复杂词汇；三是礼貌，即使用礼貌用语。

以下提供一些常用的写作案例。

The necessary things in communicating with clients in English are to achieve the following: Firstly, clarity, that is, using affirmative and accurate words, and having clear content and main ideas. Secondly, conciseness, expressing ideas clearly in short sentences and avoiding using complex vocabulary as much as possible. Thirdly, politeness, using polite language.

Here are some commonly used writing examples.

一、销售前沟通

Pre-sales communication

售前沟通主要是为客户解答关于产品信息（如价格、数量、库存、规格型号、用途）运费、运输等方面的问题，促使客户尽快下单。

Pre-sales communication is mainly aimed at answering customers' questions about product information (such as price, quantity, inventory, specifications and models, usage), shipping costs, transportation, and other aspects, in order to prompt customers to place orders as soon as possible.

（一）买家光顾店铺查看产品

Buyers visit the store to view products

Thank you for visiting our store, and you can find what you want from our store. If we don't have the item, please tell us and we will spare no effort to find it.

感谢光临我们的商店，您可以从我们的商店找到所需要的产品。如果我们没有您要的产品，请告诉我们，我们会不遗余力地为您找到。

（二）买家询问商品价格和库存

Buyers enquire about product prices and inventory

Thank you for your enquiry. Yes, we have this item in stock. How many do you want? Right now, we only have × color and × style left. Because they are hot selling items, the product has a high risk of selling out soon. Please place your order as soon as possible.

感谢您的咨询。是的，我们有这款商品的库存，您要多少件？现在我们只有×款和×颜色。因为它们是热销商品，所以很快就有可能售罄。请您尽快下单。

（三）鼓励买家提高订单金额和订单数量，提醒买家尽快确认订单

Encourage buyers to increase their order amount and quantity, and remind them to confirm their orders as soon as possible

Thank you for your order. If you confirm the order as soon as possible, we will send a gift to you. Recently, there are a lot of activities in our store. If the value of goods you buy count to a certain amount, we will give you a satisfied discount.

谢谢您的惠顾，如果您尽快确认订单，我们将会赠送您一份礼物。店铺最近有很多活动，如果您购买的货物价值数达到一定等级，我们会给您一个满意的折扣。

（四）货物断货对策

Measures for goods shortage

We are very sorry that item you ordered is out of stock at the moment. We will contact the factory to see when it will be available again and inform you of the result. We would like to recommend some other items of similar styles. Hope you like them too. You can click on the following link to check them. If there's anything we can help with, please feel free to contact us.

真对不起，您订购的产品目前缺货，我们会与工厂联系，看看什么时候能再次供货，并告知您。我们想推荐一些其他类似风格的商品，希望您也喜欢。您可以点击以下链接进行查看。有什么我们可以帮忙的，请随时与我们联系。

（五）提供折扣

Offer discounts

Thank you for your message. Well, if you buy both of the ×× items, we can offer you an ×% discount. Once we confirm your payment, we will ship out the items for you in time.

谢谢您的留言。好的，如果您同时购买这两种××产品，我们可以给您×%的折扣。一旦我们确认您的付款，我们将及时为您发货。

（六）买家议价

Buyer bargaining

Thank you for taking interest in our item. We are afraid we can't offer you that low price you bargained, as the price we offer has been carefully calculated and our profit margin is already very limited. However, we can offer you an ×% discount if you purchase more than × pieces in one order.

感谢您对我们的惠顾。恐怕我们不能给您还价得那么低的价格，因为我们的报价是经过仔细计算的，我们的利润已经很有限了。但如果您一次购买超过×件，我们将给您×%的折扣。

二、售中沟通

Mid-sales communication

售中沟通主要是发货确认、物流问题，告知客户产品的物流信息，以让客户掌握产品动向。

Mid-sales communication mainly involves shipment confirmation and logistics issues, informing customers of product logistics information to keep them informed of product trends.

（一）客户下单后发送确认单

After the customer places an order, send a confirmation form

Your payment for order number × has been received. We will ship it within the promised × days. After shipment, we will inform you of the tacking number. If you have any questions, please feel free to contact us.

您的订单编号为×的款项已收到，我们将在承诺的×天内发货，发货后，我们将告知您货运单号。如果您有任何问题，请随时联系我们。

（二）通知买家查看物流情况

Notify the buyer to check the logistics situation

The goods you need had been set on time. It's on the way now. Please pay attention to the delivery and sign as soon as possible. If you have any questions, please feel free to contact us.

您所购买的商品已经按时发货了，现在在路上。请注意尽快收货并签收。如果您有任何问题，请随时联系我们。

（三）海关问题

Customs issues

We received notice from the logistics company that your customs is currently conducting strict periodic inspections on large shipments. To make the goods sent to you successfully, we propose a shipment delay and seek your official consent. Please let me know as soon as possible.

我们接到物流公司的通知，贵国的海关正在对大量邮包进行严格的定期检查，为了使货物顺利地送达到贵处，我们建议延迟几天发货，希望征得您的同意。希望尽快得到您的回复。

（四）物流信息缺失对策

Countermeasures for missing logistics information

We have already sent the package on ×. Based on your feedback, we have contacted the shipping company and confirmed the issue. We have got back the original package and resent it. New tracking number is ×. We apologize for the inconveniences and hope you can receive it as soon as possible. If you have any problems, don't hesitate to tell us.

我们已经在×月×日发送包裹，根据您的反馈，我们已经联系货运公司并确认了问题。我们找回了原来的包裹并重新寄送，新的货运单号是×，我们对此感到十分抱歉，希望您能尽快收到。有任何疑问，请告诉我们。

（五）物流遇到问题对策

Countermeasures for logistics problems encountered

Thank you for your enquiry. We are happy to contact you. We confirm that the package was dispatched on October 16, 2015. However, it did not arrive due to shipping problems with the delivery company. We have resent your order by EMS. The new tracking number is ×. It usually takes 7 days to arrive to your destination. We are very sorry for the inconvenience. Thank you for your patience.

If you have any further questions, please feel free to contact us.

谢谢您的询问，我们很高兴与您联系。我们确认在 2015 年 10 月 16 日已寄出该包裹，然而，由于快递公司的运输问题并没有到达。我们已通过 EMS 重新发送您的包裹，新的货运单号码是×。到达您目的地通常需要 7 天的时间。我们很抱歉给您带来不便，谢谢您的耐心。

如果您有任何其他的问题，请随时联系我们。

三、售后沟通

After-sales communication

售后沟通主要是客户收到产品之后的一系列问题，包括退换货问题、买家确认收货以及买卖双方互评。

After-sales communication primarily involves a series of issues after customers receive their products, including return and exchange issues, buyers confirming receipt of goods, and mutual evaluations between buyers and sellers.

（一）退换货问题对策

Countermeasures for return and exchange issues

We are sorry for the inconveniences. If you are not satisfied with the product, you can return it back to us. We will give you a replacement or give you full return. We hope to do business with you for a long time. We will give you a big discount in your next order.

很抱歉给您带来了不便。如果不满意产品，您可以把产品退回，我们将为您更换或者全额退款。我们希望和您长期合作。当您下次购买时，我们将给您一个大的折扣。

（二）买家确认收货

The buyer confirms receipt of goods

We are very happy that you have received the order. Thanks for your support. We hope that you are satisfied with the items and look forward to doing more business with you in future.

By the way, it would be highly appreciated if you could leave us a positive feedback. This will be a great encouragement for us. If there's anything we can help with, don't hesitate to tell us.

我们很高兴地看到您已收到货，感谢您的支持。希望您对产品满意，并期待着在将来与您做更多的生意。

顺便说一句，如果您可以给我们一个积极的反馈，我们会非常感激，因为这对我们来说是一个很大的鼓励。如果有什么我们可以帮助的，不要犹豫，请告诉我们。

（三）买家收货后投诉产品有损坏

The buyer complained about product damage after receiving the goods

We are very sorry to hear that the product sent to you were damaged. We did carefully check the packaging before shipping it to you. The damage likely occurred during the transportation. We apologize for any inconvenience caused. We will give you more discounts on your next purchase with us. Thanks for your understanding.

很抱歉听到发给您的产品有残损，我们在发货时再三确定了包装没有问题才给您发货的。残损可能发生在运输过程中，我们因为带给您的不便深表歉意。当您下次从我们这里购买时，我们将会给您更多的折扣。感谢您的谅解。

（四）完成交易表示感谢，并希望买家下次能够再次光临的对策

Thanks for completing the transaction and hope the buyer can come back again in the future

Thank you for your purchase. We have prepared some gifts for you. We will give you a small gift after the discount if you purchase other products next time. Sincerely hope you like it.

谢谢您的购买，我们为您准备了一些礼物。如果您下次购买其他产品，我们会在打折的基础上再送您一份小礼品，真诚希望您能喜欢。

（五）收到买家好评

Received positive feedback from buyers

Thank you for your positive feedback. Your encouragement will keep us movement forward. We sincerely hope to have more chances to serve you.

感谢您的积极评价。您的鼓励将使我们不断前进，我们真诚地希望能有更多的机会为您服务。

第二节 纠纷处理流程
Section 2 Dispute Resolution Process

一、基本流程

Basic process

当买家申请退款或者提出投诉时，应当先由卖家积极介入进行协商，但若在平台规定时

间内不能与买家协商一致，买家未撤销投诉，或者买卖双方对于退货退款不能达成一致意见的，则可交由平台进行裁决。

When the buyer applies for a refund or makes a complaint, the seller shall first actively mediate for negotiation. However, if no mutual agreement is reached within the platform' s designated mediation period, the buyer has not withdrawn the complaint, or the buyer and seller cannot reach an agreement on the return and refund, the platform can make a ruling.

以全球速卖通平台为例。自买家第一次提起退款申请开始第 4 天至第 15 天，若买卖双方无法协商一致，买家可以提交至平台进行裁决。系统自买家第一次提起裁决申请开始截止到第 16 天，卖家未能与买家达成退款协议，买家未取消退款申请，也未提交至平台进行裁决，系统会自动提交至平台进行纠纷裁决。

Taking the AliExpress platform as an example. From the 4th to the 15th day after the buyer first submits a refund request, if the buyer and seller cannot reach an agreement through negotiation, the buyer can submit it to the platform for arbitration. From the 16th day after the buyer first filed a ruling application, should the seller fail to reach a refund agreement with the buyer, and the buyer neither cancels the refund application nor submit it to the platform for ruling, the system would automatically submit it to the platform for dispute resolution.

若买家申请退款退货，在买家填写了退货地址的 30 天内，卖家未收到退货或收到的退货货不对版，可以提交至平台进行裁决。

If the buyer applies for a refund or return, and the seller does not receive the return or the returned goods are incorrect within 30 days after the buyer fills in the return address, the seller can submit the case to the platform for arbitration.

纠纷裁决申请产生的 2 个工作日内，全球速卖通将介入处理，参看买卖双方纠纷协商阶段以及提交纠纷裁决阶段提供的证明进行裁决。

Within 2 working days of the dispute resolution application, AliExpress will intervene and handle it, referring to the evidence provided during the dispute negotiation stage and the dispute resolution stage between the buyer and seller for resolution.

若现有证明充足，则直接给出裁决意见后，进入申诉期；若证明不足，则联系双方限期提供各自证明，全球速卖通将根据双方提供的证明给出裁决意见。

If the existing evidence is sufficient, the appeal period will begin after the ruling opinion is directly given. If the proof is insufficient, both parties shall be contacted to submit their respective proofs within a specified period, and AliExpress will issue a ruling based on the proofs provided by both parties.

如果任何方逾期未提供证明，全球速卖通按照已得证明给出裁决意见，并进入申诉期。申诉期内若补充了充足的证明，则根据补充证明进行最终裁决；若未补充有效证明，则根据裁决意见进行最终裁决；若买卖双方在申诉期内协商达成一致处理意见，全球速卖通会根据双方意见进行裁决。

If any party fails to provide proof within the deadline, AliExpress will issue a ruling based on the proof obtained and enter the appeal period. If sufficient evidence is provided during the appeal period, the final decision shall be made based on the supplementary evidence. If no valid proof is provided, the final decision shall be made based on the ruling opinion. If the buyer and seller reach a consensus during the appeal period, AliExpress will make a ruling based on the opinions of both parties.

二、纠纷裁决状态

Dispute resolution status

全球速卖通纠纷裁决的处理都在投诉举报平台进行，买卖双方都可以在该平台查看纠纷状态及做出响应。

The resolution of disputes on AliExpress is conducted through the complaint and reporting platform, where both buyers and sellers can view the dispute and respond accordingly.

三、举证说明

Evidence explanation

纠纷裁决中买卖双方的举证是非常重要的，平台主要根据举证内容来进行裁决，要注意证明的收集与保管。谁投诉谁举证，投诉方在投诉的同时，需要提供支持投诉的有效证明，平台会限期要求举证，如不能提供，平台将驳回纠纷。

The evidence presented by both the buyer and seller is crucial in dispute resolution, and the platform mainly makes decisions based on the content of the evidence. It is important to pay attention to the collection and preservation of the evidence. Whoever complains shall provide evidence. At the same time as complaining, the complainant needs to provide valid evidence to support the complaint. The platform will require evidence within a specified time limit. If unable to provide it, the platform will dismiss the dispute.

四、限期举证

Deadline for providing evidence

若投诉方举证充分，纠纷即视为成立，平台会要求卖家进行反举证，平台将以收集到的有效证明为依据进行裁决。卖家若认为裁决意见不符合实际情况，则可在申诉期内与买家进行协商或继续反举证。卖家如果无法与买家达成一致处理意见或提供反证，平台则按照裁决意见进行最后裁决。

If the complainant provides sufficient evidence, the dispute will be deemed valid, and the platform will require the seller to provide counter-evidence. The platform will make a ruling based on the collected valid evidence. If the seller believes that the ruling opinion does not match the actual situation, he may negotiate with the buyer or continue to provide counter-evidence during the designated appeal period. If the seller is unable to reach a consensus with the buyer or provide counter-evidence, the platform will make the final decision based to the ruling opinion.

五、避免产生纠纷的技巧
Tips for avoiding disputes

在交易过程中，卖家应该尽量避免纠纷的产生。买家提起的纠纷主要有两大类："未收到货"和"货物与约定不符"。针对这两大类纠纷，卖家可以分别采取相应的措施来避免。

During the transaction process, the seller should make every effort to avoid disputes. There are two main types of disputes raised by buyers: "goods not received" and "goods not as agreed". Sellers can take corresponding measures to avoid these two types of disputes.

（一）未收到货
Goods not received

为了有效避免因"未收到货"而引起的纠纷，卖家要做好选择最优物流服务商及与买家有效沟通两个方面的工作。

To effectively avoid disputes caused by "goods not received", sellers need to do a good job in selecting the best logistics service provider and effectively communicating with buyers.

1. 选择最优物流服务商
Select the best logistics service provider

国际物流往往存在很多不确定因素，如通关问题、货物运输及派送问题等，这些复杂的情况很难被控制，不可避免地会出现包裹清关延误、派送超时甚至包裹丢失，可能导致买家提起纠纷。因此，卖家应根据物流信息更新是否及时、清关能力等选择更佳的快递方式。卖家如需货代公司帮助发货，应该选择正规货代公司，尽可能选择可提供实时查询货物的物流方式。

There are often many uncertain factors in international logistics, such as customs clearance issues, goods transportation and delivery issues, etc. These complex situations are difficult to control, inevitably resulting in parcel clearance delays, delivery delays, or even parcel losses, which may prompt buyers to file disputes. Therefore, sellers should choose a better express delivery method based on whether logistics information updates are timely, customs clearance capabilities, and other factors. If sellers need the help of a freight forwarding company to ship, they should choose a legitimate freight forwarding company and try to choose a logistics method that can provide real-time tracking of the goods.

2. 与买家有效沟通
Effectively communicate with buyers

卖家要提供物流跟踪信息，物流方面出现问题要及时向买家提供包裹延误的具体情况，向买家说明原因，以获得买家谅解。包裹因关税未付被扣关，卖家要向买家解释清楚产品描述中已注明买家缴税义务。当然，卖家如果主动承担部分关税，不仅能避免物品退回，更能让买家给予高分好评。包裹无人签收而暂存于邮局时，应及时提醒买家在有效期内领取。

The seller should provide logistics tracking information, and if there are any logistics problems, he should promptly provide the specific situation of package delay to the buyer, explaining the reasons to obtain the buyer's understanding. If the package was detained due to unpaid customs duties, the seller needs to explain clearly to the buyer that the buyer's tax obligations are stated in the product description. Of course, if the seller takes the initiative to bear some of the tariffs, it can not only avoid the return of the item but also earn high praise from the buyer. When a package is temporarily stored at the post office without being signed for, the buyer should be promptly reminded to collect it within the validity period.

（二）货物与约定不符

Goods not as agreed

要避免"货物与约定不符"产生的纠纷，卖家需要做好三个方面的工作：规范产品描述、保证产品质量、杜绝假货。

To avoid disputes arising from "goods not as agreed", sellers need to do three things: standardize product descriptions, ensure product quality, and eliminate counterfeit goods.

1. 规范产品描述

Standardize product descriptions

描述产品时，务必基于事实，全面而细致地描述产品。例如，电子类产品需将产品功能给予全面说明，避免买家收到货后因无法合理使用而提起纠纷；又如，服饰、鞋类使用尺码表要标明，以便买家选择，避免买家收到货后因尺寸不合适而提起纠纷等。建议卖家在产品描述中注明货运方式、可送达地区、预期所需的运输时间。此外，卖家还要在产品描述中向买家解释海关清关、缴税、产品退回责任和承担方等方面的问题。

When describing a product, it is essential to provide a comprehensive and detailed description based on facts. For example, electronic products need to provide comprehensive explanations of their functions to avoid disputes arising from unreasonable use by buyers after receiving the goods. Similarly, the size chart for clothing and footwear should be clearly marked for buyers to choose from, in order to avoid disputes caused by inappropriate sizes after receiving the goods. Sellers are advised to specify the shipping method, delivery area, and expected shipping time in the product description. In addition, the seller should explain to the buyer in the product description issues such as customs clearance, tax payment, product return responsibility, and the responsible party.

2. 保证产品质量

Ensure product quality

在发货前，卖家要对产品进行充分的检测，包括产品的外观是否完好，产品的功能是否正常，产品是否存在短装，产品邮寄时的包装是否抗压、抗摔及是否适合长途运输等。如果发现产品存在质量问题，应联系厂家或上游供应商进行更换，避免因退换货产生纠纷，因为在外贸交易中退换货会产生极高的运输成本。

Before shipping, the seller needs to conduct a thorough inspection of the product, including whether the appearance is intact, whether functionality is normal, whether there is short shipment, whether the packaging is compression-resistant, impact-resistant, and suitable for long-distance transportation. If quality problems are found with the product, the manufacturer or upstream supplier should be contacted for replacement to avoid disputes arising from returns and exchanges, as returns and exchanges in foreign trade transactions can incur extremely high transportation costs.

3. 杜绝假货，保护第三方知识产权

Eliminate counterfeit goods and protect third-party intellectual property rights

假如买家投诉卖家“销售假货”，而卖家无法提供产品的授权证明，卖家将会被全球速卖通处罚。平台直接裁定为卖家全责的情况，就是涉及第三方知识产权且无法提供授权证明的产品。

If a buyer complains that the seller is “selling counterfeit goods” and the seller is unable to provide authorization proof for the product, the seller will be penalized by AliExpress. The situation where the platform directly rules that the seller is fully responsible refers to products that involve third-party intellectual property and cannot provide authorization proof.

六、解决纠纷需注意的问题

Issues to be noted in resolving disputes

一旦产生纠纷，卖家要采取积极的态度去解决，尽量降低纠纷对自己造成的负面影响。卖家需要做好以下几个方面工作。

Once a dispute arises, the seller should adopt a proactive attitude to resolve it and minimize the negative impact of the dispute on themselves. Sellers need to do the following tasks well.

（一）及时沟通

Timely communication

纠纷具有较强的时效性，卖家如果不能及时做出回应，会逐渐形成不利局面。当卖家收到买家的疑问或负面反馈时，一定要第一时间回复，与买家进行友好协商。

Disputes have strong timeliness, and if sellers cannot respond in a timely manner, it will gradually lead to unfavorable situations. When sellers receive buyers' enquiries or negative feedback, they must respond promptly and engage in friendly negotiations with buyers.

若当买家迟迟未收到货物，卖家在可承受范围内可以给买家重新发送货物或采取其他替代方案。若买家对货物质量不满，卖家应与买家进行友好协商，让买家感觉到被重视，认识到卖家有解决问题的意愿，让纠纷解决有一个好的基础。

If the buyer has not received the goods for a long time, the seller can resend the goods to the buyer or adopt other alternative solutions within the acceptable range. If the buyer is dissatisfied with the quality of the goods, the seller should engage in friendly negotiations with the buyer to make them feel valued and recognize the seller's willingness to solve the problem, thereby establishing a good foundation for dispute resolution.

（二）保持礼貌

Maintain politeness

卖家应始终牢记以和为贵，就事论事，不意气用事，礼貌对待买家。不礼貌的态度会导致买家恼怒，甚至不配合纠纷解决。

Sellers should always remember that harmony is paramount, focus on the facts, avoid emotional reactions, and treat buyers politely. An impolite attitude can make buyers become angry and even lead them to refuse cooperation in disputes resolution.

（三）态度专业

Professional attitude

卖家与买家沟通要有专业的态度，英文表达力求完整、正确，应对买家所在国家和地区有一定的了解，了解海外买家的消费习惯以及相关政策、法律规定。

Sellers should have a professional attitude when communicating with buyers, strive for complete and correct English expression, have a certain understanding of the buyers' country and region, and understand the consumption habits of overseas buyers along with relevant policies and legal regulations.

沟通时要注意买家心理的变化。当买家不满意时，卖家应尽量满足买家一些其他的合理需求，引导买家保留订单。当买家要求退款时，尽量引导买家达成部分退款，避免全额退款退货。卖家应努力做到“尽管产品不能让买家满意，态度也要让买家无可挑剔”。

Sellers should pay attention to the psychological shifts of buyers when communicating. If a buyer expresses dissatisfaction, the seller should try to meet some other reasonable needs of the buyer and guide the buyer to keep the order. When a buyer requests a refund, the seller should persuade the buyer to receive a partial refund rather than full reimbursements. Sellers should strive to “maintain an impeccable attitude towards buyers, even when the product may not satisfy buyers”.

（四）将心比心

Empathize with others

卖家应多站在买家的角度考虑问题，出现问题要想办法解决，而不只是考虑自己的利益。“己所不欲，勿施于人”，谁都不愿意无故承受损失。卖家在可承受范围内尽量让买家减少损失，也会为自己赢得更多的合作机会。

Sellers should consider problems from the perspective of buyers, and find solutions when problems arise, rather than just considering their own interests. “Do unto others as you would have them do unto you.” No one is willing to bear losses for no reason. Sellers should try their best to minimize losses for buyers within their acceptable range, which will also help them win more opportunities for cooperation.

（五）保留证据

Retain evidence

卖家应尽量保留交易过程中的有效信息，出现纠纷时，这些信息作为证据，可帮助平台公平解决问题。

Sellers should try to retain valid information during the transaction process. In case of disputes, this information can be used as evidence to help the platform fairly resolve the issue.

第三节 重点短语与句型
Section 3 Key Phrases and Sentence Patterns

一、常用单词与短语
Common words and phrases

1. cross-border e-commerce customer communication 跨境电商客户沟通
2. intellectual property rights 知识产权
3. customer communication template 客户沟通模板
4. pre-sales communication 售前沟通
5. product information 产品信息
6. shipping costs 运费
7. inventory 库存
8. specifications and models 规格型号
9. usage 用途
10. place orders 下单
11. buyers visit the store 买家光顾店铺
12. order amount 订单金额
13. confirm orders 确认订单
14. goods shortage 货物断货
15. offer discounts 提供折扣
16. buyer bargaining 买家议价
17. mid-sales communication 售中沟通
18. logistics 物流
19. customs issues 海关问题
20. missing logistics information 物流信息缺失
21. logistics problems 物流问题
22. after-sales communication 售后沟通
23. return and exchange 退换货
24. customer confirms receipt 客户确认收货
25. product damage 产品损坏
26. positive feedback 积极评价
27. dispute resolution process 纠纷处理流程
28. basic process 基本流程
29. refund 退款
30. complaint 投诉
31. arbitration 裁决

32. dispute resolution status 纠纷裁决状态
33. evidence explanation 举证说明
34. deadline for providing evidence 限期举证
35. counter-evidence 反举证，反驳证据
36. tips for avoiding disputes 避免产生纠纷的技巧
37. goods not received 未收到货
38. effective communication 有效沟通
39. best logistics company 最优物流公司
40. goods not as agreed 货物与约定不符
41. product description 产品描述
42. customs clearance 海关清关
43. tax payment 缴税
44. product return 产品退回
45. eliminate counterfeit goods 杜绝假货
46. issues to be noted 需注意的问题
47. timely communication 及时沟通
48. empathize with others 将心比心

二、常用句型
Common sentence patterns

1. Hello, my dear friend, thank you for visiting our store.
您好，我亲爱的朋友，感谢您光临我们的商店。

2. If we don't have the item, please tell us and we will spare no effort to find it.
如果我们没有您要的商品，请告诉我们，我们会不遗余力地为您找到。

3. Thank you for your enquiry. Yes, we have this item in stock.
感谢您的咨询。是的，我们有这款商品的库存。

4. Because they are hot selling items, the product has a high risk of selling out soon.
因为它们是热销商品，所以很快就有可能售罄。

5. Thank you for your order. If you confirm the order as soon as possible, we will send a gift to you.
感谢您的订单，如果您能尽快确认订单，我们会赠送您一份礼物。

6. We are very sorry that item you ordered is out of stock at the moment.
非常抱歉，您订购的商品目前缺货。

7. We will contact the factory to see when it will be available again.
我们会联系工厂查看何时能再次供货。

8. We can offer you an ×% discount. Once we confirm your payment, we will ship out the items for you in time.
我们可以为您提供×%的折扣，一旦我们确认您的付款，我们会及时为您发货。

9. We are afraid we can't offer you that low price you bargained.

恐怕我们不能给您还价得那么低的价格。

10. After the customer places an order, send a confirmation form.

客户下单后发送确认单。

11. Your payment for item × has been received.

您对商品×的付款已收到。

12. The goods you need had been set on time. It's on the way now.

您需要的商品已经按时发出，现在在路上。

13. We received notice from the logistics company that your customs is currently conducting strict periodic inspections on large shipments.

我们接到物流公司的通知，现在贵国的海关对大量邮包进行定期的严格检查。

14. We have contacted the shipping company and confirmed the problem.

我们已经联系了货运公司并确认了问题。

15. We would like to confirm whether we sent the package on 16th, Oct. 2015.

我们想确认我们是否在 2015 年 10 月 16 日寄出了包裹。

16. If you are not satisfied with the products, we are sorry for the inconveniences.

如果您对产品不满意，我们为带来的不便表示歉意。

17. You can return the goods back to us.

您可以将商品退回给我们。

18. We are very happy that you have received the order.

我们很高兴您已经收到订单。

19. We hope that you are satisfied with the items and look forward to doing more business with you in future.

我们希望您对商品感到满意，并期待未来与您进行更多的生意。

20. It would be highly appreciated if you could leave us positive feedback.

如果您能给我们留下积极反馈，我们将不胜感激。

21. We are very sorry to hear that the product sent to you were damaged.

很抱歉听到发给您的产品有残损。

22. We will give you more discounts on your next purchase with us.

当您下次从我们这里购买时，我们将会给您更多的折扣。

23. Thank you for your purchase. We have prepared you some gifts which will be sent you along with the goods.

感谢您的购买，我们为您准备了一些赠品，将随商品一起发送给您。

24. Thank you for your positive comment.

感谢您的积极评价。

25. Your encouragement will keep us moving forward.

您的鼓励将使我们不断前进。

26. When the buyer applies for a refund or makes a complaint, the seller should first actively

mediate for negotiation.

当买家申请退款或提出投诉时，卖家应首先积极介入进行协商。

27. If the buyer and seller cannot reach an agreement within the platform's specified time, the platform can make a ruling.

如果买家和卖家不能在平台规定的时间内达成协议，平台可以做出裁决。

28. From the 4th to the 15th day after the buyer first submits a refund request, if the buyer and seller cannot reach an agreement through negotiation, the buyer can submit it to the platform for arbitration.

从买家第一次提交退款申请的第 4 天至第 15 天，如果买家和卖家不能通过协商达成一致，买家可以提交给平台进行仲裁。

29. Within 2 working days of the dispute resolution application, AliExpress will intervene and handle it.

纠纷裁决申请产生的 2 个工作日内，全球速卖通将介入处理。

30. If the existing evidence is sufficient, the appeal period will begin after the ruling opinion is directly given.

如果现有证据充足，平台直接给出裁决意见后，将进入申诉期。

31. If any party fails to provide proof within the deadline, AliExpress will issue a ruling based on the proof obtained and enter the appeal period.

如果任何一方未能在截止日期前提供证据，全球速卖通将根据已获得的证据做出裁决，并进入申诉期。

32. If the buyer and seller reach a consensus during the appeal period, AliExpress will make a ruling based on the opinions of both parties.

如果买家和卖家在申诉期内达成共识，全球速卖通将根据双方的意见做出裁决。

33. The resolution of disputes on AliExpress is carried out through the complaint and reporting platform.

全球速卖通的纠纷解决是通过投诉举报平台进行的。

34. Whoever complains shall provide evidence.

谁投诉谁举证。

35. If the complainant provides sufficient evidence, the dispute will be established.

如果投诉方提供充分的证据，纠纷将成立。

36. The platform will make a ruling based on the collected valid evidence.

平台将根据收集到的有效证据做出裁决。

37. Sellers can take corresponding measures to avoid these two types of disputes.

卖家可以采取相应的措施来避免这两类纠纷。

38. To effectively avoid disputes caused by "goods not received", sellers need to do a good job in selecting the best logistics service provider and effectively communicating with buyers.

为了有效避免因“未收到货物”而引起的纠纷，卖家要做好选择最优物流服务商及与买家有效沟通两个方面的工作。

39. Sellers should provide logistics tracking information, and if there are any logistics problems, they should promptly provide the specific situation of package delay to the buyer.

卖家应提供物流跟踪信息，如果有任何物流问题，应迅速向买家提供包裹延误的具体情况。

40. When describing a product, it is essential to provide a comprehensive and detailed description based on facts.

在描述产品时，必须基于事实提供全面和详细的描述。

41. Before shipping, the seller needs to conduct a thorough inspection of the product.

在发货前，卖家需要对产品进行全面检查。

42. If a buyer complains that the seller is "selling counterfeit goods" and the seller is unable to provide authorization proof for the product, the seller will be penalized by AliExpress.

如果买家投诉卖家"销售假货"，而卖家无法提供产品的授权证明，卖家将会受到全球速卖通的处罚。

43. Sellers should adopt a proactive attitude to resolve it and minimize the negative impact of the dispute on themselves.

卖家应采取积极的态度去解决纠纷，并尽量减少纠纷对自己的负面影响。

44. When sellers receive buyers' inquiries or negative feedback, they must respond promptly and engage in friendly negotiations with buyers.

当卖家收到买家的询问或负面反馈时，他们必须及时回应并与买家进行友好协商。

45. Sellers should always remember that harmony is paramount, focus on the facts, avoid emotional reactions, and treat buyers politely.

卖家应始终牢记以和为贵，就事论事，不意气用事，礼貌对待买家。

46. Sellers should have a professional attitude when communicating with buyers.

卖家和买家在沟通时应该持有专业的态度。

47. When the buyer is not satisfied, the seller should try to meet some other reasonable needs of the buyer and guide the buyer to keep the order.

当买家不满意时，卖家应尽量满足买家的其他合理需求，并引导买家保留订单。

48. Sellers should consider problems from the perspective of buyers, and find solutions when problems arise, rather than just considering their own interests.

卖家应该从买家的角度考虑问题，并在出现问题时寻找解决方案，而不仅仅是考虑自己的利益。

49. Sellers should try to retain valid information during the transaction process.

卖家应尽量保留交易过程中的有效信息。

50. In case of disputes, this information can be used as evidence to help resolve the issue fairly.

在出现纠纷的情况下，这些信息可以用作证据，帮助公平地解决问题。

课后练习

Ⅰ. 填空题。

Fill in the blanks.

1. Pre-sales communication is mainly aimed at answering customers' questions about ____________ information (such as price, quantity, inventory, specifications, usage), shipping costs, and other aspects.

2. If we don't have the item, please tell us and we will spare no effort to ____________ it.

3. Thank you for your enquiry. Yes, we have this item in ____________. How many do you want?

4. Because they are hot selling items, the product has a high risk of ____________ out soon.

5. Thank you for your order, if you confirm the order as soon as possible, we will send some ____________.

6. We are very sorry that the item you ordered is ____________ of stock at the moment.

7. We will contact the factory to see when it will be ____________ again.

8. We can offer you an ×% discount. once we confirm your payment, we will ____________ the items for you in time.

9. If the buyer and seller cannot reach an agreement within the platform's ____________ time, the platform can make a ruling.

10. From the 4th to the 15th day after the buyer first submits a refund request, if the buyer and seller cannot reach an agreement through negotiation, the buyer can submit it to the platform for ____________.

11. The resolution of disputes on AliExpress is conducted through the ____________ reporting platform.

12. Whoever ____________ shall provide evidence.

13. Sellers should provide logistics tracking information, and if there are any logistics problems, they should promptly provide the specific situation of package ____________ to the buyer.

14. When describing a product, it is essential to provide a comprehensive and detailed description based on ____________.

15. If a buyer complains that the seller is "selling counterfeit goods" and the seller is unable to provide authorization proof for the product, the seller will be ____________ by AliExpress.

Ⅱ. 写作。

Writing.

Suppose you are the customer service representative of an online store that specializes in cross-border e-commerce. Write an email to a customer who has recently placed an order for a product that is currently out of stock. In your email, you should:

1. Express apology for the inconvenience caused by the out-of-stock situation.

2. Provide an estimated time frame for when the product might be available again.

3. Offer alternative product suggestions that are similar in style and function.

4. Include a discount offer as a gesture of goodwill for the inconvenience.

5. End the email with a polite request for the customer's understanding and any further assistance they might need.

第十一章 Chapter 11 贸易展会 Trade Fair

贸易展会是一种有组织的展览活动，旨在为特定行业的企业提供展示和演示其产品与服务的平台。它是建立和维护客户关系的有效途径之一。在数字化日益普及的今天，贸易展会是能让买家、卖家和产品实现物理结合的重要媒介，具有强大的商业影响力。贸易展会提供了一个高度灵活的环境，能够实现广泛的销售和营销目标。

学习目标

1. 了解如何在贸易展会上招待跨境电商客户。
2. 熟悉贸易展会上的商务礼仪。
3. 掌握贸易展会上与客户展开沟通的方法与技巧。

思政目标

1. 学习展会礼仪，提升个人修养。
2. 学习沟通技巧，增强沟通能力。
3. 学习展会案例，拓展市场视野。

第一节 Section 1 贸易展会礼仪与沟通 Etiquette and Communication at Trade Fairs

一、概述
Overview

国际贸易中最重要的问题是如何寻找客户。买家想知道卖家在哪里，而卖家想知道在哪里可以找到买家。

The most important issue in international trade is how to find customers. The buyer wants to know where the seller is, while the seller wants to know where to find the buyer.

一般来说，大多数商品（石油和稀有金属等极少数重要材料除外）处于买方市场。大多数国家实行外汇管制。除此之外，由于对外贸易中的出口许可和商品限制政策，出口商比进口商更难寻找客户。无论是出口公司还是生产出口商品的工厂，都应该珍惜每一个了解国外同行信息的机会，可以通过银行、外国商会、商务参赞处、交易展会、广告及互联网等渠道建立联系。

Generally speaking, most commodities (except for a few critical materials such as oil and rare metals) are in a buyer's market. Most countries implement foreign exchange controls. In addition, foreign trade policies such as export licensing and product restrictions make it more difficult for exporters to seek customers than importers. Both export companies and factories that produce goods for export should cherish every opportunity to gather information about their foreign counterparts, which can be obtained through banks, foreign chambers of commerce, commercial counselor offices, trade fairs, advertising, the Internet, and other channels.

二、贸易展会礼仪
Trade fair etiquette

贸易展会是建立和维护客户关系的有效媒介之一。它提供了高度灵活的环境，可以实现广泛的销售和营销目标。因此，在贸易展会上适当的礼仪将大大提高成功率。以下是一些贸易展会礼仪规则。

Trade fairs are one of the most effective mediums for establishing and maintaining customer relationships. They provide a highly flexible environment that can achieve a wide range of sales and marketing goals. Therefore, proper etiquette at trade fairs will greatly increase the success rate. Here are some etiquette rules for trade fairs.

（一）问候和肢体语言
Greetings and body language

以下问候和肢体语言将有助于传达专业和平易近人的态度：

（1）在展台前站起来迎接与会者。

（2）如果需要座位，请使用高凳子，以便在站立时进行眼神交流。

（3）微笑并与来自四面八方的与会者进行眼神交流。

（4）和与会者交谈，而不是与同事交谈。

（5）只有当你和一个也想坐下的客户在一起时，才坐下。

（6）不要交叉双臂或双腿。

（7）请注意展位内和您所在空间附近的其他人。

（8）请勿进入其他参展商的展位。

（9）感谢与会者在抵达和离开时花时间在您的展位上。

The following greetings and body language will help convey a professional and approachable demeanor:

(1) Stand up to greet attendees in front of the booth.

(2) If seats are needed, use tall stools that allow for eye contact at standing eye level.

(3) Smile and make eye contact with attendees approaching from all directions.

(4) Speak with attendees, not colleagues.

(5) Sit down only if you are with a client who also wants to sit.

(6) Do not cross arms or legs.

(7) Be mindful of other people in the booth and near your space.

(8) Do not enter the space of another exhibitor.

(9) Thank attendees for spending time at your booth when they arrive and leave.

(二) 展位内工作人员不得携带食物或饮料

No food or beverages for staff in the booth

常见的贸易展会礼仪违规行为之一是将食物和饮料放在展位内供个人消费。

One of the most common trade fair booth etiquette violations occurs when food and drink are kept within the booth for personal consumption.

展位内工作人员应避免在展台内进食、饮水和嚼口香糖。

Staff shall avoid eating, drinking and chewing gum within the booth.

(三) 员工工作时间

Staff working hours

贸易展会工作人员通常负责展位搭建，应该尽早到达，以确保所有材料都得到妥善展示，并为与会者做好服务。

Trade fair staff, who are usually responsible for booth construction, should arrive early enough to ensure all materials are properly displayed and ready to assist attendees.

(四) 吸引与会者

Attract attendees

与会者参加贸易展会是有原因的，因此展位工作人员快速介绍自己并精准提问是非常重要的。

Attendees come to trade fairs with specific objectives, so it is important for booth staff to quickly introduce themselves and ask precisely targeted questions.

(五) 着装要求

Dress code

展位工作人员的基本着装要求是得体而清洁，同时考虑公司文化和展会主题。

The basic dress code for booth staff is appropriate and neat, while taking into account both company culture and the theme of trade fair.

(六) 展位设置和维护

Booth setup and maintenance

不美观的箱子和用品存放在展览区外存放额外用品的位置。展览空间应该始终保持良好状态（包括地板），垃圾不应出现在视线范围内。

The unattractive boxes and supplies shall be stored in a location outside the exhibit area where additional supplies are stored. It is important that the space appear well maintained at all times (including the floor), and trash should not be anywhere within view.

第二节 贸易展会沟通案例
Section 2 Communication Cases at Trade Fairs

对话一、谈论交易会
Dialogue 1 Talking about the trade fair

罗宾斯先生和约翰正在讨论贸易展会。（A：约翰；B：罗宾斯先生）

A：早上好，罗宾斯先生。

B：早上好，约翰。最近怎么样？

A：还不错，我正在阅读一些关于贸易展会的文章。我想问您几个问题。参加贸易展会，我能得到哪些收获呢？

B：你可以通过贸易展会来推广你的产品或服务。这样你可以直接向客户展示你的产品或服务，从而获得他们的反馈和了解他们的需求。

A：我明白了。

B：此外，贸易展会也是建立新业务的好机会，因为许多潜在的客户和供应商都聚集在一个地方。

A：好的，谢谢。我想知道，如果我想参加贸易展会，最重要的是什么？

B：作为参展商，选择合适的贸易展会非常关键。如果展会过于专业或过于广泛，可能无法吸引到你的目标客户，这样参加展会是浪费时间。因此，在参加展会时，你需要明确你的目标客户群和你希望通过参展实现的目标。

A：还有其他需要注意的事项吗？

B：还有一点，你应该设定具体和可衡量的目标。如果你仔细选择展会，并给自己足够的时间来规划目标，你就有很大的机会取得商业成功。

A：很好。您真是专家，谢谢。

B：不客气，约翰。顺便说一下，现在正在举行一个 IT 贸易展会。去看看可能是个好主意，你可以了解一下行业动态。

Mr. Robbins and John are talking about trade fair. (A: John; B: Mr. Robbins)

A: Good morning, Mr. Robbins.

B: Good morning, John. How is it going?

A: Not too bad, I'm reading some articles about trade fairs. I'd like to ask you some questions. What benefits can I expect if I exhibit at trade fairs?

B: Well, you can use trade fairs to promote your products or services. They offer you a chance to demonstrate your products or services to customers face-to-face, which allow you to get feedback and find out what customers want.

A: I see.

B: Trade fairs are also good opportunities for building new business, as many potential customers and suppliers are gathered in one place.

A：OK, thank you. I wonder what's the most important thing to know about if I want to exhibit at a trade fair?

B：As an exhibitor, choosing the right trade fair is essential. If the trade fair is too specialized or too broad, it's unlikely to attract your target customers, making participation a waste of time. Therefore, when you attend a trade fair, you should make sure you know what kind of customers you want to reach and what you want to achieve.

A：Anything else I should know?

B：One more thing. You should make specific and measurable goals. If you choose your fair carefully and give yourself plenty of time to plan your goals, you'll have a good chance of doing good business.

A：Good. You really are a specialist. Thank you.

B：You're welcome, John. By the way, there's an IT trade show being held now. It might be a good idea for you to go and have a look. You'd get an idea of what's going on.

对话二、展会前获取信息
Dialogue 2　Getting information before the trade fair

在中国进出口商品交易会（又称广交会）之前，马先生正在向他的朋友王先生询问有关展会的一些有用信息。（A：马先生；B：王先生）

A：我们想让更多外国朋友了解我们的产品，所以想参加一些国际性的贸易展会。

B：这是个好主意。实际上，这是一个让人们了解我们公司和产品的绝佳机会。

A：我明白了。听说你们公司去年也参加了？

B：是的，非常成功。

A：能告诉我更多关于展会的情况吗？你觉得展会效果如何？

B：在我看来，展会非常成功。许多人对我们的产品表现出了浓厚的兴趣。

A：你觉得展会对销售有帮助吗？

B：当然，你还可以通过展会接触到很多销售人员和参展商。

A：成功的因素有哪些？能分享下你参加展会的经验吗？

B：首先，准备工作要充分。你还需要布置一个吸引人的展位，准备一些小礼物，并且可以对你的产品进行展示。

A：是的，为展会做好充分准备是确保成功的第一步。来参加这次展会的人都是来自世界各地的非常重要的人物，他们都是我们的潜在买家。我们必须热烈欢迎他们。顺便问一下，展会什么时候举行？

B：展会将于 22 日和 23 日举行，持续两天。

A：那么注册的截止日期是什么时候？

B：12 月 15 日。

A：非常感谢。

B：实际上，你可以在互联网上获取今年和明年主要展览的时间表，并且可以查看参展费用。

Before the China Import and Export Fair, Mr. Ma is asking some useful information about the Fair from his friend Mr. Wang. (A: Mr. Ma; B: Mr. Wang)

A: In order to let more foreign friends know about our products, we'd like to take part in some international trade fairs.

B: Good idea. In fact, it's really a good opportunity to let people know about our company and our products.

A: I see. I was told your company participated last year?

B: Yes. It was a great success.

A: Could you tell me more about the fair? How did the fair go?

B: In my opinion, it went well. A lot of people showed great interest in our products.

A: Do you think the show will help your sales?

B: Yes, definitely. You can contact a lot of salesmen and exhibitors through the trade fairs, too.

A: What are the factors for success? Can you share your experience in attending the trade fair?

B: Well, the first thing is a good preparation. You also need to design an attractive display of the booth, prepare some small gifts and make a presentation of your products as well.

A: Yes. Making good preparations for a trade fair is the first step to ensure success. The people coming to this show are all very important people from all over the world, and they are our potential buyers. We must roll out the red carpet to extend our warmest welcome. By the way, when will the fair be held?

B: The fair is to be held on the 22nd and the 23rd for two days.

A: What's the deadline for registration?

B: December 15.

A: Thank you very much.

B: Actually, you can get the main fairs schedule for this year and next year from the Internet and you can check the cost of attendance as well.

对话三、展会期间

Dialogue 3 During the trade fair

史密斯先生来到了李女士的展位，李女士正在向史密斯先生介绍产品相关信息。(A：李女士；B：史密斯先生)

A：早上好，先生，欢迎光临我们的展位。这些是我们最新研发的产品样品，有多种型号、尺寸和颜色供您选择。请随意看看。

B：谢谢。

A：我们大厅里还有一个研讨会，我们的工程师将为您进行产品演示。看完演示后，您就会知道如何使用我们的产品。

B：我很想看看。

(观看演示后)

A：您觉得我们的产品怎么样？

B：非常新颖。

A：我们参加展会的主要目的是推广我们的产品。这确实是一个让人们了解我们公司的好机会，同时我们也从其他参展商那里学到了一些东西。

B：中国产品确实很好，但价格太高了。

A：嗯，我们当然首先要考虑质量。当然，如果您想大量购买，我们可以给您一个折扣。我们也希望尽快与您进行商务洽谈。

B：好的，我会考虑的。嗯，我想先去其他展位看看，找一些我想订购的其他产品，然后我会回来。

A：请便。

B：我能要一个这些样品吗？

A：抱歉，这是最后一批样品了。但我稍后会为您准备一些。请给我您的名片好吗？

B：好的，这是我的名片。

A：这是我的名片。您也可以在我们给您的宣传册或商业目录中找到我们的电话号码和电子邮件地址。您住在哪家酒店？您的房间号是多少？我今晚会把样品送到您的酒店。

B：好的。我会写下来给你。

A：晚上见。

B：到时候见。

Mr. Smith has come to the booth of Ms. Li, and Ms. Li is introducing something about the products to Mr. Smith. (A: Ms. Li; B: Mr. Smith)

A: Good morning, sir, welcome to our booth. These are the samples of our newly-developed products. There are different models, sizes and colors for you to choose from. Please have a look.

B: Thank you.

A: We also have a symposium in the hall. Our engineer will give you a demonstration. After seeing the demonstration, you'll know how to use our products.

B: I'd love to watch it.

(After watching)

A: What do you think of our products?

B: Very innovative.

A: Our main purpose for coming to the fair is to promote our products. It's really a good opportunity to let people know about our company while learning from other exhibitors.

B: The Chinese products are really good, but the prices are quite high.

A: Well, we should consider the quality first. Of course, if you want to buy a large quantity, we can give you a discount. We also hope to have a business talk with you soon.

B: OK, I'll think it over. Well, I'd like to visit other booths first to find some other items I'd like to order, then I'll come back.

A: You may, please.

B: May I have one of these samples?

A: Sorry. They are the only ones left. But I'll get some for you later. May I have your name card please?

B：Yes, here is my business card.

A：This is mine. You can also find our telephone number and email address in the brochure I have given you or from the business directory. Which hotel are you staying at? What's your room number? I'll send the samples to your hotel this evening.

B：OK. I'll write it down for you.

A：See you this evening.

B：See you then.

对话四、展会结束后获取反馈

Dialogue 4 Getting feedback information after the fair

为了下次贸易展会的进一步改进，魏女士正在尝试从她的买家那里获取一些反馈信息。（A：魏女士；B：马先生）

A：早上好，马先生，自从上次展会结束后，我一直在尝试联系您。我对展会上看到的产品印象非常深刻。

B：非常感谢。今天我能为您做些什么？

A：今天我首先在这里感谢您对我们在展会上产品的关注。

B：不用谢。

A：请给我们一些建议来改进。

B：嗯，首先我们应该感谢您在展会上向我们展示了您最新的产品。我从展会上购买的产品销售情况很好。但是关于包装，尤其是外包装，恐怕您需要做一些改进。

A：是的。感谢您的及时反馈。我们将尽力满足您的需求。我也希望我们能够保持联系，并在未来密切合作。

B：当然。

A：您计划参加明年的展会吗？

B：当然。我们将在展会期间在中心位置拥有相同的展位，如果您去那里，您不会错过的。

A：好的，没问题。您认为我们是否也应该参加其他一些展会，例如中国东部家具博览会，或者其他博览会？

B：是的，我认为应该。我们省与南非的贸易量正在增长，尤其是在家用电器方面。我们也希望逐步扩大与外国国家的经济合作。

A：好主意。下一次家用电器展会仍然在琶洲新综合体举行。您现在可以开始准备了。

B：好的，谢谢您的分享。

For further improvement of the next trade fair, Ms. Wei is trying to get some feedback information from her buyer after the fair.（A：Ms. Wei；B：Mr. Ma）

A：Good morning, Mr. Ma, I have been trying to contact you since the trade fair. I was very impressed with what I had seen at the exhibition.

B：Thank you very much. What can I do for you today?

A: Today I'm here first to thank you for your interest in our products at the trade fair.

B: Don't mention it.

A: Please give us some suggestions for improvement.

B: Well, first we should say thank you very much for showing us your latest products at the fair. The products I bought from you at the fair are selling well. But as to the packaging, especially the outer packing, I'm afraid you need to do something.

A: Yes. Thank you for your timely feedback. We'll try our best to meet your needs. I also hope we'll keep in touch with each other and cooperate closely in the future.

B: Sure.

A: Do you plan to go to the fair next year?

B: Definitely. We shall have the same booth in the center during the show, you can't miss it if you go there.

A: Sure, no problem. Do you think we should attend some other fairs, too, such as the East China Furniture Expo, or some other Expos?

B: Yes, I think so. The business volume of our province with South Africa is growing, especially in household electrical appliances. We also hope gradually to enlarge the scope of economic cooperation with foreign countries.

A: Good idea. The next fair for household electrical appliances will still be in the New Complex at Pazhou. You may start preparations now.

B: OK, thanks for sharing.

第三节 Section 3　重点短语与句型 Key Phrases and Sentence Patterns

一、常用单词与短语 Common words and phrases

1. trade fair　贸易展会
2. etiquette　礼仪
3. rich assortment　花色繁多
4. attractive and durable　美观耐用
5. complete in specifications　规格齐全
6. modern and elegant in fashion　样式新颖大方
7. ranks first among similar products　居同类产品之首
8. buyer's market　买方市场
9. foreign exchange controls　外汇管制
10. a sound business partner　很好的贸易伙伴

11. business scope 经营范围
12. commercial credit 商业信用
13. to form a picture of the company 对公司的粗略了解
14. foreign chambers of commerce 外国商会
15. Business Advisory Offices 商务顾问办公室
16. trade fairs and exhibitions 交易会和展览
17. sales and marketing goals 销售和营销目标
18. body language 肢体语言
19. eye contact 眼神交流
20. booth space 展位空间
21. exhibitors 参展商
22. staff working hours 员工工作时间
23. booth construction 展位搭建
24. dress code 着装要求
25. company uniforms 公司制服
26. trade fair booth theme 贸易展位主题
27. booth setup 展位设置
28. attracting attendees 吸引与会者
29. products and services 产品与服务
30. IT trade show IT 贸易展
31. the China Import and Export Fair 广交会
32. registration deadline 注册截止日期
33. exposition schedule 展会日程
34. cost of attendance 参展费用
35. to have a very high regard for... 对……有很高的评价
36. to hold something in the highest esteem 对……推崇备至
37. trade reputation 贸易声誉

二、常用句型

Common sentence patterns

1. The most important issue in international trade is how to find customers.
国际贸易中最重要的问题是如何寻找客户。

2. The buyer wants to know where the seller is, while the seller wants to know where to find the buyer.
买家想知道卖家在哪里，而卖家想知道在哪里可以找到买家。

3. Exporters have a harder time seeking customers than importers.
出口商比进口商更难寻求客户。

4. Trade fairs are one of the most effective media for establishing and maintaining customer

relationships.

贸易展会是建立和维护客户关系的最有效媒介之一。

5. Proper etiquette at trade fairs will greatly increase the success rate.

在贸易展会上适当的礼仪将大大提高成功率。

6. Attendees are looking to the exhibit staff for a reason to spend time at that booth.

与会者希望展览工作人员有理由在该展位停留。

7. No food or beverages for staff in the booth.

展位内工作人员不得携带食物或饮料。

8. Trade fair staff are usually responsible for booth construction and should arrive early.

贸易展工作人员通常负责展位搭建，他们应该尽早到达。

9. It is important to highlight the exhibition time and ensure that representatives remain at the booth after the scheduled time has ended.

重要的是要突出展会时间，并确保在预定时间结束后，代表仍留在展位上。

10. It is important for booth staff to quickly introduce themselves and ask attendees questions.

展台工作人员快速介绍自己并快速向与会者提问是非常重要的。

11. Clothing helps to enhance the theme of trade fair booths and should also be seen as a sign of respect for exhibition organizers and attendees.

服装有助于强化贸易展展位主题，也应被视为对展会组织者和与会者的尊重。

12. It is important that the space appear well maintained at all times, and trash should not be anywhere within view.

展览空间应该始终保持良好状态，垃圾不应出现在视线范围内。

13. I'm reading some articles about trade fairs. I'd like to ask you some questions.

我正在阅读一些关于贸易展会的文章，想问你一些问题。

14. What benefits can I expect if I exhibit at trade fairs?

参加贸易展会，我能得到哪些收获呢?

15. You can use trade fairs to promote your products or services.

你可以利用贸易展会来推广你的产品或服务。

16. Trade fairs are also good opportunities for building new business.

贸易展会也为你提供了建立新业务的好机会。

17. As an exhibitor, choosing the right trade fair is essential.

作为参展商，选择合适的贸易展会是至关重要的。

18. You should make specific and measurable goals.

你应该设定具体和可衡量的目标。

19. We'd like to take part in some international trade fairs in order to let more foreign friends know about our products.

我们希望参加一些国际贸易展会，以便让更多外国朋友了解我们的产品。

20. Did your company participate last year?

你们公司去年参加了吗?

21. In my opinion, it went well.

我认为展会进行得很顺利。

22. Do you think the fair will help your sales?

你们认为展会对你们的销售有帮助吗？

23. You can contact a lot of salesmen and exhibitors through the trade fairs.

你们可以通过贸易展会接触很多销售人员和参展商。

24. You also need to prepare some small gifts.

你们也需要准备一些小礼物。

25. You can make a presentation of your products as well.

你们可以为产品做一个展示。

26. The people coming to this show are all very important people from all over the world, and they are our potential buyers.

展会的参展人员都是来自世界各地的重要人士，他们是我们的潜在买家。

27. The exhibition is to be held on the 22nd and the 23rd for two days.

展会将在 22 日和 23 日举行两天。

28. The deadline for registration is December 15.

注册截止日期是 12 月 15 日。

29. You can get the main exhibitions scheduled for this year and next year from the Internet and you can check the cost of attendance as well.

您可以从互联网上获取今年和明年的主要展览日程表，也可以查看参会费用。

30. Good morning, sir, welcome to our booth. These are the samples of our newly developed products.

先生，早上好，欢迎来到我们的展位，这些是我们新开发产品的样品。

31. We also have a symposium in the hall. Our engineer will give you a demonstration.

我们还将在大厅举办一个研讨会，我们的工程师将为您做演示。

32. Our main purpose for coming to the fair is to let more people know about our products.

我们来参加展会的主要目的是让更多人了解我们的产品。

33. Through the fair we learned something from other exhibitors.

通过展会我们还从其他参展商那里学到了一些东西。

34. The Chinese products are really good, but the prices are too high.

中国产品确实不错，但价格太高了。

35. We should consider the quality first. Of course, if you want to buy a large quantity, we can give you a discount.

我们应该首先考虑质量。当然，如果您想大批量购买，我们可以给您折扣。

36. We also hope to have a business talk with you soon.

我们也希望尽快与您进行商务洽谈。

37. I'd like to go to other booths to see more first and find some other items I'd like to order, and then I'll come back.

我想先去其他展位看看，挑选一些需要订购的品类，之后再回来找您。

38. Can I have one of these samples?

我可以拿一个样品吗？

39. Sorry, they are the only ones left, but I'll get some for you later.

对不起，这些样品只剩最后几个了，但我稍后会为您准备一些。

40. May I have your name card please?

请给我您的名片好吗？

41. This is mine. You can also find our telephone number and email address in the brochure I have given you or from the business directory.

这是我的名片，您也可以在我们给您的宣传册或商业目录中找到我们的电话号码和电子邮件地址。

42. Which hotel are you staying at? What's your room number?

您住在哪家酒店？房间号是多少？

43. I'll send the samples to your hotel this evening.

我今晚会把样品送到您的酒店。

44. For further improvement at the next trade fair, I'm trying to get some feedback information from my buyer.

为了进一步改进下一次贸易展会，我正在尝试从买家那里获取一些反馈信息。

45. I was very impressed with what I had seen at the exhibition.

我对您在展会上展示的最新产品印象深刻。

46. Thank you for your interest in our products at the trade fair.

感谢您在展会上对我们产品的关注。

47. Please give us some suggestions for improvement.

请给我们一些改进建议。

48. We should say thank you very much for showing us your latest products at the show.

我们应该感谢您在展会上向我们展示了最新产品。

49. The goods I bought from you at the fair are selling well.

我从您那里购买的产品销售得很好。

50. But as to the packaging, especially the outer packing, I'm afraid you need to do something.

但是关于包装，尤其是外包装，我认为你们需要做一些改进。

51. Thank you for your timely feedback. We'll try our best to meet your needs.

感谢您的及时反馈，我们会尽力满足您的需求。

52. I also hope we'll keep in touch with each other and cooperate closely in the future.

我也希望我们能保持联系，并在未来密切合作。

53. Do you plan to go to the fair next year?

你们计划明年参加展会吗？

54. Definitely, we shall have the same booth in the center during the show. You can't miss it if you go there.

当然，我们将在展会中心拥有相同的展位。如果您去那里，就不可能错过它。

55. Do you think we should attend some other fairs, too, such as the East China Furniture Expo or some other expos?

你们认为我们还应该参加其他一些展会吗？比如中国东部家具博览会或其他一些博览会？

56. Yes, I think so. The business volume of our province with South Africa is growing, especially in household electrical appliances.

是的，我认为应该。我们省与南非的业务量正在增长，尤其是在家用电器方面。

57. We also hope gradually to enlarge the scope of economic cooperation with foreign countries.

我们也希望逐步扩大与外国的经济合作范围。

课后练习

Ⅰ. 选词填空。

Fill in the blanks with the appropriate words.

(stored; construction; find; mediums; buyer's; booth)

1. The most important issue in international trade is how to ____________ customers.

2. Generally speaking, most commodities are in a ____________ market.

3. Trade fairs are one of the most effective ____________ for establishing and maintaining customer relationships.

4. One of the most common trade fair booth etiquette violations occurs when food and drink are kept within the ____________ for personal consumption.

5. Trade fair staff, who are usually responsible for booth ____________, should arrive early.

6. The unattractive boxes and supplies, shall be stored in a location outside the exhibit area where additional supplies are ____________.

Ⅱ. 简答题。

Short answer questions.

1. Why is it essential for exhibitors to choose the right trade fair?

2. What are some key etiquette rules that exhibitors should follow at trade fairs to enhance their interaction with attendees?

Ⅲ. 写作题。

Writing.

As the marketing manager of a company, you are responsible for organizing your company's participation in an upcoming international trade fair. Write a report detailing how you will prepare for this trade fair, including design, product selection, staff arrangements, and expected goals. In your report, you should:

1. Describe the theme and layout of the booth design, and how it will attract the attention of potential customers.

2. Explain how you will select the products to be displayed, highlighting the company's core products and technological advantages.

3. Discuss how you will arrange the exhibition staff, including their responsibilities and training plans.

第十二章 商务谈判
Chapter 12 Business Negotiation

谈判无处不在。在现代社会中，随着人们交往日益密切，需要谈判协调的事务也大大增多，谈判成为必须具备的基本能力。商务谈判作为一种有效的协调手段，越来越多地被运用到社会生活的各个领域。随着国际标准化活动的迅猛发展，商务谈判在国际标准化活动中不仅是推动标准制定的关键步骤，更是促进国际经济合作与发展的重要桥梁。本章内容主要包括商务谈判的内涵与特点、商务谈判的基本流程、商务谈判的技巧、国际标准提案谈判案例等几部分内容，通过对商务谈判在参与国际标准化活动中的应用案例分析，帮助学生了解、运用商务谈判高效开展国际标准化活动。

学习目标

1. 掌握商务谈判的内涵与特点。
2. 熟悉商务谈判的基本流程。
3. 熟悉商务谈判的技巧。
4. 了解国际标准提案谈判信文的写作方法。

思政目标

1. 了解法律法规，增强法律意识。
2. 注重团队协作，培养团队合作精神。

第一节 商务谈判概述
Section 1 Overview of Business Negotiations

一、商务谈判的内涵与特点
The connotation and characteristics of business negotiation

（一）商务谈判的内涵
Connotation of business negotiation

商务谈判是指不同利益群体之间，为了实现各自的经济利益目标，就涉及双方利益的标的物或问题，通过沟通、协商、妥协等方式，达成双方均可接受的协议或合同的过程。它不仅仅是简单的讨价还价，更是一个涉及经济、法律、文化、心理等多方面因素的综合性交流与博弈过程，旨在通过合理的资源配置和利益分配，实现双方或多方的共赢局面，促进商业活动的顺利开展和经济的持续发展。

Business negotiation refers to the process between different interest groups to achieve their respective economic benefit goals, involving the subjects or issues related to both parties' interests. Through communication, consultation, compromise, and other methods, they reach an agreement or contract that is acceptable to both parties. It is not merely a simple bargaining process; rather, it is a comprehensive exchange and game involving multiple factors such as economics, law, culture, and psychology. The aim is to achieve a win-win situation for both or multiple parties through reasonable resource allocation and benefit distribution, thereby promoting the smooth conduct of business activities and the sustainable development of the economy.

（二）商务谈判的特点

Characteristics of business negotiation

1. 利益性

Interest orientation

商务谈判的核心目的是获取经济利益。各方参与谈判都是为了满足自身在成本、利润、市场份额、资源获取等方面的利益需求。

The core purpose of business negotiation is to obtain economic benefits. All parties involved in the negotiation aim to satisfy their own interests in terms of cost, profit, market share, resource acquisition, and other needs.

2. 复杂性

Complexity

首先，谈判主体可能来自不同的地区、国家，具有不同的文化背景、价值观和商业习惯，这增加了沟通与理解的难度。其次，谈判内容往往涉及复杂的技术、法律、财务等专业知识，需要谈判人员具备跨领域的知识储备和专业素养。最后，谈判过程中受到市场环境、政治局势、行业竞争等多种外部因素的影响，这些因素的动态变化使得谈判局势更加复杂难测，需要谈判者能够敏锐地捕捉信息并及时调整策略。

Firstly, the negotiating parties may come from different regions and countries, with diverse cultural backgrounds, values, and business practices, which increases the difficulty of communication and understanding. Secondly, the content of the negotiations often involves complex technical, legal, and financial expertise, requiring negotiators to have cross-domain knowledge and professional qualities. Finally, the negotiation process is influenced by various external factors such as market environment, political situation, and industry competition. The dynamic changes in these factors make the negotiation situation more complex and unpredictable, requiring negotiators to be able to keenly capture information and adjust strategies in a timely manner.

3. 易变性

Volatility

商务谈判过程中，各种情况随时可能发生变化。一方面，谈判双方的态度、立场和需求可能因内部决策调整、外部信息影响等因素而改变；另一方面，市场行情、竞争对手动态等外部环境的变化也会对谈判产生冲击，导致谈判的方向、重点和节奏发生变化。

In the process of business negotiations, various situations can change at any time. On one hand, the attitudes, positions, and needs of the negotiating parties may change due to internal decision adjustments and external information influences; on the other hand, changes in the external environment such as market conditions and competitor dynamics can also impact the negotiations, leading to changes in the direction, focus, and pace of the negotiations.

4. 合作性与竞争性并存

Coexistence of cooperation and competition

虽然谈判各方都有各自的利益目标，但在现代商务活动中，纯粹的竞争关系往往难以达成理想的谈判结果。因此，谈判过程中既有竞争的一面，各方都想争取更多的利益份额；又有合作的一面，因为只有通过合作，实现资源互补、风险共担，才能创造更大的价值，实现共同的商业目标。

Although all negotiating parties have their own interest objectives, in modern business activities, a purely competitive relationship often fails to achieve ideal negotiation outcomes. Therefore, the negotiation process involves both competitive and cooperative aspects. On one hand, each party wants to strive for a larger share of benefits; on the other hand, there is a need for cooperation, as only through collaboration, by complementing resources and sharing risks, can greater value be created and common business goals be achieved.

二、商务谈判的基本流程

Basic process of business negotiation

(一) 商务谈判准备工作

Preparations for business negotiation

1. 收集与分析信息

Collect and analyze information

全面收集对方的基本信息，包括企业规模、经营状况、财务状况、市场声誉、企业文化等，以便了解对方的实力和可能的谈判立场。深入研究谈判标的物的相关信息，如产品或服务的技术参数、质量标准、市场价格波动范围、行业竞争态势等，为确定合理的谈判目标和策略提供依据。同时，关注宏观环境信息，如国家政策法规、经济形势、行业发展趋势等，这些因素可能对谈判产生间接但重要的影响。

Thoroughly gather basic information about the other party, including the scale of the enterprise, operational status, financial condition, market reputation, and corporate culture, in order to understand their strength and potential negotiation positions. Delve into the relevant information about the subject of negotiation, such as the technical specifications of products or services, quality standards, market price fluctuation ranges, and industry competitive landscape, to provide a basis for setting reasonable negotiation objectives and strategies. At the same time, pay attention to macro-environmental information, such as national policies and regulations, economic conditions, and industry development trends, as these factors may have an indirect but significant impact on the negotiation.

2. 确定谈判目标与策略

Set negotiation objectives and strategies

谈判目标应分为不同层次，包括理想目标、可接受目标和最低限度目标。理想目标是在谈判中争取达到的最优结果，但具有一定的挑战性；可接受目标是在正常情况下通过合理谈判能够实现的目标，具有较高的可行性；最低限度目标是谈判的底线，一旦突破这个底线，谈判可能陷入僵局甚至破裂。根据谈判目标和对对方的信息分析，制定相应的谈判策略，如报价策略、让步策略、僵局处理策略等。

Negotiation objectives should be divided into different levels, including the ideal objective, the acceptable objective and the minimum objective. The ideal objective is the best result that one strives to achieve in the negotiation, but it is somewhat challenging; the acceptable objective is the objective that can be achieved through reasonable negotiation under normal circumstances and is highly feasible; the minimum objective is the bottom line in the negotiation, and once this line is breached, the negotiation may reach an impasse or even collapse. Based on the negotiation objectives and the analysis of the other party's information, formulate corresponding negotiation strategies such as bidding strategies, concession strategies, and deadlock resolution strategies.

3. 组建谈判团队

Build a negotiation team

高效的谈判团队应包括主谈判手、技术专家、财务专家、法律顾问等不同角色。主谈判手负责掌控谈判节奏、协调团队成员、与对方进行主要的沟通和协商，需要具备出色的沟通能力、应变能力和决策能力；技术专家能够解答谈判中涉及的技术问题，确保谈判在技术层面的准确性和可行性；财务专家负责对谈判中的成本、价格、利润等财务因素进行分析和核算，为谈判提供财务支持和建议；法律顾问则保障谈判过程和协议的合法性，防范法律风险，审查合同条款的法律合规性。

An effective negotiation team should include various roles such as the lead negotiator, technical experts, financial experts, and legal advisors. The lead negotiator is responsible for controlling the pace of the negotiation, coordinating team members, and conducting the main communication and consultation with the other party, requiring excellent communication skills, adaptability, and decision-making abilities. Technical experts can answer technical questions involved in the negotiation to ensure the accuracy and feasibility of the negotiation on the technical level. Financial experts are responsible for analyzing and calculating financial factors such as costs, prices, and profits in the negotiation, providing financial support and advice. Legal advisors ensure the legality of the negotiation process and agreements, guard against legal risks, and review the legal compliance of contract terms.

4. 制定谈判计划与议程

Formulate negotiation plans and agendas

谈判计划应详细规划谈判的步骤、时间安排和资源分配，明确各个阶段的主要任务和目标。谈判议程则确定谈判的先后顺序和讨论的议题，一般包括开场致辞、谈判主题的讨论、中场休息、关键问题的磋商、结束阶段等环节。合理的谈判议程可以引导谈判的方向，掌握谈判的主动权，营造良好的谈判氛围。

The negotiation plan should detail the steps, scheduling, and resource allocation of the negotiation, clarifying the main tasks and objectives at each stage. The negotiation agenda determines the order of discussion and the topics to be covered, typically including opening remarks, discussion of negotiation topics, breaks, consultation on key issues, and the concluding phase. A well-structured negotiation agenda can guide the direction of the negotiation, take the initiative, and create a favorable atmosphere for the negotiation.

（二）商务谈判的四个阶段

The four phases of business negotiation

1. 开局阶段

Opening phase

这是谈判的起始阶段，双方通过见面寒暄、自我介绍等方式营造轻松友好的谈判氛围，同时初步了解对方的谈判风格和态度。在这一阶段，双方一般不会直接切入正题，而是进行一些非实质性的交流，如谈论天气、时事新闻、行业动态等，以缓解紧张情绪，建立初步的信任关系。

This is the initial phase of the negotiation, where both parties create a relaxed and friendly atmosphere through greetings, self-introductions, and other means, while also gaining an initial understanding of each other's negotiation style and attitude. During this stage, parties generally do not dive directly into the main subject but engage in some non-substantive communication, such as discussing the weather, current events, and industry trends, to alleviate tension, and establish an initial trust relationship.

2. 磋商阶段

Consultation phase

这是谈判的核心阶段，双方围绕谈判的核心议题展开实质性的讨论和交锋。首先是报价环节，双方分别提出自己的交易条件和价格主张，这一过程中可能会出现试探性报价、虚盘报价等策略性行为。随后进入讨价还价阶段，双方就价格、质量、数量、交货期、付款方式等关键条款进行反复协商和妥协，各自运用各种谈判技巧和策略，试图说服对方接受自己的观点和条件，争取更大的利益空间。

This is the core phase of the negotiation, where both parties engage in substantive discussions and exchanges around the key issues of the negotiation. Initially, there is a bidding phase where both sides present their transaction conditions and price positions; this process may involve strategic behaviors such as probing bids and non-firm quotes. Following this, the bargaining phase begins, where both parties repeatedly negotiate and compromise on key terms such as price, quality, quantity, delivery time, and payment methods. Each side employs various negotiation skills and strategies to persuade the other to accept their viewpoints and conditions, striving for greater leverage in the negotiation.

3. 休会阶段

Recess phase

当谈判进行到一定阶段，双方可能会因为意见分歧较大、谈判气氛紧张或者需要内部协商等原因，宣布休会。在休会期间，双方各自回到自己的阵营，对谈判的进展情况进行总结和分析，重新评估谈判策略和目标，调整谈判方案，或者与上级领导沟通汇报，获取进一步的指示和授权。

When negotiations reach a certain point, the parties may declare a recess due to significant disagreements, tense negotiation atmosphere, or the need for internal consultation. During the recess, each party returns to their own camp to summarize and analyze the progress of the negotiations, reassess negotiation strategies and objectives, adjust negotiation plans, or communicate and report to higher authorities to obtain further instructions and authorization.

4. 结束阶段

Conclusion phase

经过休会后的调整和准备，双方再次回到谈判桌前，进入最后冲刺阶段。在这一阶段，双方都意识到谈判即将进入尾声，因此会更加积极地寻求达成协议的机会，往往会在一些关键问题上做出最后的让步和妥协，以推动谈判的最终达成。这一阶段的谈判节奏可能会加快，双方的态度也会更加务实和灵活。

After adjustments and preparations following the recess, both parties return to the negotiation table and enter the final sprint phase. In this stage, both parties realize that the negotiation is nearing its end, so they become more proactive in seeking opportunities to reach an agreement, often making final concessions and compromises on key issues to facilitate the conclusion of the negotiation. The pace of negotiation in this stage may quicken, and both sides' attitudes become more pragmatic and flexible.

（三）商务谈判收尾事项

Conclusion matters in business negotiation

1. 达成协议与签约

Reaching an agreement and signing

当双方就所有谈判议题达成一致意见后，应及时起草和签订书面协议或合同，将谈判成果以法律文件的形式固定下来，明确双方的权利和义务。协议内容应详细、准确、完整，涵盖谈判的各个方面，包括交易标的、价格、数量、质量标准、交货期、付款方式、违约责任、争议解决方式等条款，避免出现模糊不清或漏洞，以免日后引发纠纷。在签订协议之前，双方应仔细审查协议的每一项条款，确保其符合谈判的最终结果和各自的利益诉求。例如，在一场技术转让谈判结束后，双方的法律顾问共同起草了技术转让合同，明确了转让的技术内容、使用范围、转让费用、技术支持与培训责任、保密条款、知识产权归属以及违约责任等重要内容。双方的高层管理人员对合同进行了认真审核和签字确认，标志着技术转让交易正式达成，双方将按照合同约定履行各自的义务，实现技术的转移和价值的创造。

Once both parties have reached a consensus on all negotiation issues, it is important to promptly draft and sign a written agreement or contract to solidify the negotiation outcomes in the form of a legal document, clarifying the rights and obligations of both parties. The content of the agreement should be detailed, accurate, and complete, covering all aspects of the negotiation, including terms such as the subject of the transaction, price, quantity, quality standards, delivery time, payment methods, breach of contract liability, and dispute resolution methods. This helps to avoid ambiguity or loopholes that could lead to disputes in the future. Before signing the agreement, both parties should carefully review each term to ensure it aligns with the final negotiation results and their respective interests. For example, after a technology transfer negotiation concludes, the legal advisors of both parties jointly draft a technology transfer contract, specifying important content such as the scope of technology transferred, usage range, transfer fees, technical support and training responsibilities, confidentiality clauses, intellectual property ownership, and breach of contract liability. The senior management of both parties carefully review and sign the contract, signifying the official conclusion of the technology transfer transaction. Both parties will fulfill their respective obligations as stipulated in the contract, achieving the transfer of technology and the creation of value.

2. 谈判总结与评估

Negotiation summary and evaluation

谈判结束后，无论谈判结果如何，双方都应对谈判过程进行总结与评估。回顾谈判的目标设定、策略运用、团队协作、信息沟通等方面的表现，分析成功的经验和不足之处，为今后的谈判提供参考和借鉴。通过总结与评估，可以发现谈判过程中存在的问题和潜在的改进空间，有助于提高谈判团队的整体素质和谈判能力，提升企业在未来商务谈判中的竞争力和成功率。

After the negotiation concludes, regardless of the outcome, both parties should summarize and evaluate the negotiation process. Review the performance in aspects such as goal setting, strategy application, team collaboration, and information communication, analyze the successful experiences and shortcomings, and provide references and lessons for future negotiations. Through summary and evaluation, problems in the negotiation process and potential areas for improvement can be identified, which helps to enhance the overall quality and negotiation capabilities of the negotiation team, and improve the competitiveness and success rate of the company in future business negotiations.

3. 后续跟进与关系维护

Follow-up and relationship maintenance

即使谈判已经结束并签订了协议，双方仍应保持良好的沟通与合作关系，进行后续跟进工作。对于协议的履行情况进行监督和协调，确保双方按照合同约定履行各自的义务，及时解决履行过程中出现的问题和纠纷。同时，通过定期的回访、交流等方式，维护与对方的合作关系，为未来可能的进一步合作创造机会。

Even after the negotiation has concluded and an agreement has been signed, both parties should maintain good communication and cooperation, and carry out follow-up work. They should monitor and coordinate the fulfillment of the agreement to ensure that both sides perform their respective obligations as stipulated in the contract and resolve any issues and disputes that arise during the fulfillment process in a timely manner. At the same time, by conducting regular visits and exchanges, they maintain the cooperative relationship with each other, creating opportunities for further cooperation in the future.

第二节　商务谈判技巧
Section 2　Business Negotiation Skills

一、语言表达技巧
Language expression skills

（一）清晰准确
Clear and accurate

在商务谈判中，使用清晰、简洁且准确的语言至关重要。避免模糊不清、含混其词的表达，以免引起对方的误解。例如，在阐述产品的规格参数时，应明确具体的数值、单位和标准，像“这款设备的功率为500瓦特，误差范围在±5%以内，符合国际电工委员会（IEC）的标准”，而不是使用“大概”“也许”等不确定的词汇描述，让对方能够精准地把握信息，减少因信息误差导致的谈判障碍。

In business negotiations, using clear, concise, and accurate language is crucial. Avoid ambiguous or vague expressions to prevent misunderstandings. For example, when describing the specifications of a product, specify the exact values, units, and standards, such as “The power of this device is 500 watts, with a tolerance of ±5%, and it complies with the standards of the International Electrotechnical Commission (IEC),” rather than using uncertain terms like “approximately” or “maybe,” allowing the other party to grasp the information precisely and reducing negotiation obstacles caused by information errors.

（二）灵活应变
Flexible response

谈判过程中局势多变，需要谈判者具备灵活的语言应变能力。当遇到对方提出的尖锐问题或突发情况时，能够迅速组织语言，巧妙回应。比如，对方突然质疑产品的质量可靠性，谈判者可以回答：“我们非常理解您对质量的关注，事实上，我们的产品不仅通过了严格的内部质量检测体系，还获得了行业权威机构的认证，并且在多个大型项目中稳定运行，有着良好的口碑。我们可以为您提供详细的质量检测报告和客户使用反馈，以消除您的疑虑。”通过这种灵活且有针对性的回应，既化解了对方的质疑，又展示了己方的优势。

The situation in the negotiation process is changeable, requiring the negotiator to have flexible language adaptability. When encountering sharp questions from the other party or unexpected situations, one must be able to quickly organize language and respond cleverly. For example, if the other party suddenly questions the reliability of product quality, the negotiator can reply: "We fully understand your concern about quality. In fact, our products have not only passed a rigorous internal quality control system but have also obtained certification from industry authoritative institutions and have been stably operating in many large-scale projects, earning a good reputation. We can provide you with detailed quality test reports and customer feedback to alleviate your doubts." Through this flexible and targeted response, not only is the other party's doubt resolved, but one's own advantages are also demonstrated.

（三）礼貌得体

Polite and appropriate

礼貌的语言是建立良好谈判关系的基础。使用恰当的礼貌用语，如"请""谢谢""非常抱歉"等，尊重对方的意见和立场，避免使用冒犯性或刺激性的语言。即使在双方意见分歧较大时，也应以礼相待，例如："我理解您的观点，但从我们的角度来看，可能存在一些不同的考虑因素，希望我们能够心平气和地进一步探讨，找到双方都能接受的解决方案，非常感谢您的理解和配合。"这种礼貌得体的沟通方式有助于营造和谐的谈判氛围，增加对方合作的意愿。

Polite language is the foundation of establishing a good negotiation relationship. Using appropriate polite expressions, such as "please" "thank you" and "I' m sorry", respecting the other party' s opinions and positions, and avoiding offensive or provocative language is essential. Even when there are significant differences in opinions, one should treat each other with courtesy, for example: "I understand your point of view, but from our perspective, there may be some different considerations. I hope we can calmly further discuss and find a solution acceptable to both parties. Thank you very much for your understanding and cooperation." This polite and appropriate mode of communication helps to create a harmonious negotiation atmosphere and increases the willingness of the other party to cooperate.

二、倾听技巧

Listening skills

（一）专注耐心

Focused and patient

全身心地投入对方的讲述中，保持专注，不轻易打断对方。通过眼神交流、点头等方式给予对方积极的反馈，让对方感受到被尊重和重视。例如，在对方阐述合作方案时，谈判者应放下手中的其他事务，专注地看着对方，适时地点头表示认同，耐心地听完对方的全部内容，不因为急于表达自己的观点而中途插话，这样才能全面准确地理解对方的意图和需求。

Devote yourself fully to the other party's narrative, maintaining focus and not interrupting them lightly. Provide positive feedback through eye contact and nodding, making the other party feel respected and valued. For example, when the other party is presenting a cooperation proposal, the negotiator should put aside other matters, look at the speaker attentively, nod at appropriate times to show agreement, and patiently listen to the entire content without interrupting to express their own opinions too soon. Only by doing so, can one fully and accurately understand the other party' s intentions and needs.

（二）理解关键信息

Understanding key information

在倾听过程中，善于捕捉对方话语中的关键信息，如核心观点、利益诉求、潜在担忧等。例如，对方提到“我们对产品的交付时间有较高的要求，因为这关系到我们后续一系列项目的启动，如果延迟交付可能会给我们带来较大的损失”，这里的“交付时间”就是关键信息，谈判者要敏锐地抓住这一点，并在后续的谈判中重点讨论和协商解决方案，围绕对方关心的关键问题展开对话，提高谈判的针对性和效率。

During the listening process, it is important to be good at capturing key information in the other party's speech, such as core viewpoints, interest demands, and potential concerns. For example, when the other party says, "We have high requirements for the product delivery time because it is related to the launch of our subsequent series of projects, and any delay in delivery may cause us significant losses," the "delivery time" here is key information. Negotiators should keenly seize on this point and focus on discussing and negotiating solutions in subsequent negotiations, focusing the conversation on the key issues that the other party cares about to enhance the relevance and efficiency of the negotiation.

（三）分析隐含意思

Interpreting underlying meanings

除了理解字面意思，还要善于分析对方话语背后的隐含意思。有时对方不会直接表达自己的真实想法，而是通过一些委婉或间接的方式暗示。比如，对方说“我们之前合作的供应商在价格方面给了我们一定的优惠，而且售后服务也很到位”，这可能隐含着对方希望在本次谈判中获得类似的价格优惠和优质服务，谈判者要能够洞察这些隐含信息，从而调整自己的谈判策略，更好地满足对方的期望，推动谈判进程。

In addition to understanding the literal meaning, it is also important to be good at analyzing the implied meanings behind the other party's words. Sometimes the other party will not directly express their true thoughts but will hint at them through some tactful or indirect means. For example, if the other party says, "The supplier we cooperated with before gave us some discounts on prices, and the after-sales service was also very good," this may imply that they hope to receive similar price concessions and high-quality service in this negotiation. Negotiators should be able to perceive these implied messages in order to adjust their negotiation strategies, better meet the other party's expectations, and advance the negotiation process.

三、提问技巧

Questioning skills

（一）开放式提问

Open-ended questions

通过开放式问题，如“您对我们的产品有哪些方面的期望和要求？”“您认为在这个项目中，最重要的成功因素是什么？”等，鼓励对方充分表达自己的想法和观点，获取更多的信息。这种提问方式可以让谈判者深入了解对方的需求、动机和利益关注点，为后续的谈判策略制定提供丰富的依据。例如，在与潜在合作伙伴探讨合作意向时，使用开放式提问可以引导对方详细阐述其对合作模式、市场前景、双方优势互补等方面的看法，从而帮助谈判者发现双方的共同利益点和潜在的合作机会。

By asking open-ended questions, such as "What are your expectations and requirements for our products?" or "What do you think are the most important factors for success in this project?", we encourage the other party to fully express their thoughts and opinions, gaining more information. This type of questioning allows negotiators to gain a deeper understanding of the other party's needs, motivations, and interests, providing a rich basis for formulating subsequent negotiation strategies. For example, when discussing cooperation intentions with potential partners, using open-ended questions can guide the other party to elaborate on their views regarding the cooperation mode, market prospects, and how both parties' strengths can complement each other, thereby helping negotiators identify common interests and potential cooperation opportunities.

（二）封闭式提问

Closed-ended questions

封闭式问题用于确认特定的信息或事实，如"您是否同意我们提出的价格方案?""您能否在本月底前完成产品的交付?"等，要求对方给出明确的"是"或"否"的回答。这种提问方式在谈判中可以起到明确立场、缩小讨论范围、推动谈判进程的作用。例如，当谈判进入到关键条款的确认阶段，通过封闭式提问可以快速确定双方在某些问题上是否达成一致，避免在已经明确的问题上过多纠缠，集中精力解决尚未达成共识的关键问题。

Closed-ended questions are used to confirm specific information or facts, such as "Do you agree with the price proposal we put forward?" and "Can you complete the delivery of the products by the end of this month?" etc. They require the other party to give a definite "yes" or "no" answer. This type of questioning can play a role in clarifying positions, narrowing the scope of discussion and promoting the negotiation process in negotiations. For example, when the negotiation enters the stage of confirming key terms, closed-ended questions can quickly determine whether the two sides have reached an agreement on certain issues, avoid getting overly entangled in issues that have already been clarified, and concentrate on resolving the key issues on which no consensus has yet been reached.

（三）引导式提问

Leading questions

引导式提问旨在引导对方朝着自己期望的方向思考和回答问题，例如"您看，如果我们在产品质量上提供额外的保障措施，您是否会考虑增加采购量呢?"这种提问方式巧妙地将己方的提议与对方的利益联系起来，通过暗示和引导，增加对方接受己方观点的可能性。在谈判中，合理运用引导式提问可以在不引起对方反感的前提下，有效地影响对方的决策思维，促进谈判朝着有利于己方的方向发展。

Leading questions are designed to guide the other party to think and respond in the direction one desires. For example, "You see, if we provide additional quality assurance measures for our products, would you consider increasing your purchase volume?" This type of questioning subtly links one's proposals to the other party's interests, increasing the likelihood of them accepting one's viewpoint through implication and guidance. In negotiations, the reasonable use of leading questions can effectively influence the other party's decision-making thinking without causing resentment, promoting the negotiation to develop in a direction favorable to one's own side.

四、妥协技巧
Compromise skills

（一）适时适度妥协
Timely and moderate compromise

知道何时以及在多大程度上做出妥协是商务谈判中的关键技巧。在谈判过程中，当双方陷入僵局或者对方提出的要求具有一定合理性时，适时地做出妥协可以打破僵局，推动谈判继续进行。但妥协要适度，不能损害己方的根本利益。例如，在价格谈判中，如果对方对价格的下压幅度在己方可承受的范围内，并且对方在其他方面如付款方式、采购数量等有一定的让步空间，那么可以考虑适当降低价格，以换取对方在其他条款上的妥协，实现双方利益的平衡。

Knowing when and to what extent to make compromises is a key skill in business negotiations. During the negotiation process, when both parties reach a deadlock or the other party's demands are somewhat reasonable, making timely compromises can break the deadlock and push the negotiation forward. However, compromises should be moderate and not harm one's fundamental interests. For example, in price negotiations, if the other party's pressure on the price is within an acceptable range for oneself, and the other party has some room for concessions in other areas such as payment methods and purchase quantities, then it may be worth considering a slight price reduction in exchange for the other party's concessions on other terms, achieving a balance of interests for both sides.

（二）交换妥协条件
Exchange of concessions

妥协并不意味着单方面的让步，而是要通过交换条件来实现双方的共赢。例如，甲方希望乙方提前交付货物，乙方可以提出在提前交付的前提下，甲方需要支付一定比例的加急费用或者增加采购订单的数量。这种以妥协换妥协的方式，既满足了对方的部分需求，又保障了己方的利益，使双方都能在谈判中有所收获，从而增强合作的意愿和信心。

Compromise does not mean a one-sided concession, but rather achieving a win-win situation for both parties through the exchange of conditions. For example, Party A wants Party B to deliver goods in advance; Party B can propose that, on the condition of early delivery, Party A needs to pay a certain percentage of expedited fees or increase the quantity of the purchase order. This method of compromise for compromise not only meets some of the other party's needs but also protects one's own interests, allowing both sides to gain something in the negotiation, thereby enhancing the willingness and confidence to cooperate.

（三）妥协的艺术
Art of compromise

妥协的方式和时机需要巧妙把握，要让对方感受到己方的诚意和合作态度，同时也要让对方明白己方的妥协是有底线和原则的。例如，在谈判中，可以先表示对对方需求的理解和重视，然后提出己方在其他方面的困难和限制，最后提出一个双方都能接受的妥协方案，如“我们非常理解您对产品质量的高要求，也愿意在这方面加大投入，但这可能会导致成本上升，我们希望您能在交货期上给予我们一定的灵活性，这样我们可以在保证质量的前提下，尽快为您提供产品，您看这样是否可行?”通过这种方式，将妥协包装成一个双方共同解决问题的方案，使谈判更加顺利和富有成效。

The way and timing of compromise need to be skillfully grasped. It is important to let the other party feel our sincerity and cooperative attitude, while also making it clear that our compromise has boundaries and principles. For example, in negotiations, one can first express understanding and importance regarding the other party's needs, then present our difficulties and limitations in other areas, and finally propose a compromise solution that is acceptable to both parties, such as, "We fully understand your high requirements for product quality and are willing to invest more in this area, but this may lead to increased costs. We hope you can provide us with some flexibility in the delivery schedule so that we can provide you with the products as soon as possible while ensuring quality. How does that sound?" In this way, compromise is packaged as a solution for both parties to jointly address the problem, making negotiations smoother and more effective.

五、僵局处理技巧
Deadlock handling techniques

(一) 暂时休会
Temporary recess

当谈判陷入僵局时，提议暂时休会是一种常见且有效的方法。休会可以让双方冷静下来，缓解紧张的气氛，同时也为双方提供时间重新审视自己的立场和策略，分析僵局产生的原因，并寻找解决方案。例如，在一场关于合作权益分配的谈判中，双方在股权比例和利润分成上僵持不下，此时谈判者可以提议休会半小时，让双方各自回到团队中进行内部讨论和协商，调整方案，为后续的谈判寻找新的突破口。

When negotiations reach a deadlock, proposing a temporary recess is a common and effective method. A recess allows both parties to calm down, alleviating the tense atmosphere, while also providing time for both sides to reassess their positions and strategies, analyze the reasons for the deadlock, and seek solutions. For example, in a negotiation regarding the distribution of cooperative equity, if both parties are at an impasse over equity ratios and profit sharing, the negotiator can propose a half-hour recess, allowing both sides to return to their teams for internal discussion and negotiation, adjusting their proposals to find new breakthroughs for the subsequent negotiations.

(二) 更换谈判人员
Change of negotiators

如果僵局是由双方谈判人员之间的个性冲突、沟通不畅或者思维定式导致的，可以考虑更换谈判人员。新的谈判人员可能会带来新的思路和方法，打破原有的僵局。例如，在一场长期的技术引进谈判中，由于双方的技术专家在技术细节和知识产权问题上各执一词，谈判陷入僵局，此时双方可以更换技术专家，由更具沟通能力和灵活性的专业人员接替，从新的角度重新探讨问题，推动谈判继续进行。

If the deadlock is caused by personality conflicts, poor communication, or fixed thinking between the negotiators of both parties, it may be considered to replace the negotiators. New negotiators may bring new ideas and methods to break the original deadlock. For example, in a long-term technology introduction negotiation, if the technical experts from both sides are at odds over technical details and intellectual property issues, the negotiation may reach a deadlock. At this point, both parties can replace their technical experts with professionals who have better communication skills and flexibility, allowing them to re-examine the issues from a new perspective and promote the continuation of the negotiation.

（三）引入第三方

Introducing a third party

在一些复杂的谈判中，引入第三方作为调解人或仲裁者可以帮助解决僵局。第三方可以凭借其公正、专业的形象和丰富的经验，客观地分析双方的立场和利益诉求，提出合理的解决方案或调解建议，促进双方达成共识。例如，在国际商务仲裁中，双方可以共同指定一个权威的国际仲裁机构，由其根据相关法律法规和商业惯例，对双方的争议进行裁决，为解决僵局提供公正、有效的途径，确保谈判能够继续进行或达成一个双方都能接受的结果。

In some complex negotiations, introducing a third party as a mediator or arbitrator can help break the deadlock. The third party can objectively analyze both sides' positions and interests, leveraging their impartial and professional image along with rich experience to propose reasonable solutions or mediation suggestions, facilitating consensus between the two parties. For example, in international business arbitration, both parties can jointly appoint an authoritative international arbitration institution, which will adjudicate the disputes based on relevant laws, regulations, and business practices, providing a fair and effective way to resolve the deadlock and ensuring that negotiations can continue or reach an outcome acceptable to both sides.

第三节 Section 3　商务谈判案例——国际标准提案谈判

Business Negotiation Case — International Standard Proposal and Negotiation

一、商务谈判在国际标准化活动中的重要作用

The role of business negotiation in international standardization activities

商务谈判是国际标准化活动中的核心环节。在国际舞台上，各国的经济、文化和技术背景各不相同，对于标准的制定和采纳往往存在不同的看法和需求。因此，商务谈判成了一个关键的平台，各国可以在这里就标准的各项条款进行深入讨论，寻求共同点和解决方案，最终达成共识。这种共识不仅是国际标准化活动顺利进行的基础，也是确保标准能够在全球范

围内得到广泛接受和采纳的重要保障。

Business negotiations are a core component of international standardization activities. On the global stage, countries have diverse economic, cultural, and technological backgrounds, which often lead to differing views and needs regarding the establishment and adoption of standards. Therefore, business negotiations serve as a crucial platform where countries can engage in in-depth discussions on various terms of the standards, seek common ground, and find solutions to reach a consensus. This consensus is not only fundamental to the smooth progress of international standardization activities but also a vital assurance for the standards to be widely accepted and adopted globally.

商务谈判有助于平衡各方利益，减少贸易摩擦。在国际标准化活动中，各国往往都希望自己的利益得到最大程度的保障。通过商务谈判，各国可以就标准的具体条款进行深入的交流和协商，寻求利益的平衡和妥协。这种平衡和妥协有助于减少贸易摩擦，促进国际贸易的顺利进行。同时，商务谈判还可以为各国提供一个互相了解和学习的机会，有助于提升各国的国际视野和合作意识。

Business negotiations help to balance the interests of all parties and reduce trade friction. In international standardization activities, countries typically strive to ensure their interests are maximized. Through business negotiations, they can communicate and consult on the specific terms of the standards, seeking a balance and compromise of interests. This balance and compromise can help reduce trade friction and facilitate the smooth conduct of international trade. Additionally, business negotiations offer opportunities for countries to understand and learn from each other, enhancing their international perspectives and cooperative awareness.

商务谈判也是国际标准化活动中技术和经验交流的重要平台，各国可以就标准的技术细节、制定经验等进行深入的交流和分享。这种交流和分享有助于各国了解国际最新的技术动态和发展趋势，提升自身的技术水平和产业竞争力。同时，商务谈判还可以促进各国之间的技术合作和创新合作，推动全球技术进步和产业升级。

Business negotiations are also an important platform for the exchange of technology and experience in international standardization activities. Countries can engage in in-depth communication and sharing regarding the technical details and formulation experiences of standards. This communication and sharing help countries understand the latest international technological trends and developments, improving their technical levels and industrial competitiveness. Moreover, business negotiations can promote technological and innovative cooperation between countries, driving global technological advancement and industrial upgrading.

商务谈判在国际标准化活动中的重要作用还体现在其对于国际经济合作的推动和促进作用上。通过商务谈判，各国可以就国际标准化活动中的各种问题进行深入讨论和协商，寻求共同的解决方案和发展方向。这种合作和协商有助于加强各国之间的经济联系和合作，推动全球经济的繁荣和发展。同时，商务谈判还可以为各国提供一个互相了解和学习的机会，有助于提升各国的国际影响力和话语权。

The significant role of business negotiations in international standardization activities is also reflected in their ability to promote and facilitate international economic cooperation. Through business negotiations, countries can discuss and consult on various issues in international standardization activities, seeking common solutions and directions for development. This cooperation and consultation help strengthen economic ties and cooperation between countries, promoting global economic prosperity and development. Furthermore, business negotiations provide opportunities for countries to understand and learn from each other, enhancing their international influence and voice.

综上所述，商务谈判在国际标准化活动中具有不可替代的作用。它不仅是推动标准制定的关键步骤，也是促进国际经济合作与发展的重要桥梁。在未来的国际标准化活动中，我们应该更加重视商务谈判的作用，加强各国之间的交流和合作，共同推动全球经济的繁荣和发展。

In summary, business negotiations have an irreplaceable role in international standardization activities. They are not only a key step in promoting the formulation of standards but also an important bridge for promoting international economic cooperation and development. In future international standardization activities, we should place greater emphasis on the role of business negotiations, strengthen communication and cooperation between countries, and jointly promote the prosperity and development of the global economy.

二、国际标准提案谈判案例

International standard proposal and negotiation cases

当今时代，全球能源格局正经历着深刻变革，能源结构转型步伐持续加快，能源数字化浪潮汹涌来袭。这一系列变革促使供热管网领域呈现出蓬勃发展之势，新产品、新技术与新理论持续迭代，为行业进步持续赋能。中国在全球供热领域占据重要地位，拥有规模宏大的城镇集中供热系统，北方地区的集中供热规模更是居世界首位，远超其他国家。中国供热行业技术研发与实践应用方面成果丰硕，多项技术达到国际先进水平。在全球供热技术持续发展、国际交流合作日益频繁的态势下，供热管网领域的国际标准化工作愈发凸显其重要性。对供热管网领域的术语和定义达成共识是开展此项工作的首要环节。

In the current era, the global energy pattern is undergoing profound changes. The transformation pace of the energy structure is accelerating continuously, and the wave of energy digitalization is surging. This series of changes has driven the heating pipeline network field to present a booming development trend. New products, new technologies and new theories are continuously iterating, providing continuous impetus for the progress of the industry. China occupies an important position in the global heating field. It has a large-scale urban central heating system, and the central heating scale in northern China ranks first in the world, far exceeding that of other countries. In terms of technological research and development and practical application, China's heating industry has achieved fruitful results, and many technologies have reached the international advanced level. Against the backdrop of the continuous development of global heating technologies and the increasingly frequent international exchanges and cooperation, the international standardization work in the heating pipeline network field is becoming more and more prominent in its importance. Reaching a consensus on the terms and definitions in the heating pipeline network field is the primary step to carry out this work.

2021 年，我国向国际标准化组织（ISO）提交了关于供热管网（Heat Supply Network，HSN）的新标准提案，该提案涉及热供应管道系统的设计、建造、集成、控制和调节领域，是由我国发起的首个供热管网领域国际标准提案。2024 年 5 月，国际标准提案《供热管网—术语和定义—第 1 部分：系统》在 ISO 正式批准立项，实现了供热管网领域国际标准项目“零”的突破，也标志着中国在供热管网领域国际标准化工作取得实质性的进展。回顾历时近三年的提案历程，并非一帆风顺。提案初期，HSN 提案在国际上赢得了部分国家的认可与支持，为提案的推进奠定了一定基础，然而由于各国供热行业发展水平参差不齐、利益诉求存在差异等诸多因素，提案也遭遇了来自不同方面的反对声音。特别是在对 HSN 提案投票后，有些国家对提案是肯定性答复，也有国家质疑提案相关内容。

In 2021, China submitted a new standard proposal on the Heat Supply Network (HSN) to the International Organization for Standardization (ISO). This proposal covered the fields of the design, construction, integration, control and regulation of heating supply pipeline system, and it was the first international standard proposal in the field of heat supply network initiated by China. In May 2024, the international standard proposal *Heat Supply Network – Vocabulary – Part 1: System* was officially approved and established as a project by the ISO, achieving a breakthrough from zero for international standard projects in the field of heat supply network and also marking that China has made substantial progress in the international standardization work in the field of heat supply network. Looking back on the nearly three-year proposal process, it was not all smooth sailing. In the early stage of the proposal, the HSN proposal won the recognition and support of some countries in the international arena, which laid a certain foundation for the promotion of the proposal. However, due to many factors such as the uneven development levels of the heating industries in different countries and the differences in interest demands, the proposal also encountered objections from different aspects. Especially after the voting on the HSN proposal, some countries gave affirmative replies to the proposal, while others raised doubts about the relevant contents of the proposal.

针对以上情况，SAC① 对重点国家和反对提案的相关国家发送邮件，征求这些国家对提案的支持，范例如下：

In response to the above situation, SAC sent emails to key countries and countries that opposed the proposal, soliciting their support for the proposal. Examples are as follows:

范例1

（重点国家邮件）

Dear ×××,

Hope this letter finds you well.

In August 2021, SAC has submitted a new proposal to ISO on establishing a Technical Committee

① SAC，全称为 Standardization Administration of the People's Republic of China，即中国国家标准化管理委员会。——编者注

(TC) for "Heat Supply Network" (HSN). The proposed TC will focus on standardization in design, construction, integration, control and regulation of heating supply pipeline system. The proposal has entered the stage of ISO member voting.

We will work closely with experts all around the world to develop low-carbon, energy-efficient, safe and smart heating networks, with the goals of reducing energy consumption, improving operational safety and reliability, and increasing energy efficiency, thus help to achieve the requirements in ISO 2030 Strategy and the UN Sustainable Development Goals for clean energy transition and infrastructure construction development.

As the proposer of the new ISO/TC, China Urban Construction Design & Research Institute Co., Ltd (CUCD), has undertaken hundreds of foreign aid construction projects in Africa since 2005. CUCD is contributing its wisdom and strength to green development in African countries continuously.

We are all part of the global village. To achieve the common goal of low-carbon and sustainable development, we would like to take this opportunity to invite you to participate in this work and vote for ISO/TS/P 301 proposal on "Heat Supply Network". Your support would be the most appreciated. Please reply to me if there is any progress or questions. Looking forward to hearing from you.

Best regards,

×××

范例2

(重点国家邮件)

Dear ×××,

Hope the letter finds you well.

At the end of August, SAC submitted an application to ISO for the establishment of the ISO Heat Supply Network (HSN) Technical Committee (ISO/TC). This committee will focus on the standardization of design, construction, integration, control and regulation of heating supply pipeline system. The proposal has entered the stage of ISO member voting.

According to the procedural requirements of ISO, we organized two ZOOM① meetings on 26th and 28th October. There were two experts from your country attending the meetings. We had a good communication. Mr. Jurgen Rose expressed his support for the proposal and expect to cooperate on smart heat meter in the future. Mr. Sonke kraft attended two meetings and paid high attention to the proposal.

① ZOOM 是一款专业的办公视频会议软件。——编者注

We have common technical basis in terms of heating supply network. The technical integration in this standardization field will promote the efficient use of products such as heating pipelines, pumps and valves and will contribute to low-carbon, energy-saving and sustainable development.

Therefore, we would like to ask you to support China's proposal (HSN) and we expect to cooperate and promote the relevant international standards together. We appreciate your support very much. If you have any questions, please contact us.

Sincerely,

×××

范例3

(反对国家邮件)

Dear ×××,

Hope this email finds you well.

As you have already known that SAC submitted a new technical activity proposal on Heat Supply Network (HSN) which passed the vote with 30 approvals from ISO members. We noticed you cast negative feedback on the vote. SAC attaches great attention after receiving your comments and would like to provide more information for further discussion. Your main concerns focus on the questions about the need for new technical field where relevant EN standards already exists.

SAC would like to indicate that the scope of this new proposal covers the heating pipe network from the heat source to the heat users. Energy system will not be covered under the working scope of this new TC. And the proposed ISO/TC HSN places emphasis on the integration and utilization of the pipeline, valves, fittings, etc. There will be no overlapping with the existing ISO TCs. Undoubtedly, EN standards prepared by CEN/TC107 represents the advanced level of heating technology in Europe. However, due to the design concept, as well as the regional and national differences in infrastructure, raw materials, manufacturing technology, construction technology, it is necessary to develop international standards with global consensus from all regions to meet the global needs. For example, most district heating pipes apply according to EN253 which specifies requirements up to DN1200. In China, pipes up to DN1600 are installed. This is the original intention and purpose of this proposal.

An important part of the proposed ISO/TC is to extract the commonalities and basic content of the heating supply network in terms of design, construction and operation based on global features, so as to formulate international standards. Besides, this established new TC intends to closely cooperate with CEN/TC107 to jointly promote the international standardization of HSN. By doing so, it will help to increase the influence of advanced European heating technology, promote the worldwide development of heating supply network technology and achieve the common carbon reduction target.

I hope the above information can help you to better understand the necessity and importance of the proposal. And we do hope you can support this proposal for the TMB ballot and actively participate in the follow-up activities.

Please feel free to reach out to me if there is any enquiry. And wish you a Happy New Year and may the joy, health and prosperity come with you in the coming year!

All the best,

×××

第四节　重点短语与句型
Section 4　Key Phrases and Sentence Patterns

一、常用单词与短语
Common words and phrases

1. business negotiation　商务谈判
2. domestic business　国内贸易，国内商务
3. financial interest　经济利益
4. terms and conditions　（合同）条款和条件
5. discounted price　折扣价
6. time limit　期限，时限
7. a package of　一揽子，一包
8. participate in　参与，参加
9. be beneficial to　有利于，有益
10. cope with　应对，处理
11. win-win　双赢的
12. bilateral negotiation　双边谈判
13. multilateral negotiations　多边谈判
14. host field negotiation　主场谈判
15. guest field negotiation　客场谈判
16. neutral field negotiation　中立谈判
17. soft-typed negotiation　软式谈判
18. hard-typed negotiation　硬式谈判
19. principle-based negotiation　原则式谈判
20. information collection　信息收集
21. preparation for negotiation team　谈判小组准备
22. long-term relationship　长期关系

23. get the initiative　获得主动权
24. in turn　反过来，依次，轮流地
25. make an effort　做出努力
26. throw a stone to clear the road strategy　投石问路策略
27. picky strategy　吹毛求疵策略
28. concession phase　让步阶段
29. target price maximization　目标价格最大化
30. positive and negative concessions　积极让步和消极让步
31. central link　中心环节
32. practical stage　实践阶段
33. negotiating subject　谈判主题
34. common ground　共同基础，一致之处
35. consultation phase　磋商阶段
36. quality assurance　品质保证
37. legal regulations　法律条例
38. opening price　开盘价格
39. close a deal　达成交易
40. set a target　制定目标
41. usual practice　惯例
42. psychological expectation　心理预期
43. reserve price　保留价格，最低价格
44. downward trend　下跌趋势，向下趋势
45. meet expectation　符合预期
46. reach an agreement　达成协议，达成共识
47. cut the losses　减少损失
48. close a deal　成交
49. confirm the agreement　确认协议
50. observe the contract　遵守合同
51. commercial integrity　商业诚信
52. final say　最终决定权
53. good cop, bad cop tactic　红白脸战术
54. negotiation strategy　谈判策略
55. communication style　沟通方式
56. social etiquette　社交礼仪
57. treatment of contractual disputes　合同纠纷的处理方式
58. negotiation suspension　谈判中止

二、常用句型
Common sentence patterns

1. Our... is much admired in the world market and enjoys a wide acceptance in many countries.
我们生产的……在世界范围内受到赞誉，畅销许多国家。
2. We are pleased to give you a quotation for our commodities.
我们很高兴给贵方报价。
3. I am confident our offer is in line with the prevailing market price.
我确信我们的报价符合市场价。
4. I can give you a discount of 15% if you make payment in advance.
你们如果提前支付货款，可以给你们打八五折。
5. Actually, this price leaves us no profit at all.
其实，这个价格让我们毫无利润可言。
6. Our price is reasonable and realistic.
我们的价格是现实合理的。
7. Our price is based on reasonable profit instead of wild speculation.
我方报价是以合理的利润为根据的，而不是漫天要价。
8. To start the ball rolling, let's meet each other halfway.
为了达成交易，我们各让一步吧。
9. I hope you can offer us the most competitive price.
希望你们能给我们最有竞争力的价格。
10. The price is on the high side.
价格偏高了。
11. The price is too high to be acceptable.
价格太高，无法接受。
12. Your price is about 15% higher than that of some other suppliers.
你们的价格比其他的一些供应商还要高出15%。
13. You are really good partners to do business with.
你们真的是很好的商业合作伙伴。
14. Your price is much higher than that of the current market.
你们的报价比目前的市场价格高很多。
15. It will be rather difficult for us to push our sales if we buy it at this price.
如果我们以这个价钱购买，将很难推销。
16. If you hold on to your price, it is not necessary for us to have further discussion.
如果你方坚持你们的报价，我们没有必要再做进一步的商讨。
17. I don't think it is wise for us to insist on our own prices.
我想我们双方都坚持各自的价格是不明智的。

18. Even if it is so, there is a big gap between our prices.

即便如此，我们的价格差距还是太大了。

19. It is well known that our products are of top quality and enjoy a good reputation these years.

众所周知，近年来我们的产品一直是质量上乘，并有良好的声誉。

20. Well, shall we get down to our business?

好吧，我们进入正题好吗？

21. Let's go back to the price.

我们接着谈价格好吗？

22. Our counter offer is well founded.

我方的还盘还是很合理的。

23. Your price is beyond our reach.

贵方的价格我方承受不起。

24. Frankly speaking, your counter offer can hardly cover our production costs. I'm afraid that we can do nothing to make further reduction at the price, since we have already got the lowest price.

坦率地说，你们的还价勉强支付生产成本。恐怕我们无法再降价了，这已经是最低价了。

25. You should know that all companies are cutting their prices down so that they can get a larger market share.

你方应该知道为了获得更大的市场份额，所有的公司都在降价。

26. We may reconsider the price if your order is big enough.

如果你方订量大，我们可以重新考虑价格。

27. I'm afraid I'll have to take it up with our general manager.

恐怕我得征求我们总经理的意见。

28. We are thinking of appointing a local sales agent to help push our sales.

我公司考虑在当地指定一位销售代理，以帮助我公司的推销。

29. We wish to be agent for the goods you are exporting.

我们愿意担任你们出口商品的代理。

30. We usually deal on an 8% trade discount basis with an additional quantity discount for orders over 1,000 pieces.

我们通常给8%的行业折扣，对于超过1000件的订货，还另外有数量折扣。

31. I wonder if we can make payment for this order by documentary collection.

我想知道我们是否能以跟单托收的方式付款。

32. We only accept payment by irrevocable letter of credit payable against shipping document.

我们只接受不可撤销的凭装运单据付款的信用证。

33. We have especially reinforced our packing in order to minimize the extent of any possible damage to the goods.

我们已经强化包装，将货物遭受损害的可能性降到最低。

34. The packaging material depends on the goods you have ordered.

包装材料的选择要根据你所订购的货物来决定。

35. Good quality and competitive prices would mean nothing if goods cannot be put on the market in time.

如果商品无法及时进入市场，就算品质再好，价格再有竞争力，都没有用。

36. That is the best we can do. We cannot go any further if you still make no concessions.

这是我们能做的最好的了。如果你方依旧不做出让步，我们很难再继续谈下去。

37. Many other suppliers offered us lower prices than yours.

很多其他的供应商出的价格都比你方低。

38. The prices of raw materials have risen considerably, so we cannot keep our original prices and have to adjust the prices accordingly.

因为原材料价格涨得相当厉害，所以我们无法保持原价，不得不对价格做相应的调整。

39. All the prices are subject to our final confirmation.

所有的价格都要得到我方的最后确认。

40. If one party fails to execute the contract, the other party has the right to cancel it, and the loss resulting from the fact should be undertaken by the party breaching the contract.

如果一方未能履约，另一方有权取消合约，据此造成的损失由违约方负担。

41. Both of us should abide by the terms and conditions of this contract.

我们双方均应信守合同中的条款和条件。

42. I'll draw up an agreement at once.

我立刻起草一份合同。

43. Since everything is ready, we can sign the contract today.

既然所有事情就绪，我们今天就可以签订合同。

44. It is necessary to include a Force Majeure term in this contract.

合同中加入不可抗力条款是很有必要的。

课后练习

Ⅰ. 判断题。

Please determine whether the following statements are True or False.

1. When negotiating with the counter-party, you only need to focus on your own benefit and interest. (　　)

2. Both parties should try to understand each other's point of view before making decision. (　　)

3. Negotiation object is the combination of the topics of negotiation and various material elements. (　　)

4. There are there goals in negotiation plan: the ideal objective, the acceptable objective and the minimum objective. (　　)

5. Besides considering the negotiation team and information collection before the negotiation, we

also need to consider the negotiating time and place. (　　)

6. In order to create a relaxed atmosphere at the opening stage of the negotiations, we often talk about some topics, such as weather, politics, religions and interests. (　　)

Ⅱ. 将下列句子翻译为英文。

Translate the following sentences into English.

1. 真正意义上谈判的成功是实现双赢。

2. 谈判开局阶段需要营造良好的开局氛围，这样有利于谈判的开展。

3. 发生不可抗力事件，生产和交货可能会受到影响。我们对此产生的任何损失或损坏不予负责。

4. 你们必须在每份合同内都写明货物内容、数量和单价。

5. 你们目前面临着与许多供应商竞争，他们的报价比你们的要低很多。

6. 考虑到我们大量增加的生产成本，我们的价格一点儿也不过分。

7. 或许我们对目前市场价格的趋势各自持有不同的观点。

8. 如果是这样的话，我们不能再进行这笔交易了。

9. 我建议签一个两年的合同。

10. 这样高的价格我们很难获得利益。为了做成交易，我们为什么不各让一步呢?

11. 考虑到我们的进一步合作，我方决定给你方百分之五的折扣。

12. 我很高兴我们最终在价格上取得了一致意见。

13. 我们希望您能在交货期上给予我们一定的灵活性，这样我们可以在保证质量的前提下，尽快为您提供产品。

Ⅲ. 根据以下内容写一封信文。

Write an English letter according to the following particulars.

如您所知，我方提交了一份关于电子商务欺诈的新提案，该提案获得了国际标准化组织(ISO)成员的32票赞成，得以通过表决。同时，我们注意到在表决过程中也出现了一些不同的反馈声音，我方在收到相关意见后高度重视，愿意提供更多信息以供进一步讨论。

REFERENCES 参考文献

［1］李亚，李军．国际经济与贸易专业综合实训：函电与单证［M］．大连：东北财经大学出版社，2021.

［2］逯宇铎，陈璇．跨境电子商务［M］．北京：机械工业出版社，2020.

［3］刘刚．进出口业务英语函电［M］．北京：北京理工大学出版社，2015.

［4］杜昌忠，林丽华．职场商务英语沟通［M］．上海：复旦大学出版社，2014.

［5］孙圣勇．国际贸易文书实务［M］．北京：国防工业出版社，2011.

［6］易露霞，刘洁，尤彧聪．外贸英语函电［M］．4 版．北京：清华大学出版社，2020.

［7］马述忠，卢传胜，丁红朝，等．跨境电商理论与实务［M］．杭州：浙江大学出版社，2018.

［8］王健．跨境电子商务［M］．北京：机械工业出版社，2020.

［9］李贺．报关实务［M］．2 版．上海：上海财经大学出版社，2018.

［10］冯潮前．跨境电子商务支付与结算实验教程［M］．杭州：浙江大学出版社，2016.

［11］胡秋华，吴思乐．世纪商务英语外贸函电［M］．4 版．大连：大连理工大学出版社，2019.

［12］王黎明．外贸英语函电［M］．4 版．北京：机械工业出版社，2022.

［13］吴石梅，李子丹，张彤，等．商务英语函电［M］．北京：清华大学出版社，2021.

［14］王珍．外贸英语函电［M］．3 版．大连：大连理工大学出版社，2021.

［15］马俊，毕劲芳，马欣玥．国际商务谈判理论与实战（双语版）［M］．北京：清华大学出版社，2021.

［16］吴思乐．世纪商务英语谈判口语［M］．5 版．大连：大连理工大学出版社，2023.